Shelter from the Texas Heat

Shelter from the Texas Heat

BOBBI KORNBLIT

PTP
Peach Twig Press

Shelter from the Texas Heat: a novel

Printed in the United States of America

ISBN:978-0-615-53861-7

Library of Congress Control Number: 2011917686
Kornblit, Bobbi
Shelter from the Texas Heat: a novel

1.Women's—Fiction. 2. Texas—Fiction. 3. Jewish—Fiction.
4. Civil rights movements—Fiction.

DISCLAIMER

This book is a work of fiction. Names of historically significant people, events, and places have been used to provide a framework for the story. All other characters and events are products of the author's imagination and are used fictitiously. Any resemblance of the fictitious characters and fictional events to actual people and events is completely coincidental. In all cases, historical facts have been included with as much accuracy as possible in the fictive setting. Neither the author nor the publisher assumes any responsibility for errors.

PTP
Peach Twig Press

www.PeachTwigPress.com
Post Office Box 720060
Atlanta, Georgia 30358

DEDICATION

Polly, my mother

Lolly, my friend

And to the memory of Simon—my safe haven

Shelter from the Texas Heat

"I think that my biggest achievement is that after going through a rather difficult time, I consider myself comparatively sane. I'm proud of that."

—Jacqueline Kennedy Onassis ca. 1970

"Women are like tea bags. We don't know our own true strength until we are in hot water."

—Eleanor Roosevelt (1884–1962)

PROLOGUE

"Put on a little lipstick. It'll make a world of difference!"

Rachel's mother's advice still rolled around in her mind after years of hearing it repeated in countless situations. Familiar as it was, Rachel knew it would take more than a swipe of red to cover the numbness in her heart.

She thought her mother was great at telling her what to do, but somehow Rosy's role as a sage didn't fit with their tumultuous home life when Rachel was young—when her mother couldn't handle her difficult father and didn't quite follow her own advice.

Dealing with the world these days wasn't any easier for Rachel. Sometimes she didn't sleep, or slept too much, but often joked about how she never missed a meal.

Her only salvo was swimming, submerging in the water. In the early mornings, she swam laps, mindlessly plowing along the black-striped lane with even strokes—anything to keep from thinking.

Rachel always attempted to complete eighteen round-trips. Eighteen for the Hebrew letter *chai,* for "life."

When she finished or couldn't go any farther, she dove to the bottom and grazed the drain grate with her fingertips, only coming up when her lungs felt like stretched party balloons on the verge of exploding. She gasped for air, needing to breathe, wanting to live, even though she knew that everyone doesn't get the choice.

One morning, she flipped on her back and floated in the quiet, soothing water, gazing at banks of lazy clouds in the gunmetal February sky drifting across the glass-paneled roof that enclosed the indoor pool. Suddenly, a streak of light blazed across the sky—a shooting star rocketing to Earth—like a biblical sign from ancient days when mankind tried to decipher the meaning of life by looking to the heavens.

For a matter of seconds she stared, mesmerized by the light show that burst into a trio of bright trails soaring across the surface of the pool, reflected in the glass ceiling.

Rachel darted up the slick steps and headed toward the corner of the pavilion to get a better look at the flashes as they sped out of her line of vision. When she turned, silky trails of white smoke were the only evidence—ethereal markers in the sky.

Her cell phone rang, perched on a nearby chair. She skidded on the wet pool deck, running to catch her phone before voicemail kicked in.

"Rach, did you see it? Oh my God! The Space Shuttle Columbia flew right over Dallas and blasted into bits! I just heard it on the news in Austin," her best friend, P.J., blurted.

Rachel struggled to catch her breath. "You're not going to believe this: I watched it right above me! Can't talk now, I'm dripping wet. I'll call you later." She headed back toward the deep end.

Rachel had been dazzled by the display in the morning sky. Then she realized the light show that had given her a moment's joy actually meant the descent into grief and darkness for someone else—a place she knew only too well.

She thought, *Yes, I've seen it all before.*

Rachel's world had exploded and pushed her over the edge.

ALL CHOKED UP

CHAPTER 1

"I USED TO BE a good wife, a good mother, a loyal friend, but then everything started spinning out of control," Rachel Frank berated herself almost daily. It seemed like ages ago when things were different.

When she was a dutiful corporate wife, she attended functions to show her support for her husband of twenty-five years, Michael—who she truly believed was completely trustworthy.

At a charity dinner at a hotel in downtown Dallas, she fidgeted with the rhinestone buttons on her cocktail suit, thinking formal dinners tend to be long, boring affairs that drag on with speeches made to disinterested audiences who are busy carrying on their own private conversations. She scanned the menu at the banquet, and *Petit Artichaut a la Provence* brought a wary smile to her face. Her husband's client across the table raised his eyebrows like an insect's antennae. She wondered if he thought she was flirting with him or perhaps was tipsy from the flowing champagne during the cocktail hour. To shake things up, she announced, "I've never completely trusted artichokes ever since I was a kid in Texas. Vegetables aren't supposed to be evil, but I'd swear this one is downright mean and green." She shot him a glance, and he winked before digging into his appetizer.

Rachel looked down at her plate and could only see spikes sharp enough to draw blood and leaves as thick as armor—thinking how they give up the delicious secret of their fleshy hearts only after being dumped in scalding water.

Michael was busy discussing zoning ordinances with his client. They quieted down as the keynote speaker took center stage.

Dr. Clara Amparo reached the lectern to deliver her opening remarks: "Ladies and gentlemen, thank you for your generous contributions that help provide shelter for women who live in the shadow of fear. In America, a woman is severely beaten in her own home every fifteen seconds. I'm here to tell you that over half of married couples experience violent episodes over the course of their marriage."

The tuxedoed waiter whispered to Rachel, "Madame, is the *Artichaut a la Provence* not to your liking?"

"Gosh no, it looks super!" The cluster of greens remained untouched on her plate. Then she confidently selected the correct appetizer fork and began to savor the delicate morsels that had been relieved of their thorny armor—not like the first time she ever encountered those ornery thistles in the early sixties when she was an eleven-year-old at the weekend ranch of her best friend, P.J. Rutherford—one of the few memories of her childhood that always made her smile.

P.J. and Rachel met in homeroom at North Dallas Elementary. Both were painfully thin and equally plain, except for Rachel's flaming red hair. They were as close as sisters—someone else's sisters, not hers.

Whenever possible, Rachel would escape from the chaos of her household by hanging out with P.J. Papa fought with Mama and her two sisters picked on her in turn. Her mother always said, "When I married your father on V-J Day, one war ended and another one started." Her parents tied the knot at the end of WWII and then started taking potshots at each other shortly thereafter.

P.J. invited Rachel to spend the weekend at her family's ranch, only about an hour away from their mansion in North Dallas. Rachel's father used to say that Russell Rutherford "had more money than

Carter's got little liver pills." Although a herd of American Brahman cattle lazily grazed in the pastures, the Rutherfords used their spread to entertain business associates and society friends.

Upon her arrival, Patty Jane Rutherford's high-pitched twang chirped, "Rach, this is it, the Double R."

"Not exactly what I figured a ranch would be like," Rachel said, eyeing the immense compound of buildings.

"Most the ones I know aren't much different," P.J. replied with a shrug. The girls walked past the rock bottom swimming pool lined with boulders that led to a waterfall. Heat waves rippled from the concrete deck, and Rachel looked longingly at the cascading water.

They headed to the guesthouse where they would be at liberty to make all the noise they wanted without disturbing the adults. In the sweltering midday sun, a man with gleaming mahogany skin, dressed neatly in black slacks and jacket with a starched shirt and bow tie, headed toward them.

"Let's go say hi to Maddy," P.J. said.

He was toting Rachel's baby blue Samsonite suitcase, and tiny beads of sweat clung to the deep furrows in his brow. The girls met up with him in front of the guesthouse. He held the door open, clutching the suitcase while balancing a brown and white striped garment bag in the other hand. He unzipped the bag and hung up P.J.'s crisp yellow sundress with the Neiman Marcus price tag dangling from the collar.

Rachel clicked open the latches of her suitcase and retrieved her cotton underwear from the puckered pouch. She unpacked her best shorts with her name printed clearly in black ink inside the waistband—Rachel Miller—and carefully unwrapped her Keds from their cocoon of white tissue paper.

"Now, young gals, dinner's ready at six, so don't y'all be late." Madison walked to the door, catching the screen frame before it slammed shut.

"Rach, let's pretend we're roommates and this is our college dorm," P.J. called down from the top bunk bed. "I hope we're always together. Friends forever!" P.J. 's bony feet dangled near Rachel's face.

"Me, too! I'm not so sure they have bunks in college, and get your smelly feet out of my face! If this is supposed to be school, let's play first and study later."

They shimmied into their swimsuits. Rachel's sisters always teased her about being as flat as a pancake, so she hated for them to see her undressed. But she wasn't too embarrassed around P.J. because she hadn't developed either. Rachel's mom couldn't understand her youngest daughter's modesty because she liked to parade around the house in her bra shaped like a pair of satin ice cream cones.

Rachel crammed her wiry helmet of red hair into a daisy-covered swim cap, and P.J. stretched a light blue one that matched her eyes over her silky blonde ponytail. They plunged into the pool to escape the unrelenting heat. The water deliciously tingled every nerve in Rachel's body.

"Marco!" P.J. called out.

"Polo!" Rachel responded in their watery hide-and-seek.

With her eyes scrunched shut, P.J.'s toothpick arms flailed, trying to catch her pal who was flitting around the pool.

Mama had always encouraged Rachel to swim because it was supposed to be good for her asthma; the velvety, moist air on the water's surface flowed more easily into her lungs. But the sudden starts and quick blind chases of their game made her chest feel as tight as the rubber swim cap squeezing her skull. Rachel feared she'd probably gotten too much sun on her freckled face, and P.J.'s alabaster skin had slowly baked from horsing around in the water.

They hoisted themselves out of the pool and dripped dry on the chaise lounges, like a couple of horny toads sunning on the rocks. The hot, thick air hummed with the sounds of distant tractors and buzzing gnats. P.J. got up and stood in front of her best friend, blocking the afternoon sun. "Ready? Race you to the bunkhouse!"

Rachel leapt out of her chair and they sprinted across the deck. P.J. won by a sunburned nose. Once inside the cabin, Rachel's eyes struggled to adjust to the dim light, and the musty scent of cedar clung to her nostrils. Swirling grained patterns on the wall panels reminded her of the animal shapes she enjoyed searching for in clouds, but the knotholes were the eyes of lurking, menacing beasts.

Rachel decided there was no need to finish drying off because they had to shower before dressing for dinner with P.J.'s parents in the main house. She traced the white outline of the straps that crisscrossed her one-piece. Every part of her body that had been exposed to the sun's rays glowed an ominous pink hue. The specks across the bridge of her nose seemed to have burst into full bloom, spreading like the wildflowers in the pasture.

At the bathroom mirror, Rachel corralled her mass of hair into a ponytail. The deep cling-clang-cling of an iron triangle signaled suppertime, and P.J. flew around the room, throwing on her clothes like a fireman rushing into gear to fight an inferno. She flung open the screen door, banging it against the cedar siding, and shouted, "Ready, on your mark . . . Get set . . . Go!"

Rachel gasped for air when they entered the main house, trying to recover from the foot race, her lungs assaulted by the crisp air-conditioning. She whipped out a small white bottle from her shorts pocket and deeply inhaled a squirt of medicinal spray. In spite of her asthma and aching sunburn, she was glad to be away from home, relieved to not to hear Papa's shouting for a few days.

"This here's your special spot, Miss Patty Jane," Madison said.

He ushered Rachel to a chair carved with a five-pointed star and two entwined Rs. "Thank you, Mr. Madison," Rachel said. The concrete block started to ease off her chest as the medicine began to kick in.

"Madison's his first name. You can call him Maddy," P.J. said.

The furry cowhide seats scratched Rachel's newly sunburned legs. Maddy scooted her closer to the table covered with an unfamiliar assortment of silverware at each setting, which confused Rachel. The two armchairs at the opposite ends of the table remained empty.

Strains of Elvis Presley crooning his hit "Please Release Me" wafted above a gentle gurgle. Rachel spotted an oil well fountain in the corner and was mesmerized by the miniature gusher. Then a pair of double doors swung open and Mrs. Rutherford appeared, followed by her husband, a boulder of a man. Maddy flew to escort her to the table. He was careful not to catch her flowing chiffon dress on the hoof-footed chairs. Her chestnut hair, swirled and lacquered high above her head, was adorned with a jeweled honeybee. Rachel gawked at Russell Rutherford's looming frame from top to bottom, settling on his boots that looked like a pair of rattlesnakes.

P.J. lightly tapped her on the jaw. "You could catch flies like that!"

"Dinner's served, y'all" Madison announced with a flourish.

"Aren't you supposed to say 'chow-time' or 'grub's on'?" Rachel whispered to P.J.

She giggled stealthily behind her hand and said, "Mother likes to think of herself as Elizabeth Taylor in *Giant*."

Lynda Gayle Rutherford fixed a steady gaze on her daughter's guest, and then a smile flashed across her frozen face. "Patricia Jane, did you show Rachel around the Double R?"

P.J. nodded. "Uh huh."

"I take it that you mean 'yes, ma'am' with that grunt. Rachel, Mr. Rutherford and I are delighted you could join Patricia Jane for the weekend. Madison, tell Elena we're ready now."

Big Russ grinned as large as Texas. "Welcome, Rachel, darlin'. Hope y'all have more fun than a coyote in a hen house. I saw you eyeballing my Charlie Parker boots—best maker of manly footwear the good Lord ever created. And how's my little Patty-cake?" His voice sweetened and he winked at his daughter. "Come over here and give Daddy a peck."

She started to get up, but her mother's steely glance signaled for her to remain seated. "Patricia Jane, please do the honor of saying grace at our table, since your little friend is of the Jewish persuasion," Mrs. Rutherford purred.

P.J. shut her eyes tightly and blurted, "Dear Lord, thank you for the cow we're about to eat. God bless Rachel, too. In Jesus' name, Amen."

Rachel panicked, staring at her plate, not sure if it was "kosher" for a Jew to be blessed by Jesus. She thought how the meals at her home weren't anything like this. Her family never said blessings before meals, and dinner wasn't exactly her favorite time of day. Mama always told her to "mind her peas and Qs" so Papa wouldn't get upset. Rachel always wondered what was wrong with peas and tried to avoid them whenever possible.

Suddenly, a woman clad in a black dress with a white pinafore emerged from the swinging door, holding a large tray. Rachel's elbow slipped, sending her fork plummeting to the floor.

Maddy stooped to pick it up. "Nothin' to worry 'bout. I'll get you another one while Elena keeps on passing the chokes."

On each small plate, she placed a large green prickly vegetable on a bed of baby lettuce garnished with a yellow rose carved out of lemon peel. Maddy flanked Rachel, distributing little silver bowls of melted butter. After a while, he discretely slipped her a fresh fork. She started to tackle the artichoke although uncertain of how to get past the thorns. Rachel remembered what Mama had said: "Eat everything you're served." Armed with the large fork, she stabbed a thick leaf and stuffed it into her mouth, chewing, but barely making a dent.

Rachel prayed no one would address her while her mouth was full of what tasted like a garden weed. Then a brainstorm hit: She surreptitiously spit the wad into her hand and shoved it into the breast pocket of her new white shirt.

"Rachel, dear," Mrs. Rutherford began, "you pluck one petal at a time from the artichoke and dunk it into the lemon-butter sauce. Use your two front teeth to scrape the meaty part."

Rachel felt her face redden deeper than her fresh sunburn at the mere mention of her overbite that was encased in braces. "Yes, ma'am," she said and began to scrape at the rubbery leaves, watching P.J. following suit.

"When you've removed all the greens, discard the fibrous choke, carve out the heart, and dip this delicacy into the butter sauce with your cocktail fork."

Cocktail fork? Rachel wondered. P.J. had a tiny fork in her clutches, so Rachel grabbed hers and was about to stage her next attack on the artichoke when she noticed a feathery green outline on her pocket. As the faint streak became a runny stain that branded the front of her chest, her heart sank as the green mark appeared like a slowly revealed image on a magic eight ball. She grabbed a doily embroidered with crimson double Rs—just the right size to soak up the offending juices and hoped to stop the spread before someone noticed. She thought dinnertime with the Rutherfords wasn't turning out to be much better than at her house, but at least no one was yelling . . . so far.

The meal was finally coming to an end when Elena served generous pieces of pecan pie and then watched from the corner near the fountain as Rachel eagerly cracked the crunchy topping to get to the thick, syrupy filling.

"Pie's great, Elena. *Muy deliciosa,*" P.J. said.

"That'll be all, Elena," Mrs. Rutherford said, not actually eating her dessert, just moving it around her plate.

"Elena, darlin', you make a pecan pie better than a blue-thumbed carpenter can spank nails," Mr. Rutherford exclaimed, with crumbs sprinkled on the corners of his upturned mouth. "Patty-cake, why don't y'all run on and start your camp-out in the guesthouse?"

"All right, Daddy. See ya in the mornin'. Night, Mother."

"Thank you very much, Mrs. Rutherford," Rachel parroted, glad she was about to make her escape. Then she heard the sound of freedom: wood scraping against wood as Maddy pulled out her chair from the dinner table.

When the girls walked back toward their room, the evening air felt as heavy as a blanket and the stars hung high in the sky. They stopped to lie on the chaises for a while and then dashed around the pool deck catching lightning bugs in empty salsa jars. Full of guilt, Rachel released her prey because she knew how awful it felt to be trapped.

Later that night, while lying on the bunk bed below P.J., Rachel mulled over the odd meal she had just eaten: the weird, spiky vegetable and the meat from a cow that P.J. had probably known since it was a calf. Rachel was glad not to hear crying like at home and listened to P.J. exhaling softly in little puffs like a guardian angel above her.

NIGHT FLIGHT

CHAPTER 2

AT THE CHARITY DINNER, Dr. Amparo's rich voice filled the room: "In the Dallas-Fort Worth Metroplex, less than five hundred beds provide a safe haven for women and children who must flee from their homes—from their spouses. At Hideaway Hotel, we give them a new start. We call it a hotel instead of a home because we want these women to get back on their feet and check out—into a safe, new life."

The shelter director's words landed in the pit of Rachel's stomach. Her cheeks felt flushed and she dabbed a napkin to her forehead.

Michael gently squeezed her hand. "Rachel, are you okay? Hot flashes again?" he whispered.

"I'm fine," she said and continued to wipe her brow. The squeal of the amplifier shrilled in her ears.

Dr. Amparo stood center stage in the ballroom, imploring the audience to pay attention to the plight of women. "Can we count on each and every one of you to become the village for these displaced citizens of our world? Let Luella Perkins, a success story from Hideaway Hotel, tell you in her own words what your contributions have meant to her and her three daughters."

A woman in a simple skirt and sweater took the microphone. In a throaty voice, she said, "Hello, everyone, my name's Luella Perkins. I'm here tonight because my husband, Raymond, couldn't find me to kill me."

"Can you believe she's spilling her guts to a bunch of strangers?" Rachel whispered to Michael. She hadn't mustered the courage to tell her husband the whole truth about her turbulent life in her youth. She tried to bury the memories of her father's behavior, but with Luella's poignant story, they started racing to the surface. "I just didn't feel like going out tonight, Michael." She took a sip of champagne, but the cool bubbles didn't stop the heat rising in her. "I know tonight's a big deal to your client since it's his favorite cause. It was nice of Trent to invite us to his table." She reached over and gave Michael a quiet kiss.

Luella Perkins faced the audience and began her tale of spousal abuse. She took a deep breath and said, "Hideaway Hotel gave me the chance for a new life. I thought there was no hope for me and my kids. I just couldn't break the cycle of abuse until I found that little piece of heaven on earth, and Dr. Clara Amparo and her staff literally saved my life."

"Saved my life," echoed in Rachel's mind. *I found safety and love when I married Michael.*

As a girl, she had looked for security when she spent time with P.J. Even today, she pictured her best friend as that shy girl who rarely spoke up around adults. Rachel and P.J. shared their own private jokes, like the conspiratorial glances they exchanged after the bovine invocation at the ranch house dinner.

Growing up, Rachel's family ate meat fairly often because it was plentiful in Dallas and cheaper than chicken at the A&P grocery store. When Mama dared to make meatloaf or some other sensible dish, such as Frito-pie casserole, she and her two sisters, Hedy and Lenora, temporarily united in their refusal to eat it—one of the rare instances they ever agreed on anything.

Rosy always prepared a well-balanced meal: a salad, some meat, a starch and dessert—usually Jell-O, banana pudding, or occasionally icebox pie. Rachel had relished the smells of the kitchen when her mother scurried about to get supper ready on time for when her father got home from the plant.

"Mama, how about Dr. Pepper tonight?" Rachel asked.

"All that sugar will rot your teeth. Dallas tap water's got fluoride in it—good enough for us." She commanded in rapid fire, "Hedy, set the table; Lenora, make sure your room's clean before dinner; and Rachel, get your homework done before you come to the table."

Hedy, a tomboy who was beginning to notice boys, haphazardly bunched the silverware in a pile at each setting. Glancing over, Mama instructed her, "Nice people put the knives and spoons on the right and the fork on the left."

In their house, there was only one knife and only one fork. No tiny tines to confuse the issue like at P.J.'s fancy dinner table.

Silvery strands of gray slipped in front of Mama's eyes as she whipped the potatoes. Once her thick mahogany tresses had framed her striking heart-shaped face. She had been considered the most beautiful Jewish girl in Dallas in her day. Boys asked her out for lunch, afternoon sodas, and nighttime dates as soon as she was allowed to ride in a car without a chaperone. She had her pick of any boy at Cedar Ridge High. Although her name was Sharon Rosenshein, everyone called her Rosy. It suited her personality.

Rachel often rummaged through the boxes of old photos with torn edges where some adoring beau had wrapped his beefy arm around her mother's tiny waist. In one of her favorite shots, teenaged Rosy stands in a seductive pose like a movie siren with heavily rouged lips. Sunlight glints the dark tendrils caressing the straps of her bathing suit that accentuates her curves. Rosy could have had any man she desired.

Rachel longed for a safe place, for a happy family like on her favorite television program, *Father Knows Best.* But danger always hovered over her low-slung house in North Dallas, like a brewing Texas thunderstorm.

Rachel's father always had a number of reasons to start fighting with her mother; Rosy could never do anything that pleased Danny. Sometimes the smallest thing would set him off.

"Did you pick up my cigarettes?" he would ask.

"Meant to, but I forgot—I had to get carpool, and then Rachel came down with an asthma attack, so we went straight home."

"Godammit, I ask you to do one thing, and you can't even manage it!" Papa screamed, his face reddened and his eyes narrowed with anger.

He pulled her arm and dragged her into their bedroom. "This drawer's where they belong, and it's empty, bitch! I only ask you to pick up my fucking cigarettes. Is that too much?"

From her adjacent room Rachel could hear a deep thud of a weight against a wall, like a sack of potatoes dropped on the kitchen counter.

"When I say do something, I mean it. You hear?"

Rachel didn't hear any other voices except Papa's bellowing from behind the closed door.

"I'm sick and tired of all of your lazy shit. You had plenty of time to go flirt with the pharmacist, but couldn't go get my Lucky Strikes. Well, this is the last time you're going to forget to get them, I'll guarantee it!" he hollered.

Heavy footsteps marched down the hall. Then the front door slammed, causing tremors on the shelf with Rachel's collection of porcelain animals above her bed.

Mama flipped the switch of the bedroom overhead light. Rachel squinted, unaccustomed to the glare, and focused on the rhinestone-tipped sunglasses that sparkled around her mother's face. Rachel had seen Hollywood stars in magazines wearing them indoors, but her mother never did.

"Quick, get up and let's go, girls!" Mama called from the doorway of the room that Rachel shared with Hedy.

"Where to?" Rachel asked.

"Leaving your Papa. Hedy, help your sister put a pair of blue jeans and a shirt in her bag, and don't forget your toothbrush."

"Hedy, should we put on our sunglasses, too?" Rachel asked as she climbed out of bed.

"Shut up and get ready, stupid!" Hedy said in her scariest voice. "We're leaving now. Get your own damn things ready!"

Mama moved on to the next bedroom. "Lenora, get some clothes on. Let's go! . . . Now!"

"Where's Papa?" Lenora mumbled and settled back under the covers.

"Out to get cigarettes," Mama replied from the dim hallway. "Lenora, get up—now!"

Heavy-lidded, Lenora finally emerged from her room, clutching her overnight duffel and her record case. To smooth the kinks, her thick black hair was coiled around orange juice cans she had covered with a paisley scarf for the car ride.

"Leave the records. We'll get them later," Mama said.

"Can Gypsy go, too?" Rachel asked. P.J. had given her the miniature ceramic horse from her vast collection at the ranch. Rachel longed to call her friend to say she was going away, but it was the middle of the night and she was forbidden to use the phone at such a late hour.

"Okay, take Gypsy, but make sure you wrap her in plenty of tissue so she won't break. Girls, let's go. Go get into the car!" Mama said in a cracked voice. She bent the blinds, tipping her sunglasses to peer out the window. The street was still and dark—no sign of Papa's new white Chevrolet Impala.

Mama put her small blue suitcase into the trunk and slammed it shut. Rachel and her sisters climbed into the car, stumbling over each other like the Three Stooges.

Lenora yelled, "You two creeps get in the back. I'm oldest, so I get the front."

Hedy and Rachel claimed their respective territory on each side of the hump. Hedy covertly mouthed to Rachel, "Coo-dees."

"I am rubber and you are glue," Rachel shot back.

Mama shouted, her hand flailing in the back seat like a feral animal, "Knock it off! Rachel, shame on you for taunting your sister. No talking—that means everyone!"

Hedy grinned so widely that the hole from her missing back molar showed.

Mama dug her hand in her pocketbook and fished for the car keys, glancing down the street and then looking back into her purse. "Where in the Sam Hill are they?" she muttered. "Stay here and lock the car doors. I'll be back in a sec."

She darted back into the house and hunted for her keys. Rachel could see her mother through the kitchen window; the refrigerator clock glowed while her search became more frantic. She finally spotted her keys on the kitchen table next to the aspirin bottle and grabbed them before making a dash for the car.

The girls waited for their mother to return to the car. Rachel feared that their escape from their father was getting off to a rocky start. Lenora leaned over and unlocked the driver's side door for Mama to get in. She shoved the key in the ignition, but the Ford Fairlane only sputtered and coughed like one of Rachel's asthma attacks. Rachel peered out the back window and saw the wide-set headlights of Papa's car at the end of the block, heading their way, sending shivers through her body.

Mama stomped on the pedal a few times, whispering, "Come on, come on!" The engine clattered, then started. She burned rubber, tearing into the street and headed in the opposite direction from the oncoming lights. The three sisters didn't utter a sound, stunned by their mother's wild driving and fear of their father.

Mama turned right on Preston Road without obeying the stop sign. The girls had never witnessed her running a traffic sign before. She wove between the few cars that were on the road at that late hour and then quickly swerved onto a quiet side street. She passed a few houses and then pulled into a gravel driveway and cut the headlights. Four heads turned simultaneously to watch the white car turn onto the street. Rachel ducked down in the back, holding her breath while Papa sped by in a blur of light. He passed the driveway where they were hiding in the open but kept going until his red taillights were tiny embers.

A porch lantern flashed on, flooding the front of the house and driveway in a dangerous white beam. A figure appeared from inside, barely visible from behind the screen door. The eerie light streaming into the car revealed Mama's face. Her eye was swollen almost shut and looked as dark as the shadows across her right cheek.

"Mama, he's going to catch us. Let's go!" Rachel pleaded.

Gravel popped and scattered as her mother pulled onto the street. Sharply turning left, they were back on Preston Road.

"Where are we going now?" Hedy broke the silence in a quivering voice.

"You wouldn't like it if *I* drove the way you are," Lenora taunted.

"We're leaving your father. You know this isn't the first time he's done some bad stuff. We need a hotel tonight, then I'll figure out what comes next tomorrow."

Rachel thought she heard soft sobs from Hedy, but it was too dark to see her face.

"Rachel, you're awfully quiet back there, honey bun. You all right?"

"I'm okay, Mama." The faint squeal of wheezing punctuated her words.

"Hedy, get her inhaler out of my purse and give it to your sister."

She rummaged around. "It's not back here, Mama. Lenora must have it up front."

Lenora felt blindly on the floor and located the purse. She reached in and found the small plastic bottle. "Here, catch!" She tossed it into the back seat. "You're such a big baby, Rachel, always looking for attention."

The inhaler flew past Rachel and became lodged somewhere between the bed pillows and the clothes. The whistling in her chest grew louder. She gulped for air, her panic steadily building.

Hedy reached between the crevices of the back seat and retrieved the bottle. "Here, Squirt, take a squirt."

Rachel breathed deeply, inhaling the medicinal cloud that stung the back of her throat. The vice around her bronchial tubes slowly began to loosen.

Her mother just kept driving. Lenora dozed in the front seat, slumped against the passenger door. They passed deserted shopping centers and restaurants. At times, Mama hesitated at some hotels but then continuing driving. Rachel suspected they had passed the same streets before, noticing the same stores they had whizzed by earlier. Then Mama slowed down and pulled into the parking lot of the Thunderbird Motel on Greenville Avenue, a street dotted with neon signs from dance halls and bars. "Vacancy" flashed in red, like a beacon of hope on the plate glass window.

"Lenora, wake up, we're here. Girls, stay in the car while I check in. Lock the doors! And don't open them to anyone until I come back," Mama said.

She rang the buzzer. Through the window, the three sisters watched their mother talking to a scraggly man in the lobby. She handed him her charge-a-plate and then he gave her a key with an object attached to it.

Mama approached the car, her lips tightly drawn. She opened the door and said, "Our room is on the second floor near that outside staircase." She tossed Lenora the key with a large blue plastic thunderbird dangling from it. "Take your stuff and go open the room—Number 207. I'll get the two girls and their things. Go ahead, sweetie. We'll be right up."

After another spray of the epinephrine, Rachel's chest opened up— the delicate airways expanded. She slowly climbed the stairs, clutching her overnight bag while dragging her pillow. She couldn't wait to unwrap Gypsy to find out if the horse's tail was still intact after the wild ride. Hedy and Mama were behind her, almost banging into each other when they stopped at the doorway to gawk at the room. Sad, filthy curtains hung lopsided from a few loose metal hooks. Multicolored lights from the taverns across the street streamed through the gaps where the fabric panels didn't meet. The waffled spreads on the two double beds were a suspicious shade of gray, and Rachel wondered if they had once been white and cheerful.

Mama let out a sigh that grazed her throat. She straightened her back and exclaimed, "Super! Lenora and I'll bunk together. It'll be fun. You two take the other bed. Rachel, honey, what are you standing there for?" Mama's knee gently pushed Rachel into the room. "It's just fine. Besides, we won't be here very long." A weak smile emerged from the lines on her face. She put down her suitcase and then neatly folded back the spread. She plopped on the bed closest to the door and flipped off her shoes, sending them like little missiles across the room. "Let's get ready for bed, girls."

Rachel slipped into her pajamas with the little cows leaping over the moon and got under the covers. She always thought about her best friend whenever she put on her PJs.

Mama walked over in her bare feet on the stained shag carpet, leaving footprint impressions. She made the rounds, kissing each of her daughters. Rachel felt comforted by her soft lips against hers, but Lenora only offered her cheek to her mother.

Mama climbed in next to Lenora and said, "Better not kick in your sleep!" She reached to turn off the lamp with the crumpled shade and then removed her sunglasses, placing them on the nightstand. She whispered, "Don't worry, little ones, we're safe here."

Rachel felt the scratchiness of the sheets soften as she drifted toward sleep.

A heavy fist slamming against wood shattered the quiet. "Open up this fucking door! I know you're in there!"

How in the world did Papa find us? Rachel wondered in disbelief. She started to whimper, and Hedy's warm legs touched hers under the covers. Lenora sat up, eyes wide and unblinking, while Mama crept slowly toward the door.

"Danny, go away. Quit yelling and just leave," she called back in a trembling voice.

"You're coming home with me *now!* I'm not leaving without you. What the fuck do you think you're doing, Rosy?" He banged again on the flimsy door, rattling its wooden jam that suddenly seemed like cardboard. "Open this damn door. I'm your husband!"

Someone in the next room shouted from behind the thin walls, "Y'all, keep it down! We're trying to get some shut-eye here!"

Mama looked around the room and didn't spot a phone. "Sorry, sweeties, when the man at the desk said we could use the lobby phone, I never imagined we wouldn't have one in our room. No way to call for help." She crouched next to the door and pleaded, "Danny, don't keep yelling. Calm down and we'll talk."

"I'm okay now. Just come on home with me. This is no place for our girls. You can keep the chain on. Just open the door so I can hear you better," he said, his sharp tone softened.

She flipped the latch and cracked the door so the safety chain allowed about four inches of air between the two of them. "Rosy, I'm not going to hurt you. Things will be different. Let me prove it to you. I don't want to lose you and my girls. There's nothing to be afraid of." He pressed on the door. The chain held tight and straight.

"Please don't let him in. I figured we were finally safe," Rachel whispered like a prayer. In the dim light streaming through the door, she got a good look at her mother's right eye, swollen and deep purple like a bunch of rotten grapes.

Dark fingerprints had emerged around Rosy's smooth left arm. She grasped the tarnished chain and slid it along the track. It dropped, hanging limply. The door swung open and Danny stood in the doorway, his muscular body silhouetted against the neon street signs. Wet streaks on his cheeks glistened in a rainbow of colors.

One foot at a time, as if in slow motion, he moved into the room. "Okay, we're heading home. Leave everything and get into my car now. Game's up! Rosy, get a move on!"

"Papa, can we change into our jeans first?" Rachel asked, trying to make her lip quit quivering. She sat frozen on the bed.

"Just come home in your PJs. It's okay, Red. I'll come back tomorrow and get your stuff."

He grabbed his reluctant wife's arm tightly and pulled her down the stairs, her feet tripping on each other, but she kept going. The girls followed one after the other—Lenora first, then Rachel headed down. Hedy's damp hand rested on her neck as they slowly descended the flight of stairs. The three sisters hunkered down in the back of the Chevy. Lenora got the hump, but this time she didn't complain. Rosy sat up front. They rode in silence, afraid to speak, with only the sound of Rachel's labored breathing in the backseat.

The next morning the parents dropped off their daughters at religious school, saying they would retrieve what was left behind at the hotel while they were in class. At a quarter to twelve, Papa drove through the parking lot, making his way to the front of the passenger loading area. The girls piled in and took a short trip across the street to Jake's Steaks and Shakes for lunch where other families from the synagogue frequented. The Millers passed by the turquoise and hot pink vinyl booths but just kept walking to their table, eyes forward. Mama wore her sunglasses and didn't wish anyone good *Shabbas*, as she usually did on the Sabbath.

When they returned home, Rachel went to put away her things, but when she reached the bottom of her overnight bag, a sick feeling washed over her. Two things were missing: her pillow and Gypsy. She tore through the bag again, but her prized possession wasn't there— the horse that P.J. had given her. She flew into the den and pleaded with her mother, "I need Gypsy. She's gone. We've got to go back and get her. Ple-e-ase, let's go save her before they throw her away!" Rachel's sobs slurred her words.

Mama just stared out the window. "Sorry, honey bun. I'm afraid we can't ever go back there again."

BUILDING BLOCKS

CHAPTER 3

M ICHAEL EYED RACHEL with concern while the rest of the group was focused on Luella Perkins's moving presentation. "Rach, we can get out of here if you want," he said, squeezing her hand under the table.

"All right, meet me in the lobby in a couple of minutes." She feared a loose tear might betray her uncontrollable feelings. She nodded her excuses to their tablemates, and Michael's client Trent winked again when his wife wasn't looking.

As Rachel barreled into the ladies room, the click of her heels on the marble floor pounded in her ears, like a tiny firing squad. She slid the lock on a stall and sat on the down-turned lid, racked with sobs. In the distorted reflection on the metal door, her freckles peeked out from under the layer of foundation, and rivulets of mascara streaked down her cheeks.

Got to get a hold of myself. She tried to quell the emotion that had built up like an oil well spewing all to kingdom come. *What the heck am I crying about? The past is over. I love my daughter and husband, and Michael's the one man I can trust.* But the tears kept coming.

The glare of the headlights of their Mercedes swerved into the covered portico of the hotel. The valet escorted them to the car and waited until Rachel collected herself into the passenger seat.

"Thanks, buddy," Michael said while palming him a five and collapsing into the driver's seat, his knees crunched close to the steering wheel. He fiddled with the seat controls and the rear view mirror, mumbling, "Why do valets always screw everything up?"

"Uh, so he could touch the pedals; he's not six feet like you." Rachel's mood was beginning to lighten as they swung out of the driveway onto the snarling traffic on McKinney Avenue.

Michael actually was tall, dark, and handsome—a fabled combination Rachel never thought she'd end up with. She attributed his good looks to the kindness in his dark brown eyes and in the way he carried himself. He had no excess baggage—no little blue suitcase to drag him down—while she felt she had enough to keep her own personal porter busy for a lifetime.

A gifted architect, Michael chose to build structures that are enduring and original—works meant to withstand the test of time in form and function. He graduated from Cornell but chose to hang out his shingle in his beloved Texas.

His career choice aptly fit his solid and stable nature—character traits that were part of the reason Rachel chose him for her mate. She had wanted a home that couldn't be shaken by uncontrollable and unpredictable forces, and she believed Michael was both her parachute and safety net.

Pulling off McKinney onto Harwood Street, Michael pointed out the window at his latest project. "What's so hard to understand about my rooftop design for the Rutherford Plaza?"

An abstract lattice of beams and steel cable crowned the structure. He leaned out the window to get a better look. "I designed it to represent the oil economy of the past and telecommunications of the future. They call that bank tower with green neon the 'Jolly Green Giant,' so no telling what Rutherford Plaza's nickname will be."

"'Pick-up Sticks Place'?" Rachel said, trying to coax a smile.

"People still remember the Pegasus sign on the First National Bank Tower, but that flying red horse has been gone for decades. How about something new in this town?"

"P.J.'s driving in from Austin for the Grand Opening and I can't wait to see her."

"She's the only good one in her family. Rutherford was such a bear to work with. Remember, it took forever to get the plans signed off? Thank God, they didn't insist on an oil well fountain in the new lobby!" he said.

"There's one too many of those in this world!" Rachel laughed, feeling restored, remembering the sound of the gusher fountain at her friend's ranch house.

"If you and P.J. weren't so tight, I might've scrapped the whole deal. The project's been a bitch from start to finish!"

Michael complained how he was often kept waiting at the old eight-story Rutherford Building. To add insult to injury, his design sensibilities were assaulted by the cut pile carpet with double Rs in a lobby that looked like a stampede—with a scattering of overstuffed, cowhide armchairs. And the antiquated offices were without a hint of the high-tech world.

Michael stopped for a red light and stroked her arm. "That obsolete conference room . . . and those gawd-awful red walls!"

"Yeah, Rutherford corporate crimson," Rachel replied, recalling how the trappings of the business were cloaked in that garish hue— from company jets to beer cozies. "P.J. wouldn't be caught dead in that color."

"So I'm sitting there thinking of how I can bring them into the twenty-first century, when Lynda Gayle Rutherford appears, trailed by her assistant, Mitzy, who points that I'm supposed to sit between Tweedle Dee and Tweedle Dumber, a couple of guys in polyester suits," Michael said.

"Mrs. R's running the show now. Hey, she likes you more than she ever liked me," Rachel said, thinking how her best friend's mother never really made her feel welcome.

Lynda Gayle Rutherford had assumed the catbird seat of the Rutherford empire after Russell Rutherford suffered a massive stroke caused by a tiny aneurysm that had lurked in his rotund belly for over a decade. Smoking his Cuban cigars and his predilection for plates brimming with barbecued beef ribs contributed to his decline. A couple of stiff drinks in the evening—and often in the afternoon—had fortified him against the pressures of employing thousands of people in three states, but the stress and his lifestyle finally caught up with him.

After depositing her husband into the most upscale care facility in Dallas, Lynda Gayle picked up the reins of the business while he languished in a hospital bed.

Michael conceded that Lynda Gayle had big plans for the company, which he discovered was seeded with her money. The irony that Rachel's closest friend's mother was her husband's biggest client hadn't escaped her. She always walked a fine tightrope to protect her relationship with P.J. and preserve Michael's association with the challenging Mrs. R.

Michael and Rachel pulled onto their street and aimed the remote at the gate. Reflections of the wrought iron spread across the hood of their car. The gate swung open wide, and then the doors to the three-car garage revealed spaces for Rachel's Beemer, Michael's Mercedes sedan, and their daughter Missy's new white Mustang convertible.

Rachel and Michael had surprised her with the Mustang as a high school graduation present months in advance of the actual ceremony. She shrieked with joy when she walked into the garage and found it in place of the eight-year-old Volvo she'd been driving for the past two years. Her first car had been a safe and reliable vehicle, but in her words, it wasn't exactly "the bomb."

The top of the gleaming Mustang was rolled back. Missy gleefully examined her vanity plates, "M-I-S-T-X-S." "Oh my God, is this for real?" she squealed.

Missy gathered her strawberry blonde hair into a ponytail and pulled the thick, straight lock through the back of The University of Texas baseball cap her parents had left on the car seat for her. She climbed into the palomino bucket seat to test the fit and turned the key to rev the engine. "Thanks, Mom and Dad. You two really rock!" Forgetting to kiss them goodbye, she roared into the street. "I'm going to show Jillian. She'll just die when she sees my car!" she called out from the open sports car.

Missy's relationship with Jillian paralleled that of Rachel and P.J.— friends for life. The two resembled each other and some people mistook them for sisters. Missy never corrected the mistaken identity because she was an only child and craved having a sibling. Rachel would tell her: "Believe me, the fantasy of having sisters beats the reality."

When Missy drove away, Michael said, "Let her go show her best friend. Did you expect her to be seen riding around with us?"

"No, not really. But I don't think we could have given her anything better for her graduation." Michael and Rachel high-fived each other as they watched their daughter disappear down the road.

Their moment of glory was as short-lived as a fireworks display. A few weeks later, Missy screamed, "You're the worst parents on this friggin' planet! I can't believe you're not letting me go to the all-night party! What century do you live in? This isn't like the Dark Ages when you were growing up."

"Melissa, no seventeen-year-old daughter of mine's going to stay out all night in a hotel room after prom. No way!" Visions of "ruffies," underage sex, and potential lawsuits spun through Rachel's head.

"Everybody does it. It's totally safe—we'll all be in the hotel together. I promise, nothing's going to happen," Missy switched gears, pleading in her most angelic voice.

"That's right! Nothing *is* going to happen because you'll be home by two, that's late enough. End of discussion!" Rachel shouted and wondered, *When did I become my mother?*

Missy stormed out of the room and slammed her bedroom door. Her plans for the prom involved three couples; the girls were splitting the limo and the boys were handling the prom tickets. With the cost of the dresses, hair, makeup, nails, shoes, and limo, the evening would set the girls back some considerable cash. Rachel and Michael were amenable to paying for the transportation so the kids wouldn't be driving around after hours. Although they felt it would have been more responsible to forbid Missy, they finally caved in to their daughter's pleas. Rachel wanted to keep her safe—just like her mother had tried to do on the late night escape from her father through the streets of Dallas.

CHAPTER 4

WHEN MELISSA WAS BORN, Michael and Rachel paid tribute to the last titian-haired ancestor before Rachel—grandmother Bubbie Malka Rosenshein—by naming their daughter "Melissa." Following the Jewish tradition, they honored a departed loved one, not the living. There are no juniors, seconds or "Tripps" for Jews.

Her paternal grandmother, Marlena, contended that Missy was actually named after her, even though it wasn't exactly "kosher" to do so because she was still alive. She pulled Rachel aside and averred it again at Missy's baby naming.

A month after her child was born, friends and family assembled for a *Simchat Bat* service to rejoice the arrival of a daughter. Rachel was free to pick any date, unfettered by the restrictions of a male birth that require a circumcision rite on the eighth day of life. From the beginning, she was sure that having a girl would be much easier than raising a boy.

On a tangerine and rose-tinged October evening, the setting sun signaled it was time for the service to begin. The proud new parents made their way through the maze of cars from the parking lot toward the entrance of the synagogue. Rachel clutched a ceremonial spice box in one hand and enlaced her husband's fingers with the other. Michael cradled Missy in the crook of his arm. Rachel dismissed the tight knot in her stomach as a case of stage fright before having to be on display in front of the congregation.

Her heartbeat slowed to a steady trot from a gallop when they entered the synagogue. The soaring white walls of the sanctuary eased her tension. Rows of Stars of David—deftly woven in silver and gold threads—adorned the arc of the covenant. Above the altar, a twisted brass lantern cradled the flame of the Everlasting Light that twinkled with the continuity of a faith that has lasted for generations.

Michael grabbed a purple yarmulke from the basket at the entrance, and Rachel stood on tiptoes to center the precariously tilting cap on his head of full, dark hair. They entered the sanctuary that was buzzing like a beehive, with the chatter of *kibitzing* people who were busy greeting each other and snatching bits of gossip.

Missy looked resplendent in her lavender velvet frock with a matching bow clipped to her few wisps of strawberry blonde hair. Michael and Rachel promenaded down the aisle with their daughter safely nestled in her father's arms. The brass spice box decorated with enamel hearts and six-pointed stars felt cool in Rachel's hand. The rabbi had suggested the use of spices as metaphors for the parents' hopes and dreams for their child, which at first had seemed like an odd tangent, but during the months of planning, they grew to embrace the concept.

Michael and Rachel nodded and smiled at the congregation comprised mainly of their friends and family. Wafting strains of the organ gradually stifled the conversations.

Rachel looked around the room, fixated on how different it was from when she was young. Her parents hadn't held a baby naming ceremony for her. She had burst into the world two months ahead of schedule, a little blue prune weighing less than three pounds. With premature lungs starved for air, she was rushed into an incubator—her cocoon for three months.

Her life had been as fragile as a twig. In the chaos of trying to stabilize a critically ill infant, her birth certificate was filled out only with "Baby Girl" where the first name should have appeared. Her parents hadn't settled on what to call her, and the first days were filled with fear the infant would lose her battle to survive. About a month after she was born, when they were sure that she was going to make it, they decided on Rachel Laura, in honor of her Great Aunt Rivka—just about the only thing they ever agreed on.

Only when Rosy enrolled her youngest daughter in elementary school did she discover that the name on Rachel's birth certificate was still "Baby Girl Miller." The document was eventually legally amended, and Rachel finally received an official name that had been overlooked in her parents' endless battles.

Rachel longed for Missy to have a proper welcome into this world. Melissa Janelle Frank deserved more than the first few months of life in a Tupperware container with air vents, deprived of the touch of loving hands and the taste of mother's milk.

Michael and Rachel decided to hold the baby naming at a *Havdalah* service on Saturday night, the celebration of the end of Shabbat. Rabbi Sachs wore a tweed sports jacket with leather elbow patches instead of priestly robes, and his yarmulke was attached with a silver hairpin.

He took Missy from Michael's arms and whispered in her ear, bouncing slightly to calm her. He looked into Missy's face while he recited the opening prayer: "We distinguish the Shabbat from the mundane days of the week. It celebrates the sacred from the secular. We're especially joyous to welcome Melissa Janelle Frank into a covenant with God and the Jewish people." He held aloft a silver chalice and recited a blessing over the wine. Missy's light green eyes followed the goblet. She gurgled like it was part of a game. The rabbi handed the baby to Michael and stepped back, taking his seat on the chair to the side, leaving Rachel at the microphone.

Family and friends had been asked to select a spice and write a little paragraph about how it pertained to the baby's future. Rachel had typed all of their comments and mailed scripts of the service with instructions for the participants to rehearse their parts.

She knew hers by heart but carried the paper in case she got the jitters. Rachel smoothed the folded white sheets on the lectern and recited, "We light the candles and say prayers over the wine, but only at *Havdalah* do we bless aromatic spices, *besamim*. These delicious scents are intended to boost our spirits and dispel the sadness in our lives." She glanced around the room and smiled at Mama, who was sitting on the first row near Rachel's two sisters and their families. P.J. and her husband, Juan, were seated on the second row.

Rachel's breathing felt labored when she spotted the empty seat next to her mother. A thought kept floating up to the surface that couldn't be pushed back. After the divorce, Papa hadn't been a part of the important milestones of her life, and now he wasn't there for her child. She picked up her notes to keep her place in the service, but the letters blurred. With the back of her hand, she pressed an insistent tear resting on her cheekbone.

She inhaled deeply and continued, "This spice box should remain with Missy for the rest of her life. We'll ask some of you to come forward and fill it with spices that will remind her of the joy, hope and love that surround her today and always. Michael, you're first."

The scent of talcum and baby oil floated in the air. Michael handed Missy to his wife, and the baby's Pillsbury doughboy legs flailed about, revealing her purple velvet panties trimmed with white lace. He took the spice box, opened the hinge, and sprinkled a few flakes of rosemary into it, saying, "This fragrant herb is to stimulate her quest for knowledge. Try to learn something new each day and keep an open mind."

Rachel felt like her whole world was next to her on the altar. Michael's lips brushed against the tufts on the top of Missy's head. She giggled at her father's touch.

Mama was next in line to add her spice. Her friend Irene's deep, gravelly whisper could be heard for several rows. "It was such a *shanda* at first, the shame of it. I don't know how Rosy ever had the nerve to show herself in public after the split. I'm not sure she ever got a *ghet,* a *real* Jewish decree. Funny though, she's never seemed happier—a real poster child for divorce." People nearby shushed her to be quiet, since her voice carried loudly.

Rosy had lost the look in her eyes of a fox that was being chased by the hounds. After years of living alone, she had regained her energy and spirit. Her beauty had dimmed like that of an aging film star, yet there were traces she was once stunning. Golden frosted streaks replaced the dull gray strands that used to outline her face.

Michael held out his hand to escort his mother-in-law up the three steps to the altar. Her legs were still shapely, and some of the older men in the congregation sat a little straighter as she climbed the stairs in her leopard high heels. She smiled with bright red lips and adjusted the microphone. Beaming at her newest grandchild, she said, "My darling little Melissa, I fill your spice box with thyme—for courage to get you through the tough times that I hope will be few and far between." She shook a bottle of green herbs. "Know that all things improve with thyme." Rosy smiled with satisfaction at her pun, stopping short of taking a bow, just tilting her head before returning to her seat.

Rachel thought about how her mother enjoyed every day of her life to the fullest.

P.J. and Juan worked their way down the long wooden pew to the aisle. Hedy and Lenora huddled together whispering as Rachel's friends prepared to speak on the altar. Hedy's husband, Walter, held their son Jack in his lap, who was fidgeting. Lenora had haltingly apologized that her husband was out of town, but he was rarely present at family gatherings.

Rachel's siblings glared at her and then shifted their focus on P.J. and Juan. A wave of guilt flooded over Rachel, figuring from her siblings' reactions, she had made huge misstep to schedule her best friend before them. Although her sisters were inconsistent about when blood was thicker than water, and she surmised this was one of those times.

Five-year-old Jack bolted from his seat and darted down the aisle. Hedy ran after him, calling, "Jack, get your little *tushie* back in your seat right now!"

From the pulpit, P.J.'s light blue eyes glistened, catching the rays from the Everlasting Light. Juan stood at her side and rested his hand on her shoulder. In a strong, clear voice she said, "This is my first time to be part of a Jewish service. I do believe in miracles, and I see one when I look at this child. I remember when Rachel and I were little together. It's hard to believe it wasn't just yesterday."

P.J.'s porcelain fingers grasped Missy's tiny hand that reminded her of the Betsy-Wetsy baby dolls she and Rachel used to play with and change toy diapers. P.J. said, "Melissa Janelle, how about if I call you M.J.? I bring you purple lavender to spark your creativity—and to match your pretty little outfit! When you inhale the scent from the box, you can't see its color, but you can smell its exquisite aroma. As an artist, I believe you need beauty and creativity in your life so your soul can soar to amazing heights. Juan and I feel honored to be here." Together they said, "*Mazal tov!*"

Irene's foghorn voice could be overheard saying to Rosy, "Now I've heard everything—a *shiksa* and a Mexican speaking Hebrew!"

Hedy corralled her son back to his seat. Jack's shirttails had escaped from his trousers, and he dragged his tiny jacket along the carpet on the aisle. Rachel began to feel even more remorseful that others were to participate before her sisters had their turn. The two women's stares bore through her with laser-like precision.

Grandma Marlena and Grandpa Izzy tottered their way to the front. They haltingly read their parts with a delivery that sounded like a three-second delay. They recited in similar, but not totally synchronized, rhythms, "We bring our great granddaughter the staples of cooking: salt and pepper. Remember this—when families eat together, they form a bond at the end of the day."

Grandma Marlena leaned forward and said solo, "And Melissa, most of all, don't forget to tighten the lid on your horseradish bottle during the Jewish holidays!" She gave Rachel a knowing look.

Finally, Hedy and Lenora stood in front of the congregation to add their grains of knowledge and hope. Their taut voices stumbled over their lines like it was the first time they had ever laid eyes on them, clearly never having rehearsed. Missy twirled in Michael's arms during their speeches, cooing loudly. Her cascade of gurgles caused even her tense aunts to erupt into laughter, and the congregation delighted at the baby's impromptu contribution to the service.

Rachel was prepared to add the final scent to complete the spiritual mixture, without the need to refer to her script. She held the glass bottle over the brass opening as if she were pouring precious diamonds into the box. "*Gingi* means 'redhead' in Hebrew. So, my darling daughter, I bring you ginger—the spice of independence. Keep an open mind, but be strong enough to make decisions and carry them out." Her vocal chords tangled like a vine. She inhaled deeply, closed her eyes, and continued, "I pray you'll grow up to be a strong, loving woman with an independent spirit."

Rabbi Sachs's hands gently cupped Melissa's head. He sweetly incanted Hebrew prayers that had been offered from generation to generation.

Rachel bowed her head and prayed silently, "Just let her grow up to be a good person and to be proud of being Jewish." The good wishes and the spices floated through her thoughts—thyme, rosemary, and ginger—noting that all she needed was parsley and sage to complete the mixture! Her mind wandered to the times in her past with Mama and Papa and then back to the present with Michael and Missy. Then she felt a comforting surge, thinking how kind it was for P.J. and Juan to secretly practice saying "congratulations" in Hebrew as a surprise.

Grandma Marlena hugged Rachel tightly in the reception line at the Oneg supper after the baby naming. She had given Missy the velvet dress for the special occasion. A blur of people rushed around to grab a chicken wing or a piece of marble cake from the buffet tables.

Rachel's grandmother pulled her aside, intimating she had some private words of wisdom to impart. With a twinkle in her eye, she said, "Tell Melissa to always remember: It's never a *shanda* to be poor—just to dress poorly."

Rachel wrapped her arms around her grandmother's girth, laughing and jiggling.

Rachel began to realize that her child would get various kinds of advice during her lifetime—some of it valuable and some not. She deeply inhaled the bouquet of spices mingled in the box and gazed into Missy's wide-open eyes.

The people present were important to Rachel and added their spice of life to the ceremony. A hole in her heart widened when she thought about her father who wasn't there to welcome his granddaughter into the world.

Rachel hadn't had any contact with him for over eight years since he moved to California to work in the fledgling computer industry. He acquired a new family with a woman who had two boys of her own. His abandoned daughter wondered how well he treated his stepsons.

When the checks ended for Rachel's college tuition, she never heard from her father again after graduation. Papa had lived up to his obligation to educate his three daughters but was never required to pay monthly child support. Mama had only wanted to escape from a doomed marriage. She had traded her financial security for the promise that her children would get an education and be able to support themselves.

Michael and Rachel agreed on having a religious baby naming in the temple instead of at home. Rachel was brought up more a cultural Jew, while he came from a traditional Jewish home. In the rush of everyday living, they both chose to forego most of the rituals of their heritage but now wanted their child to have a connection to Judaism in her life. They never routinely lit the Sabbath candles or served braided challah bread on Friday nights before Missy was born.

When Rachel was growing up, her father only allowed the family to celebrate the big four holidays—Rosh Hashanah, Yom Kippur, Passover, and Chanukah—in the most cursory way. She used to joke that she was surprised he didn't use a stopwatch to time their Passover Seders. Her family rushed through the ritual meal, jumped immediately to the recitation of the customary four questions, downed a few cups of wine, and went directly to singing the closing song, "*Dayanu*," which states any one of God's miracles would have been enough. Rachel wondered if Papa had done anything to stay involved with her, would it have been enough?

As a child, she and her siblings weren't allowed to talk much at the table during the holidays. At one Seder when she was five-years-old, Grandma Marlena served cold red beet borscht. When Rachel took her first spoonful, it seared her mouth and her tears dripped into her bowl.

Papa continued to eat his. Noticing her reluctance, he slammed his spoon on the table and commanded, "Rachel, stop playing with your food and finish your soup right now!"

"But it's hot!" she protested, resting her spoon.

"Everyone knows borscht is cold. Not another word out of your mouth!" he escalated to a shout.

Spoonful by painful spoonful, she downed the vile broth that stung her lips. Tears ran down her face with every mouthful, but she finished the bowl.

When it was time for the next course, Rachel trailed her grandmother as she cleared the dirty dishes into the kitchen. She spotted Grandma Marlena picking up an empty, overturned bottle of red horseradish. She bent down and whispered to her maligned grandchild, "So that's why your borscht was on fire."

The grandmother went back out to collect the rest of the dishes and never uttered a word in Rachel's defense about the discovery. After that, Rachel never fully trusted Grandma Marlena again.

Sometimes Rachel complained to P.J. that she felt cheated about her father's absence in her life. In turn, P.J. confided about her never-ending struggles with her hard-as-nails mother.

FAIR GAME

CHAPTER 5

L YNDA GAYLE RUTHERFORD had become one of Michael's biggest clients over the years. Missy often wondered how her parents maintained contact with P.J.'s mother, who had little communication with her own daughter—Rachel's best friend. It was an awkward situation everyone danced around.

Michael was careful not to let slip mention of Lynda Gayle in front of P.J. The painful wounds in her heart had hardened into resentment as tough as keloids.

Missy and Rachel swore to each other that they would never let anything come between them. When Missy went away to college, they chatted on the phone several times a week, and sometimes her sorority sisters teased her about being a big baby who was still attached to her mother's umbilical cord. Rachel told her daughter they were probably jealous over their great relationship. She would answer her cell no matter where she was or what she was doing when Missy's ID scrolled across the screen. Missy's voice refreshed her mother.

Michael said, "Rachel, you and Missy blow out the phone plan every month."

"Money well spent. At least she stays in touch." Rachel was proud that the lines of communication were strong between Missy and her.

"Discussing which shade of cashmere twin set to buy for her isn't exactly quality time."

"It is when she's using our credit card! I'd rather for her to enjoy what she gets than have it sit in her closet."

"Think we'll get the card back when she graduates?"

"I want her to be independent, but it's fun to spoil her because she's so good. She never gives us a lick of trouble," Rachel said.

She was thrilled when Missy called to say she was coming home for Texas/OU football weekend with Jillian. Although Rachel had some mixed feelings because she knew from experience what a crazy—and possibly dangerous—event it was, she was happy her daughter would be back in Dallas for a couple of days.

Most people in the suburbs steered clear of downtown when the game was on. The streets transformed into a wild block party where police were the only chaperones present.

Rachel figured the pranks must have gotten much wilder and more elaborate nowadays. She and Michael unilaterally decided they would tell Missy to be back from the game by 12:30 a.m. Rachel didn't want to go through a sleepless night, wondering when Missy would get home. At school she could do whatever she wanted, but under their roof she'd have to abide by their rules.

It was music to her ears when Rachel heard the hum of the Mustang pull into the driveway from Austin. Missy flew into the house, gave her mother a quick kiss, and darted up to her room. Rachel sighed with relief that life was back to normal. Her daughter was in her room and on the phone, her natural habitat.

Michael and Rachel decided to go to the State Fair of Texas with Missy and Jillian before the girls headed over to the stadium at Fair Park. They took two separate cars so the teens could stay and party after the game.

The first time Rachel attended the Texas/OU game, she and her friend Christie drove to Dallas for the weekend. They stashed their stuff at Rachel's parents' house and bolted out the door right after they arrived. They headed to Fair Park, the site of the Cotton Bowl, passing cars covered in streamers and balloons, jam-packed with kids clad in either red for Oklahoma or burnt orange for The University of Texas. Shouts were exchanged between vehicles and body parts hung out of open windows. Although it was October, convertible tops were peeled back and students teetered on trunks, anchored by their feet resting on the back seats or on other students' shoulders.

The traffic snarled through the city streets. Rachel and Christie finally made it to their bleacher seats just in time for the kickoff. The girls were more interested in scoping out the stands for hot guys than watching the game. Rachel had never been much of a football fan, almost a cardinal sin in Texas.

In high school, she had been the head of the Pep Squad—the group of girls who weren't cool enough to be cheerleaders but had an overabundance of spirit. Rachel enjoyed creating the colorful flip card formations that P.J. would help her design on grid paper. P.J.'s private girls' school didn't have a football team, so she relished the chance to get a taste of the gridiron.

At Rachel's first college away game, The University of Texas handily won the match with their greatest rival school, the University of Oklahoma at Norman. She figured there would be hell to pay after she and Christie escaped the jammed parking lot at the stadium near the grounds of the State Fair of Texas and headed for downtown.

"Let the games begin, yee-haw!" Shelly yelled out the window.

Rachel's car swerved to the left, avoiding a car that veered into her lane. Beer was flowing in the vehicles all around her, and someone hurled a bottle at her side of the car. The barrage of exploding glass startled her, and luckily, didn't shatter the window.

Cars were stacked in row after row in gridlock. Guys got out and milled around in the middle of the street, weaving between vehicles. A boy dressed in baggy red O.U. sweats turned around on Christie's side and yanked down his pants. He wiggled his lardy butt and yelled, "Longhorns, you can kiss my ass!"

The girls laughed and were grateful that was all he showed them. They yelled back, "Better dead than red!" and burst into fits of giggles.

Christie's cheeks were flaming from laughing so hard and silly tears rolled down her face. She shouted, "Man, there's a big ass moon out tonight!"

Rachel used to look forward to going to the State Fair every year when she was a kid. When she was twelve, her family piled into Papa's white Chevy Impala with the long fins, a land boat, and took the expressway to Fair Park in South Dallas. Once they got off the highway, they passed neighborhoods that looked nothing like the manicured yards of North Dallas. They headed down Grand Avenue, passing slumped houses with wooden siding that barely had enough paint to decipher the original color. Old folks in broken-down rockers rested on their rickety porches, and children played in the yards under the shade of towering oak trees. The area was teaming with people walking the streets or hanging around their houses. Most of them were black. Rachel didn't have any friends in Dallas who weren't white. Camp was the only place she had contact with any minorities.

The family passed liquor stores and pawnshops on the way to the fair grounds. Papa pointed out that he grew up a few blocks away, where most of the Jewish families had lived before they moved to the suburbs across town in North Dallas.

When they entered the Fair, Big Tex was always there to greet them. He was an enormous cowboy, as big as an office building, measuring fifty-two feet tall. In a booming drawl he shouted, "Howdy folks! Welcome to the State Fair of Texas." His papier-mâché face beamed in a perpetual, mile-wide grin. The brass plaque at the base of the statue bragged in Texas-sized terms how it took seventy-two yards of denim to make his five-pocket jeans. Faux mother of pearl snaps fastened his red cowboy shirt with embroidered arrowheads adorning the collar. Rachel wondered where they kept him silently cooped up in storage during the year.

Big Tex had started out as a Santa for a department store Christmas display in a little town near Corsicana—billed as the world's largest Santa Claus. The Fair bought him for seven-hundred-and-fifty dollars and transformed him into the world's biggest cowboy. He made his debut at the State Fair of Texas when Rachel was a year old. She had started bawling in her stroller when she first laid eyes on the gigantic cowboy.

The Fair was divided into two sections: the exhibition halls and the midway rides. When he dropped off the kids, Papa doled out five dollars to each and forbade his daughters from playing any of the rip-off carnival games.

They were allowed to take along a pal to the midway. Hedy, Lenora and their friends snaked along the line for the Texas Sidewinder roller coaster. Rachel and P.J. agreed they were too chicken to ride it. Watching the people screaming on the loops and hairpin turns, Rachel's stomach began to flip flop, and she hadn't even gotten in line yet.

She and P.J. fibbed that we were going to check out the prized piglets in the 4-H exhibit. In an uncharacteristic fit of defiance, they went directly to the "throw-a-nickel-into-the-dish-and-win-a-baby-chick" game, never even coming close to a member of Future Farmers of America Club. The two girls tossed coin after coin onto the table full of colorful bowls, glasses, and compote dishes that gleamed like jewels under the spotlights. The shower of change created a symphony of plinks against the glass. Not one of their nickels stuck to its target. The money bounced off the dishes, spun around, and rolled onto the floor. Fluffy yellow peeping chicks, like little powder puffs, tugged at their heartstrings. Neither girl had considered an explanation if they had actually won a prize.

Coins flew through the air and missed the mark. Rachel and P.J. conceded their defeat and headed down the crowded aisles to rejoin

Rachel's sisters. Amid the intoxicating scent of cotton candy and caramel-coated peanuts, the carnival barkers called to them like sirens luring sailors to the rocks. "Wanna win this pink teddy bear, little lady? Just throw the baseball and she's yours."

Rachel plunked down two quarters on the counter and grabbed a metal bucket of balls. She lined up the stitched seams of the ball in her hand and carefully aimed at the pyramid of chipped wooden milk bottles on a dusty black platform. Soon she was addicted to the challenge and handed over dollar after dollar to the cashier in exchange for silver coins. She continued to lob balls at the milk bottles over-handed, and when that failed, under-handed. The bottles wobbled but never toppled, just like her Weeble toy family at home. She glanced at her watch, stunned to find an hour and five minutes had elapsed. She hoped she could meet up with her sisters before they discovered her ruse.

No such luck. As Rachel and P.J. crossed the bridge from the Fun Zone, they spotted Hedy and Lenora pointing at them. Hedy's eyes narrowed as she spat out, "Wait till Papa hears what you've been doing. Your goose is sunk!"

Lenora's lips curled in a smirk, "You're not supposed to gamble. You're gonna get it, Rachel!"

Panic rose from Rachel's stomach to her throat, and she began to wheeze. She sputtered, "We were just looking for the baby farm animals. We heard the chicks peeping and thought . . ."

"Oh yeah? Let's see how much money you've got left," Hedy countered.

Rachel shoved her hands deep into her jeans pockets, digging around for any stray coins that were left. P.J. walked over to Hedy, and like a magician, pulled a five-dollar bill out of her purse and waved it in Hedy's crimson face.

"Rachel asked me to hold onto her money. It's hers and you shouldn't take it away from her!" P.J. said, widening her stance.

Hedy shifted her feet and crossed her arms tightly. "I . . . I wasn't going to take her money."

P.J. smoothed her flip nonchalantly. "Rach, I'm starved. Let's go get some Fletcher's corny dogs."

Lenora took a menacing step in front of them. She spoke with a note of parental authority, "From now on, we'd better stick together. I'm in charge and Papa would want me to keep an eye on you kids. I'm hungry, so let's all go get some dogs on a stick."

Even as an adult, Rachel still drove to Fair Park every October to get a corny dog, a vice she couldn't shake. She still craved the batter at Fletcher's that fried up golden and crunchy on the outside and fluffy on the inside. She covered it with a ribbon of mustard and ate her way down the stick until she picked off the last remaining bits of crust that clung stubbornly to the wood.

When she asked Missy to accompany her, her daughter crinkled her nose and said, "Mom, how can you eat that poison-on-a-stick? It's full of nitrites and enough fat to clog anyone's arteries."

"At least I pass on ordering cheese-on-a-stick," Rachel replied, making excuses for her annual indulgence.

She and Michael entered the State Fair with Missy and Jillian. A new and improved Big Tex had added a fresh trick to his repertoire: his huge arm mechanically waved while he shouted "howdy" to the crowds. Big Tex even sported spanking new duds. His legs were bowed like a cowboy's should be from years in the saddle. His massive boots had a spit polish finish, and his belt buckle glistened in the afternoon sun.

"Curfew's twelve-thirty! If you're running late, call us," Rachel called out to Missy.

"Don't worry, Mom. We'll get home on time. You and Daddy, be good at the Fair and don't blow your money on any sucker games!"

She had heard Rachel's stories about how the grandfather Missy never knew thought the games were fixed and had repeatedly lectured that it required little skill or brainpower to win the prizes that cost a fraction of the money spent on playing for them. The mathematical odds of winning were stacked against the players, whom he said were "dumb schnooks who couldn't resist the challenge."

Rachel and Michael rode a few of the tamer rides, ate the ritual corny dogs, saw a few prized bulls, and then headed home. In their bedroom, Michael grabbed her waist, pulling her toward him. "Get any ideas from those prized bulls?" he asked.

"Yeah, they reminded me about how much BS is slung around here!" Rachel said and pretended to run away in fear of reprisal. Then she yanked off her sweater and waved it like a toreador.

He stamped his feet on the rug and charged forward shouting, *"Olé!"* They clung to each other and sank down on the carpet, making love with renewed passion—their excitement heightened at having the house to themselves, even though their daughter had been back in town only a few hours. They felt like a couple of teenagers left to their own devices while the parents were out for the evening.

After their tryst, they went downstairs to grab a snack.

Rachel looked into the refrigerator and shuffled around the food. She said, "My back is killing me from our little romp on the floor. You know, I couldn't eat another bite after my second corny dog! You look a little funny, what's up?"

"My stomach's doing flip-flops, probably due to your damned dog addiction! Let's go back upstairs. It's closer to our big bathroom!"

They listened to the game on the radio, since television coverage was blacked out for the Dallas/Ft. Worth metro area. The crowd roared behind the jubilant announcement that Texas trounced O.U. The couple turned off the radio and kissed lightly before crashing for the night.

Rachel awoke with a start around midnight. Her back felt clammy and her nightgown clung to her body. A nightmare had shaken her, but she couldn't quite remember it, noting that fast food often gave her disturbing dreams.

The house was soundless. She got out of bed, careful not to wake Michael, and tiptoed down the hall; the carpet felt soft and plush under her bare feet. The door to Missy's room was ajar and the desk lamp cast a slice of light into the hall. Rachel peeked in and found her daughter's bed empty.

Sleep eluded Rachel. The minutes dragged—soft green letters on the alarm clock glowed 12:15, 12:16, and then 12:30. She propped herself on her pillow—poised, waiting to hear the rumble of the Mustang. She got up and punched in Missy's cell phone number. No answer. 1:10, still no sign of Missy. At 1:35, she tapped Michael on the shoulder and whispered, "Honey, Missy's not home yet. She's over an hour late. I called but she didn't pick up."

He slurred his words in semi-sleep, "Maybe she's out of range. She'll be home soon." He turned over and dozed back to sleep.

Rachel's breathing grew shorter and sharper with each passing moment. Scenarios spun through her mind: Maybe Missy and Jillian had been in a wreck; maybe someone had slipped them some drugs. Her head was filled with what might have happened. She turned on the lamp on the night table.

Michael stirred, one hand shielding his eyes from the light. "What time is it, hon?" Now *he* sounded worried.

"It's late. Think we should call the police?" her voice rose on the final word. "Why didn't she call us, Michael?"

"You two use the cell at the drop of a hat. Look, Rachel, I'm sure she'll come up with some cock and bull explanation. Let's try to stay calm." Michael got up and went to the bathroom. When he returned, he sat on the edge of the bed, resting his chin in hand.

The phone rang, electrifying the tension in the room.

Michael lunged for the receiver. "Yes, officer . . ." A long pause hung in the air.

"What? . . . What?" Rachel asked between every sentence. She tried to lie still enough so she could figure out the puzzle of the one-sided conversation, wishing her heart would beat more softly.

"How long have they been there?" Michael asked. He motioned for Rachel to bring him his pants, which were lying on the floor near her blouse that had been the matador cape.

She moved closer to him, hoping to hear the voice on the other end of the line. "Is she okay?" Rachel whispered, her panic rising.

Michael angled the receiver so his wife could listen, too. "What's a Class C misdemeanor?" he asked.

More talk on the other end of the phone that Rachel couldn't make out.

"We'll be right down. . . . Yes, thanks, put her on." The thin lines on his forehead deepened in the uneven shadows of the room. "Hi, sweetheart," Michael said in a soothing, fatherly voice. "We'll talk about it when we see you. Don't cry—your mother and I are on the way." He returned the receiver to its cradle and put his arms around Rachel. "It's not all that bad. Missy's okay. She and Jillian were busted for underage drinking. I'm not surprised about Jillian—but Missy?" Michael zipped his fly and put his keys in his pocket.

"And for *that*, they put her in jail? I'm going with you!" Rachel threw on her slacks and sweater as if someone had pushed a fast-forward button.

They drove downtown in silence, both deep in thought. Rachel's pulse began to return to a normal rate. The very idea of Missy getting arrested made her madder than a hornet, but it also chilled her to the core. "Don't the police have anything better to do than to arrest kids?" she muttered under her breath.

Michael didn't respond.

Then her anger slowly focused on Missy. "What in the hell was she thinking?" We trusted her. Why'd she get into so much trouble?"

"Big-time lack of judgment."

"At least she's not hurt. I bet Jillian put her up to this."

"Rachel, let's find out what really went down and then we'll figure out the right punishment."

They completed the route to the police station without further conversation. Rachel didn't even feel like listening to the radio because she was bombarded by her thoughts.

Michael and Rachel trudged up the concrete steps and passed through the heavy metal door at the station. A desk sergeant sat behind a long counter covered with stacks of papers, a fingerprint inking pad, and a sign-in log. Michael signed their names and absentmindedly put the pen in his pocket.

"The pen—put it back!" she whispered. "You're stealing!"

He smiled for the first time since they had received the phone call and dropped the pen on the counter. Rachel turned around and didn't see Missy in the waiting room. *Please, God, don't let her be sitting in a cell with who knows what.*

"Take a seat and we'll call you in a few minutes," the sergeant said. Twenty minutes passed and they were still waiting uncomfortably in the plastic molded chairs with rickety metal legs. Rachel felt she had already counted the hours long enough during the night, but she stared at the large round clock looming above the desk counter. Finally, the sergeant looked up from his papers and said, "Mr. and Mrs. Frank, come this way."

Down flat gray corridors, past closed office doors with detectives' names on the doorplates, the nervous couple entered a holding room. Missy and Jillian were encamped in the back row of chairs, with their heads bent down as if they were dozing. A couple of dozen teens filled the room, and the smell of barf and alcohol permeated the stale air.

Detective Harris called out, "Melissa Janelle Frank. Jillian Fay Sanderson. Come up here to the front."

Missy's slouched frame snapped to attention and she lifted her head. Tears rolled down her face when she saw her parents at the front of the room, staring at her with steely faces. Jillian's folks lived farther away, so Rachel figured they were still en route. The girls worked their way up the aisle.

"I'm sorry, ya'll, really sorry," Missy sobbed. Her nose ran and started to turn red and raw.

Rachel rummaged through her purse to find a clean tissue. When she handed it to Missy, their fingers touched, but she didn't grab her hand to hold it tenderly.

Michael addressed the detective, "Exactly what happened?

"Your daughter and her friend were picked up at Cisco's Bar. A plain-clothes officer on duty for Texas/OU weekend observed Miss Sanderson drinking a cocktail and watched Melissa show an ID. The bartender questioned its validity and summoned the officer. The photo remotely looks like your daughter, but it probably belongs to one of her friends."

Missy studied the floor while he spoke and Jillian fidgeted with her hair.

"When he questioned them, your daughter had an attitude and demanded her license back. She hadn't been served yet, but under Texas law, the officer had to confiscate her ID, along with the false one Miss Sanderson finally coughed up."

"What's a Class C misdemeanor? That's what we were told Missy was charged with," Michael asked.

"It means a court date will be set. If she pleads no contest, she'll be subject to court costs, probably about a hundred dollars. Then she'll receive a probated sentence that requires community service along with state-run alcohol awareness classes. Miss Sanderson will probably have to forfeit her driver's license for a year because she was caught drinking." He turned toward Missy and Jillian and said sternly, "Even though this is a misdemeanor, you were breaking the law. This could go on your permanent record."

"Yes, sir," Missy mumbled. Her eyes were dry now, but they widened with the officer's threat. She shifted her weight, while Jillian chewed on a stringy strand of hair.

"Mr. and Mrs. Frank, you can take your daughter now. Hopefully, the punishment you'll dish out will hit home how dire the consequences could have been. Miss Sanderson, take a seat until your parents show up."

Missy and Jillian briefly hugged, whispering to each other. Jillian plodded back to her chair next to the boy with putrid stains on his orange sweatshirt. Michael and Missy signed the papers in triplicate and handed them, along with the pen, to Officer Harris.

The three of them walked down the hall in single file—Michael, Rachel, and then Missy. They passed by the desk sergeant, who never glanced up. Out the metal doors, the trio emerged into the cool night air that made the police station seem stuffy and foul by comparison.

Once they got into the car, Michael began his own interrogation. "I want to hear exactly what happened, young lady. Start from the beginning!"

A little voice arose from the back seat. "We were all hanging out after the game. Then we stopped by some parties in hotel rooms and just chilled. It's not like anyone was doing keg stands. Then Marcia, a sorority sister who's a junior, wanted a ride to Cisco's. It was about eleven-thirty, and I thought I had plenty of time to drop her off and still make it home by curfew."

"What about phoning us—and what the devil is a keg stand?" he asked.

"It's when someone stands on their head and drinks from the hose on a keg. Honest, Dad, I've never done it. I'd hurl."

"Thank God for small favors," Rachel added, running her hand over her forehead.

Missy continued between sniffles, "Marcia borrowed my cell and called her boyfriend to tell him where to meet us. I guess she stuck it back in her purse. She wanted us to come inside and wait with her until John showed up. Jillian had a fake ID, so she knew she'd get by the bouncer, but I didn't have anything."

Michael kept his eyes on the road, and Rachel didn't turn her head to the backseat to look at Missy while she told her story. Rachel's neck was still stiff from the afternoon of lovemaking on the floor, so she just let her daughter keep talking.

"Marcia handed me her sister's ID, who's blonde and twenty-two. We got in okay and scored some seats at the bar. Jillian ordered a margarita and was served—no problem. I just ordered a Coke. Then I decided to get a beer, since I had an ID that had worked at the door. The lights at the bar were pretty dim, mainly those neon beer signs, so I figured the bartender wouldn't notice it wasn't really me in the picture. When I handed it to him, he whipped out a flashlight from under the counter." Missy took a big gulp of air. "When the beam of light hit it, I knew I was toast. I asked for it back and started to get up from my stool. Instead, he handed it to an older guy in a baseball cap who was standing behind me, blocking my way to the door. He flashed a police badge and then started talking to Jillian. He made her show her driver's license, and he snatched that one, too, and made us get into the squad car, so her car is still in the parking lot a Cisco's, if it hasn't been booted by now." She sucked in a deep breath and waited for her parents to say something.

"And then what?" Michael asked.

"He said we could make a call to our parents when we got to the station."

"Melissa, this is serious stuff!" Michael barked while glancing into the rear mirror. "For one thing, you know better than to drink and drive. We trusted you, and you blew it! I could have sworn you had better judgment than to pull this kind of crap. Tomorrow your mother and I will pick up the Mustang from the club. If you didn't have to get back to school, we'd take away your keys. Rachel, want to add anything?"

Rachel turned to take a look at Missy, who appeared so small and miserable in the backseat. "Just that I am very disappointed in you. We'll talk about it tomorrow."

They drove the rest of the way home in silence.

CHAPTER 6

IT WAS ALMOST IMPOSSIBLE for Rachel to remain angry with Missy, who usually stayed on a straight path and avoided serious trouble. Rachel thought of the time she herself had strayed as a teen and felt some compassion for her daughter.

On Thursday nights, Rachel attended Cotillion, a combination of dance lessons and etiquette that most seventh graders took from a dance academy in a converted Safeway in a shopping center. The girls wore white gloves and stockings and hoped the boys they had crushes on would ask them to dance and press against them.

Feeling gawky, Rachel stared at her open closet for at least thirty minutes, imagining herself in each outfit on the dance floor.

Hedy tiptoed into their room and whispered from behind, "If you think you're going to look cool, forget it! Doesn't matter what you pick 'cause you'll still be a dork."

"Go soak your head in the toilet!" Rachel muttered under her breath, just loud enough for her tormentor to hear.

Rachel ruefully looked in the mirror. *She's probably right. I am a dork.*

Hedy had been elected cheerleader of the junior class of Preston High. As her ego swelled, she became harder to live with by the minute. A former tomboy, her fearless athleticism paid off when she finally slimmed down and filled out. Even so, when Rachel riffled through her sister's dresser drawers one day, she uncovered a stiff padded bra wrapped in a full slip. She figured Hedy wanted to make sure the boys would notice her curves through her thick cheerleader sweater.

Rachel fretted she didn't have enough tits to "lift and separate" in her Playtex Cross Your Heart bra. She contorted in the mirror to center the slit of her half-slip. Mama always said: "Good girls never leave the house without doing the slip test," instructing her daughters to stand in front of the window to check if she could see the V between their legs in the light.

Rachel snapped a plain garter belt in the front and slid it around to the back. She didn't have enough heft to wear a girdle but needed it to hold up her silky nylon stockings. She hooked the garter clips and smoothed her legs, imagining herself a model in a hosiery commercial. She lifted her plaid dress from the Sanger-Harris department store bag and admired it. Although she had been saving it for the upcoming Jewish High Holidays, she pulled it over her head and painstakingly fastened the long row of plaid fabric buttons.

She looked in the mirror. *Maybe this week Stewart will notice me.*

Mama dropped her off at the Town North Dance Academy, where her classmates were hanging around the front. P.J. sat balanced against the window ledge, looking perfect with her blonde hair combed in a uniform flip held in place by a good coating of Aqua-net. A circle pin adorned the bodice of her dress, just above where her emerging shape was visible beneath dark blue velvet. She giggled with Stewart Braverman, her hand covering her mouth, never taking her eyes off his handsome face. His muscled arm rested on the wall above where she was sitting.

Rachel called out to them from the car window, "Hi, y'all."

The couple turned her way, but only P.J. waved. Rachel struggled to get out of the car, holding her dress down in front as her legs spread apart.

P.J. walked over to her, and then the two friends entered the dance hall together, taking their seats with the other girls in a row of metal folding chairs along the wall. Carrie Anne was dressed to kill in her new outfit. Rachel's friend Christie wasn't allowed to attend Cotillion because she was devoutly religious and couldn't dance. P.J and several others were also Southern Baptists, but they did the latest steps—and Rachel had even seen P. J. take a sip of beer.

The first number at Cotillion was the waltz. The dance instructors, Mr. Jimmy and Miss Irene, picked members of the class to be their partners. Mr. Jimmy—with his slim waist and slicked black hair—extended his hand to Rachel. She grabbed his long fingers and walked to the center of the floor. Miss Irene—lithe and willowy in a cream chiffon skirt and black leotard top—selected Roy, the shortest boy in the class, at five feet. The triple stanzas of the "Blue Danube" wafted through the ballroom, mixed with the scent of English Leather and Jungle Gardenia.

"One, two, three and one, two, three, and . . ." Mr. Jimmy counted aloud while they danced, for the benefit of the other students. Rachel's teeth clenched tightly as she softly followed the count along with him, looking down at his feet. "Chin up, Rachel. A lady only looks into her partner's eyes."

He firmly clasped her waist, his guiding hand stiffened as they whirled around the room. In the midst of a spin, Rachel spotted P.J. waltzing with Stewart. The space between their dance plane was closer than hers with Mr. Jimmy. P.J. was smiling into Stewart's warm brown eyes, and they were perfectly in sync.

"Rachel, you're off count. Let the beat of the music talk to you." Mr. Jimmy stopped abruptly. "Begin again. One, two, three and one, two, three and . . ." After a few more trips sailing around the dance floor, the "Blue Danube" ended. Mr. Jimmy bowed curtly from the waist with one hand behind his back. Rachel clumsily did a short curtsey, feeling exposed in the center of the dance floor.

Mr. Jimmy announced to the crowd, "Now, let's pick up the pace with a little number by Chubby Checkers called 'The Peppermint Twist.' Remember to imagine you're squashing a bug with both feet while you are drying your back with a towel."

Rachel noted the instructions that came with Lenora's twist record said to act like you were stubbing out a cigarette, but she figured Mr. Jimmy had to clean it up for the young participants. Wishing she could dance with Stewart, her hopes were dashed when Jason asked to be her twist partner. P.J. huddled with Carrie Anne, since they weren't picked, and Stewart started doing a mean twist with Miss Irene. His hips and arms twirled in all directions like a whirligig.

After the number, Miss Irene took the microphone. "Girls, it's time for the song you've all been waiting for—the Sadie Hawkins dance. It's the great Southern tradition where a gal can ask any guy she fancies to dance. Y'all, get ready to pick your favorite partner on the count of three. One . . . Two . . . Three!"

Rachel sprinted across the dance floor—the great divide between the boys and the girls—to the row of chairs on the other side of the room. She skidded to a stop in front of Stewart, beating Carrie Anne by a fraction of a second. P.J. remained in her seat, her hands folded neatly on her lap.

As tradition dictated, Rachel asked, "Stewart, may I have the honor of this dance, please?"

"Sure, Rach. Let's get it on."

In a backwoods twang like Sadie Hawkins, Miss Irene said, "Okay, y'all, let's see your fox trot. The fellas are hot to trot, and you gals look pretty foxy."

Mr. Jimmy set the needle on the record, sending crackling scratches over the speakers playing "What is this Thing Called Love?" Stewart held Rachel closer than Mr. Jimmy had moved around the dance floor with her. The thumps in her chest seemed to drown out the music, and her armpits dampened with each verse. She wondered if Stewart could feel her heart pounding.

Rachel hoped her palms weren't damp. Stewart gripped her strongly in perfect dance position and twirled her on the turns, making her head literally spin. Her slip peaked out from under her dress when she swirled with abandon.

The notes faded and Mr. Jimmy announced, "It's time for intermission, young ladies and gentlemen. Help yourselves to punch and cookies in the lobby. Ten minutes, everyone."

Stewart kept his hand on the small of her back. As the couple headed toward the refreshment table, he whispered, "Rachel, let's get out of here."

She turned and waved meekly to P.J. across the room. P.J. looked away and sipped her punch with Carrie Anne, giggling at their private jokes.

Stewart and Rachel sneaked out the front door and headed down the alleyway where the lights from the shopping center were dim reflections in the puddles of water. Amid dumpsters and dilapidated cardboard boxes, they huddled in the dark.

He reached inside his sport coat and pulled out a cigarette. He snapped a single wooden match and a flame popped off his fingers. "Wanna drag?"

"Uh huh." Not taking her eyes off his face, Rachel took a shallow puff. The searing smoke assaulted her temperamental lungs. After a brief coughing fit, she sputtered, "I'm okay. It's just been a while since my last drag." Rachel shuddered, thinking Papa would kill her if he found out she was smoking.

Stewart wrapped his arms around her waist and pulled Rachel close to him. The stench of rotten food clung to her nostrils, and a feral animal scurried behind a box. He pressed his wet mouth next to hers. His hot, smoky tongue pushed her lips open and probed her mouth— a sensation that was sweet, and yet annoying, at the same time.

"Rachel, just breathe through your nose and open your mouth," he instructed.

Their faces tangoed to find a comfortable fit. It all seemed to be working fine until his hand inched up from her waist and slid over her barely perceptible breasts.

She pulled away, breathless, and moaned, "I've never been French kissed before, much less been felt up."

"Just let me touch you. It's cool; don't worry. I know you're into me because you picked me for the Sadie Hawkins dance."

She let his hand drift down the front of the shirtwaist, passing over the row of little buttons. Her head began to spin when she heard the Cotillion music start again. Intermission was over, but they didn't budge from the alley.

After their session of deep kissing, her lips felt raw and swollen. She noticed people shuffling out of the dance center and pulled away from his embrace. "Stewart, I've gotta go. Mama will be here any minute to pick me up."

"Okay, no sweat. See ya around, Rach." He swaggered back to his group of friends who had gathered near the curb.

P.J. brushed past Rachel when she surfaced from the alley into the light. P.J. slid into the backseat of her car, gathered the hem of her dress, and Maddy shut the door of the long white Cadillac. She looked at Rachel with still eyes through the closed window but didn't wave.

Rachel clutched her queasy stomach, wondering if she felt ill from the cigarette or from Stewart's last remarks—or from how she had treated her best friend.

Rachel learned something about her own desires that night in the alley with Stewart. She had dropped P.J. the same way Stewart ditched her after that night of petting and making out. She had pushed her friend aside when she thought P.J. would get in the way.

She didn't spend the night at P.J.'s the weekend after Cotillion. Although Rachel slept over most Saturday nights, P.J. didn't mention getting together. Instead, Rachel moped around the house, listlessly dressing and disrobing her Barbies. In Rachel's play world, her Ken doll got a little frisky flirting with the other dolls that weekend, but he remained technically faithful, so her Barbie forgave him.

In Monday morning homeroom, P.J. came up to her old friend before the class bell rang. "Want to go to Northpark Mall on Saturday?

We can go for lunch at the Mermaid counter at Neiman's and then stop by the Melody Shop to check out the guitars."

"Far out!" Rachel was relieved to know she had been missed as much as she had longed for P.J.

"I want to get the new *Joan Baez in Concert* album. She sings my new favorite song, 'Don't Think Twice, It's Alright,'" P.J. said with a smile.

Rachel knew it would take more than Stewart Braverman to destroy her friendship with P.J. Years later, when they were laughing about seeing him at her twentieth high school reunion, Rachel divulged that he had apologized for being such a jerk by never calling her after Cotillion.

Stewart had also said P.J. was wise not to have accepted his offer to go out with him, because he was just an oversexed, hormone-crazed kid who wasn't worthy of either of the girls.

With Stewart's confession, Rachel realized P.J. had never told her that Stewart asked her for a date that week after Cotillion. Rachel had expectantly watched the Princess phone on her bedside table for days, hoping to hear from him. She frequently checked to make sure it hadn't been accidentally knocked off the hook or the line hadn't suddenly gone dead.

Rachel was aware that P.J. always protected her feelings and never wanted to hurt her best friend, showing real class. P.J. was there for the important times in her life.

They had been childhood friends, and then P.J. shared in her joy when Rachel passed the threshold into motherhood. She embraced Missy as the daughter she could never have.

THE HANGOVER

CHAPTER 7

RACHEL HAD STARTED TO CALM DOWN from the trip to the police station to collect Missy, but Michael was still fuming. Once they were in the house, Missy tried to crumble the cold war between her parents with the oldest excuse in the book, whining, "Everybody uses fake IDs!"

"Well, you're not everybody, but if you keep acting this way, you certainly *will* be," Michael said, tight-jawed. "We'll continue this tomorrow. Go take a shower and let's all get to bed."

The next morning, Missy dragged downstairs and slid onto her chair at the kitchen table. She got up to make herself a bowl of her favorite cereal—fishing to gather a pile of colored marshmallow bits on her spoon. After a few scoops, she left most of it uneaten.

While washing the breakfast dishes, Rachel noticed that the smooth space between her daughter's eyebrows constricted every time the metal pots and pans banged together. Rachel tested her theory and clanged a few lids together like crashing cymbals. On cue, Missy winced in pain.

"Missy, your hangover's step number one of your punishment. I'll come up with the rest," Rachel said icily. Her suspicions that she had been drinking even before they arrived at the bar had just been confirmed by the rendition of the "1812 Overture" performed on stainless steel lids. Rachel tallied Missy's offenses in her head: She had not only gotten into trouble with the police but had also lied about drinking. Rachel was sure it was a night all of them would remember for some time to come.

"Talk about disappointment! Believe me, this isn't over yet. We need to find a lawyer, and then you've got to get back here from school to show up for court. Anything to say for yourself?"

Missy's eyes turned wet and glassy. "Mom, I'm really sorry. Everybody had beer at the party. No way I could say no, and then Marcia wanted to see John. I'm really sorry, Mommy. I swear it won't happen again."

Rachel mused how she was seldom called "Mommy" anymore—just when Missy wasn't feeling well or was in trouble and needed help. She wanted to hold out her arms to feel Missy's body pressing tightly against her but pushed back the urge, administering her on the spot version of tough love.

"You'd better turn your act around, starting right this minute! That means buckling down at school until you get back home to sort this thing out."

"Okay, Mother," Missy answered tartly, her lower lip jutting out slightly.

Rachel fretted that she was "Mother" again. She and Michael drove to the bar to pick up the Mustang, the lone vehicle in the parking lot. Missy stayed home to gather her things for the drive back to Austin. She had to wait until afternoon to pick up Jillian, who needed a ride back to campus. Rachel figured Jillian was in no better shape than Missy and wondered if the Lucky Charms had worked magic on her daughter's hangover.

Michael went his separate way to play tennis after the trip to Cisco's. Rachel was relieved the Mustang hadn't been booted or impounded. She drove it home. The car reeked like a stale ashtray, but she decided not to go down that road with Missy for the moment.

Missy piled her books and rolling duffel stuffed with clothes into the trunk. She adjusted her UT baseball cap, pulling her glossy ponytail through the back strap. The afternoon sun filtered through the rust and gold trees, setting them ablaze with color. She lowered the convertible top for the ride to Austin.

Although Rachel was still miffed, she leaned over the car door to give Missy a kiss. "Don't speed! There's a speed trap at Hillsboro near the overpass. Don't forget to call us when you get back to your room."

"Okay, Mother. I said I'm sorry." Missy gunned the engine to punctuate her response.

"Hope to God you've learned something from this whole mess. Drive carefully, honey bun." The car was already in the street, and Rachel wasn't sure if she had been heard over the roar of the V8 engine.

Rachel went upstairs and stripped the linens that still held her daughter's sweet scent. She spread out the comforter and placed Missy's teddies and beanies the way her girl liked them, lined up across the ruffled pillow shams. Although Missy wasn't a child anymore, she still decorated her bed with her favorite stuffed animals. Rachel hadn't had the heart to cover up the border of vines and sunflowers she and P.J. had painted when Missy was a baby.

Rachel cleared away enough plush toys to make room for her head and collapsed from fatigue on the bed. She fell into a deep sleep, exhausted from being awake most of the previous night.

She drifted into an off-kilter dream in which she was so small that Mama had tethered her on a leash so she wouldn't get lost in the crowds at the Texas State Fair. Rosy had dragged her closer to the gargantuan cowboy statue to read the inscription on the plaque. Baby Rachel strayed as far as the cord would stretch because Big Tex frightened her. His booming voice shouted "Howdy!" while his enormous hand swung back and forth waving to the people below. Then in a split second, a gust of wind blew up, and she heard a splintering sound. His hand plummeted to earth, about to land directly on Mama. Frozen with fear, little Rachel stood there bawling, unable to do anything to save her mother.

The slam of the front door awoke the adult Rachel at around six o'clock. Her armpits were damp, and tears stained the pillow sham. For a minute, she couldn't place where she was. The bed felt too soft and unfamiliar, then she remembered dozing off in Missy's room. She repositioned Missy's stuffed animals in a row and called out cheerily in response to Michael's greeting.

"Up for a movie before it gets too late?" he asked.

"Check what's playing while I get ready." Rachel went their room to change her blouse and freshen her makeup.

She and Michael grabbed a quick Chinese meal at the food court after the flick and returned home after nightfall. Rachel was relieved that the outdoor lights had automatically clicked on, so the house didn't look deserted when they approached. She already missed hearing Missy roaming around upstairs. Even though her daughter had been home for only two days, the swirl of activity and music that emanated from her room had made her mother feel happy. Rachel stashed her purse on her desk in the kitchen on top of a pile of unread magazines and glanced at the answering machine to see if Missy had called yet. The light was static. No messages.

CHAPTER 8

T O RACHEL, the house was like a safe nest when Missy and Michael were under its roof. But it always felt a little empty when her daughter was away at school, even though she was only four hours away by car.

She and Michael bought their home shortly after they married. Because of its prime location, they couldn't pass up the modest, low-slung ranch-style, devoid of distinguishing architectural features. Michael was eager to put his creative stamp on their living space.

Missy was born in that three-bedroom house. Rachel had carefully selected the color for the nursery: yellow, a safe choice for either a boy or a girl. At twenty-six, she was still young and healthy enough that an amniocentesis wasn't necessary, and she preferred not to have a clue about the gender. She couldn't wait to have a family of her own.

When Rachel was pregnant, she asked Michael, "What do you want—a boy or a girl?

"Hun, if it's a girl, she'd better have a good throwing arm like her mom at camp, and if it's a boy, he ought to be a whiz with crayons—like his dad and 'Aunt P.J.'"

Rachel loved Michael for his egalitarian attitude but secretly hoped for a girl to give a safe home full of love. In her dreams, she pictured dressing alike in matching mother and daughter smocked dresses. She'd even go as far as looking like an overgrown Raggedy Ann doll with her red curly locks if it would make her feel bonded with her daughter. She wondered if her child would have ginger-colored hair like hers or would inherit Michael's dark, sleek mane. She knew genetics could play a trick on them, and they could produce a towheaded blonde like P.J, since Rachel was the only recessive redhead in her family for the past two generations. But she knew in her bones that Michael would be a loving dad and her house would be full of "peas and quiet."

P.J. and Rachel painted a sunflower border that looped and trailed along the ceiling. The mom-to-be figured they could always embellish the mural with bees and snakes if a more boyish motif was needed.

P.J. had been an art major in college and now worked as a freelance illustrator. She drove in from Austin, and the two old friends spent three consecutive weekends painting and reminiscing about the past. P.J.'s whimsical brushwork floated across the walls, creating a botanical fantasyland, and Rachel filled in the outlined areas—desperately trying to color within the lines.

P.J. said, "Now that you're going to be parents, aren't you afraid you'll screw it up—like my folks did? I knew Daddy always loved me, but I never could get a grip on Mother."

"Ever have fun with your mom?" Rachel asked. "When we were little, she was always out shopping."

P.J. stroked her chin with her thumb, leaving a dueling scar of cadmium paint. "She and I never really talked about anything major. We've always been on different wavelengths—like during the summer before junior high when she was pissed off that Neiman's allowed an African-American model on the catwalk."

"I remember when she took us to lunch downtown at the Zodiac Room." Rachel wiped the paint from her friend's cheek.

"Mother ragged on and on about how 'those people need to learn their place' and she couldn't imagine a day when that *girl* could actually afford the Valentino gown she was strutting around in."

"Some bearded guy she called Mr. Stanley came over to say hi to her," Rachel said.

"She acted like he was royalty. Sweet as my hot fudge sundae, she gushed about how gorgeous the models and fashions were. I almost fell out of my chair. I found out later that he was Stanley Marcus, the storeowner, working the room and schmoozing with the biggest customers. Dallas referred to him as 'the merchant prince,'" P.J. said.

"Did you say 'schmoozing'? Not bad Yiddish for a *shiksa*. No wonder she was so nice to him. Was she trying to get a discount?"

"Who are you calling a *shiksa*? For as much time as I've spent with you, I'm almost Jewish by osmosis. And hey, Mother only buys at the beginning of the season. She wouldn't consider rummaging through the sale racks during 'Last Call' because she wants first pick."

P.J. swirled a white dollop of paint into a blob of purple, and violet emerged out of the mixture. She loaded her brush and said, "Get this for being uptight—she wouldn't even let me pierce my ears, saying that's what trashy colored girls from the wrong side of the tracks did when she was growing up in Midland. The civil rights movement never was her thing."

"Mama says that Jews and blacks need to stick together because they're both hated," Rachel added.

"How can people despise someone just because of their color? Who said white is right?"

What about your father?" Rachel asked, painting long strokes of green in the leaves.

"The company hires Latinos and blacks, but none of my folks' friends are minorities. I'll bet he's never met Maddy's family or seen Elena's house in East Dallas." P.J. sat down on the rocker with the pale yellow seat, tucking her legs under her like she used to do as a girl. "I don't know how Maddy put up with my parents all these years. In the summer of '63, he wanted to protest in Washington, D.C. My folks were planning on entertaining the CEO of a publishing house, who was coming to Dallas to negotiate buying my father's *Texas Today*

Magazine. You and I were hanging out in the den next to Daddy's office when the whole thing went down, remember?"

Maddy had knocked softly on the door to Russell Rutherford's study. "Boss, I need a little time off."

"Sorry, pal, this is an important time for us. We need you here, so you'll just have to take off later in the year."

"But, Mr. Rutherford, I've got to go out of town for a few days. Something I can't miss. I'll pick up extra days when I get back, but I gotta go."

"What's so important, Madison? When I say something, I expect you to jump like a jackrabbit."

"Well, sir, I also need an advance on my paycheck to buy two bus tickets to Washington, D.C."

"For what in hell-fire do you not only need the time off but also want some extra money, to boot?"

"I'm going to the capital of the United States. Gonna hear the Reverend Dr. Martin Luther King Jr. preach. My son Joshua's goin' with me. I'll be back by Monday morning." He looked intense, his mouth tightly set and his fists closed at his sides—determined. "My brother Arthur and his son are making the trip, too. It's already planned and I gotta go. Grandma Nettie was born a slave right before they was freed, and some things gotta change by now."

"Whoa, are you sayin' . . .?"

"No disrespect meant, sir. I'm just sayin' I'm a-goin'."

Russell Rutherford sat down in the oversized leather chair at his desk and snorted like an old Brahma bull. He opened a small drawer and pulled out a cigar. He took a silver trimmer and clipped off the tip, which rolled across his desk. His thick fingers grabbed a miniature Smith & Wesson and pulled the trigger—releasing a golden flame shooting out of the barrel. Tilting back in his chair, the springs squealed from his heft. He took a deep puff and exhaled clouds of smoke that enveloped him. "Madison, you're going to drive the old blue Caddy we keep at the ranch. That way it'll be cheaper for y'all. Have someone give you a ride out there to pick it up." He reached into his left back pants pocket and pulled out a green wad tamed by a monogrammed gold money clip and peeled off the top bill. "Here's a hundred towards the gas." He held it out, waving it in the air.

Maddy stood frozen like a statue, staring at the money. Then he relaxed his fist and slowly extended his sinewy hand. "Mr. Rutherford, I'll take you up on your offer to borrow the car. Arthur's strapped for cash right now. We'll share the driving and won't stop 'til we get there. This here hundred dollar's an advance on my salary. I'll be back by Monday mornin'."

Maddy didn't speak to P.J. or Rachel when he passed by the den. He just shook his head in disgust as he walked by them, muttering, "Like hell I'll jump like a jack rabbit."

A few days later, Rachel spent the night at P.J.'s house. Her parents dropped her off on the way to their bridge game. Her folks were on fairly solid speaking terms that week.

"I'll pick you up tomorrow at one. Be ready because we're going to Hedy's swim meet at the Jewish Community Center," Mama said.

"Can you come get me up later? Hedy won't care if I'm there, and if she loses she'll take it out on me," Rachel asked.

"That's no reason not to go, but I guess you can stay there until suppertime. Don't make me wait when I honk the horn." Mama checked her lipstick in the visor mirror.

"No way Hedy's going to lose! She's been practicing, and she's one tough little girl. You ought to start competing soon, asthma or not." Papa eyed Rachel in the rear view mirror and angrily flipped the passenger visor back in place.

Mama didn't protest; she just put her lipstick back in her purse.

"Okay, Papa, maybe next summer. Bye, I hope y'all cream everyone at bridge!" Rachel leaned over to give her mother a kiss, contorting from the back seat—just missing her father's cheek, pecking at the air instead.

They arrived at the end of the Rutherfords' driveway. The lawns of the adjacent homes were parched golden brown from the oppressive Texas summer heat. From the side of the house, a man in a forest green uniform appeared spraying green paint on the lawn from a canister strapped on his back. The freshly coated blades contrasted with the cool charcoal gray facade of the sprawling, modern house with the dark tile roof.

"Rosy, now that's what I call filthy rich: when you've got enough money to paint your friggin' St. Augustine in the middle of summer. We haven't even given our house a lick of paint in the past five years," Papa said.

Rachel bolted out of the Chevy and almost ran up the walk, careful not to step on the freshly sprayed grass. She pushed the doorbell, waited a few seconds, and then P.J. swung open the front door.

"Where's Maddy?" Rachel asked, puzzled because he usually answered the door when she came to play with P.J.

"He took a trip with his kid to Washington, D.C.—went to that church service or something in a mall where he wants to hear a reverend preach. Daddy says it's going to be on TV tomorrow." P.J. waved to Rachel's parents as their car backed away.

"Let's make sure to watch it so we can try to spot Maddy," Rachel said.

"Cool. Want to play some records in my room?"

They padded down the hall, almost sinking into the plush white wall-to-wall carpet, passing a parade of family photographic portraits signed by Olan Mills. Snapshots of the Rutherfords posing with famous people lined the walls. Rachel was sorry she didn't have a chance to study the important faces peering out from limousines or at formal dinners because she felt awkward about having someone catch her staring at their stuff.

When they got to her bedroom, P.J. shuffled through a stack of albums. "I just bought the new *Free Wheelin' Dylan*. Why didn't you bring your guitar so we could try to figure out the chords to 'Blowin' in the Wind'?"

"Let's just listen and write down the words now, and then we'll work on the music later. Too bad the lyrics don't come with the album; it sure would save a lot of time."

The nasally serenade of their musical heartthrob, Bob Dylan, filled the room. The girls pressed their ears close to the speakers and then stopped the needle so Rachel could jot down as many words as they could remember. "What's the second part?" she asked. "Play it again." The needle scratched and skipped as P.J. slid it along the vinyl while Rachel transcribed the missing lyrics.

"Do you think he's going to marry Joan Baez? They make a way cool couple," Rachel asked.

"I don't know why he'd want anybody else. She sings like an angel," P.J. answered wistfully.

After a while, they stacked a Joan Baez record on top of a Dylan album. They breathed quietly, listening side by side under the filmy white islet canopy dotted with blue flowers on the four-poster bed. Finally, Baez's soothing voice stopped. The record player clicked off, and Rachel pretended to be asleep. Then she heard P.J.'s father quietly moving through the room, and then the sound of a soft kiss so close by. He whispered, "Sweet dreams, little Patty-cake."

A tear inched down Rachel's cheek as she lay wishing her father had spoken to her as gently, and she felt a nagging sense of envy that he had never safely tucked her in bed with a goodnight kiss.

The next morning P.J. and Rachel dressed quickly and headed down the long hallway to the kitchen. Elena was fast at work whipping up eggs into a frothy mix for her *Huevos Rancheros*. Rachel was always amazed by the constant introduction of new-fangled contraptions at the Rutherfords' house. Their kitchen was the most modern of any of her other friends' homes. She watched Elena place strips of bacon on a layer of paper towels in the microwave oven, the first she had ever seen. P.J. warned they shouldn't stand too close to it while it was operating, but the temptation was too great because it was such a show to watch through the little window as the bacon shriveled and browned in a matter of seconds.

Rachel thought everything was idyllic at P.J.'s, relieved the Rutherfords never engaged in loud arguments. She noticed they occasionally went outside for discussions by the pool but surmised they weren't actually fighting. At her own house, she figured the neighbors across the street could hear her father's shouting.

P.J. and Rachel swam most of the morning and then came in to watch television in the late afternoon. P.J. said, "Daddy told me it'll be on TV in a few minutes."

Flipping past cartoons, the girls selected a channel when they saw huge crowds of people like ants swarming on a cherry pie. Rachel fiddled with the sound knob and stared into the solemn face of the news anchor who announced: "Today, Wednesday, August 28, 1963, is a momentous time in our nation's history. An estimated 250,000 Negroes and whites have gathered at our nation's capital to support the civil rights bill pending in Congress. The movement's leader, the Reverend Martin Luther King Jr., will address the crowd in a matter of minutes. Let's get a closer view of Dr. King and the people who surround him. Ladies and gentlemen, he's ready to begin."

Dr. King stood close to the jumble of microphones on a podium at the foot of the Lincoln Memorial, literally standing in the shadow of the "Great Emancipator." A hush fell over the crowd, and they stopped in their tracks when he began to speak. He talked about Lincoln's freeing the slaves. Rachel tried to absorb his powerful words that lamented the horrors of segregation and discrimination.

Russell Rutherford entered the room and eased into his favorite leather chair that made a squishing sound under his weight. P.J. and Rachel sat on the carpet, with their legs tucked behind them next to the television. They wanted to be close up in case they caught a glimpse of Maddy and Josh. They sat transfixed at the camera shot held close on Martin Luther King's face, with the occasional glimpse of men in white round caps and flowing garments who surrounded him.

His soaring and sad voiced rang out from the television, sharing his dream that the nation would live up to its ideals.

Lynda Gayle was leaning in the doorway with one manicured hand firmly planted on her hip. Her lips curled downward. "So that's what Madison went to hear? I suppose he'll rise up and quit when he comes back. And you supported his trip to this March for Jobs and Freedom? He already has a job!" Her barbs were aimed at her husband.

"Darlin', he'll be back on Monday. I spoke to Lyndon earlier today and he said this movement's growing in leaps and bounds. We'd better face the fact that the world's gonna change, whether we like it or not. Hopefully it will be a peaceful transition, and there's no way to get around it."

Rachel wondered if he had actually spoken to the vice president and was puzzled why P.J.'s mother was so irritated.

Rachel's attention was drawn back to the television when Martin Luther King Jr. quoted a familiar passage from the U.S. Constitution that she had learned last year in sixth grade. She recited the words in unison with him, "We hold these truths to be self-evident that all men are created equal."

"Well then, you'd better learn to pick up your own dry cleaning and serve your own cocktails," Lynda Gayle snapped at her husband, turning on her high heels, keys in hand. "Elena, I'm going to Lou Lattimore Boutique and I'll be back in about an hour. Make sure everything's ready for our guests tonight. Drinks on the patio at six sharp! Use the good crystal."

The gleam on P.J.'s house started to tarnish, as Rachel feared it was beginning to seem more like her own. Although P.J.'s parents didn't yell, Rachel was beginning to be able to determine they were in a form of combat nonetheless.

CHAPTER 9

AFTER FEELING DISQUIETED by the disturbing dream while dozing on Missy's bed, the Chinese meal Rachel and Michael ate at the food court after the film sat like a brick in her stomach. She couldn't erase the image of Missy in the police station, which added to her agitation. Furious and sad at the same time, Rachel wondered how things would resolve with the upcoming court date for her daughter's case.

The phone cut through her thoughts. She grabbed it, hoping to hear Missy on the line. An unfamiliar voice asked, "Is this the residence of Melissa Janelle Frank?"

"Yes, who's calling?"

"Officer Tilset from the Springland Police Force. Ma'am, are you by yourself?"

"No, why? My husband's right here. Let me put him on an extension. Something wrong, officer?" *Two calls from the police in two days. What in the world is going on?*

Michael looked around the room for the portable phone, annoyed Missy was always using it without replacing it in the cradle. He finally found it next to the TV remote on the coffee table.

"Does your daughter drive a white Ford Mustang convertible, personalized license plate 'M-I-S-T-X-S'?"

Michael answered this time and Rachel remained silent. "Yes, was she caught speeding?"

"Hillsboro, I knew it!" Rachel whispered to Michael.

"No, sir. I'm so sorry to inform you that an act of violence has been perpetrated on your daughter and her female companion. The driver was badly injured and her passenger was pronounced DOA at Springland Hospital." He let out a low sigh and then continued, "I deeply regret to have to deliver such sad news. Who was the young woman she was traveling with?"

"Jillian Sanderson. Are you saying Missy's alive and Jillian's dead?" he asked, grabbing Rachel's hand.

"Yes, sir. May I have the name of the parents of the deceased?"

"Sam and Justine Sanderson on Pemberton Lane. I can't believe this," Michael answered.

Rachel felt the room beginning to spin and she staggered toward the couch. Michael steadied her and sat beside his wife.

"What happened? How is she? Where's my daughter?" he asked frantically.

"We discovered a white Mustang at around 1800 hours, uh, six o'clock, that appears to have been forced off the spur road going into Springland. No identification was found on either of the young women. Their purses were apparently stolen from the vehicle. We ID'd the driver by running a check on the license tags. Could you tell me what your daughter was wearing?"

Rachel barely uttered, the words sticking in her throat, "She had on her UT cap when she drove away." The thought of her daughter being injured made her start sobbing uncontrollably, as if a demon were thrashing every part of her mind and body. Missy had looked so cute adjusting the hat in her rear view mirror before she drove off.

"The driver had on a University of Texas baseball cap," the officer said.

"Missy usually wore it when she rode with the top down," Michael mumbled.

"Your daughter is unconscious due to acute loss of blood and is in serious but stable condition. The bullet entered her abdomen but wasn't fatal. Miss Sanderson was shot in the head at close range by a .38-caliber pistol. They must have tried to close the convertible top, because it was dangling in midair when we found the car in a gully. Wide skid marks indicate that the young women were forced off the road by another vehicle—probably a pick-up. Might have been dark green, based on the paint scratches on the Mustang. I can show you the police report when I see you at the Springland Hospital."

"We're on our way, officer. Where do we go?" Michael scribbled down the directions. "It'll take us about two and a half hours." He hung up and locked his arms around Rachel. She could see fear in his eyes ringed with wet lashes. "Rach, why don't you stay here with your mother and I'll go find out what happened."

"I'm going with you. I'll go crazy if I stay here! Let's get on the road right now. We'll call Mama from the car."

Michael went into the kitchen and phoned Jillian's parents. He spoke in hushed tones for about a minute. Rachel could only imagine their profound grief from hearing the news of their child's death. The Sandersons had just gotten the word from the police, so Michael wasn't the first to deliver the blow. Michael and Rachel offered to give them a ride, but they refused, wanting to take their own car. Sam decided to make the trip with his older brother because Justine was too hysterical to travel; her sister-in-law would stay with her. Rachel was ashamed to feel relieved they wouldn't have to drive Sam, with his grief filling the car. Her own fear about Missy's condition would be enough of an unwanted passenger.

Within five minutes they were headed to Springland. Rachel could only conjecture that Missy had taken the turnoff to show her best friend the house on Water Street where her great-grandparents used to live. She ran through theories: Maybe Missy impulsively decided to visit old Grandpa Izzy, who was in a nursing home for the memory challenged ever since Grandma Marlena died. There were some days when he was lucid enough to recognize visitors, and Missy hadn't been there for a while. Or perhaps the girls wanted to stop for a soft drink to perk up from the monotony of driving past the flat landscape of rows of rust-colored maize and furrowed fields of black dirt. Rachel had driven that dusty back road into town countless times in her life, seldom with any traffic, with long stretches before another car rambled along.

It all seemed like a bad dream—a gigantic nightmare that wouldn't stop. Rachel decided to call her mother from the hospital after she assessed the situation and had more details. She didn't want to worry Rosy until absolutely necessary.

Rachel suddenly didn't care if they got a speeding ticket. She urged Michael to step on the gas and hoped they could make it to Springland in two hours flat. She thought Michael was driving like a bat-out-of-hell, but she felt they were actually in purgatory, not knowing the exact condition of their daughter.

At the turnoff to the farm road leading to Springland, Michael warned Rachel to close her eyes, but she kept them open. The night was dark and starless. On the poorly lit country road, a circle of glaring lights flashed up ahead. They finally got close enough to barely make out Missy's convertible slammed head-on into a deep, brushy ravine. Police cars with flashing lights from Springland and nearby Waco blocked a clear shot at seeing the vehicle. A string of flares bordered the scene and uniformed officers milled around. Michael kept driving, heading straight for the hospital. He swerved into the emergency parking section, and Rachel barely waited for him to stop the car before jumping out of the vehicle.

They burst into the hospital entrance. Michael breathlessly spit out the words to the receptionist. "Where's Melissa Frank? We're her parents."

The antiseptic smell and streaked linoleum floors lured Rachel back into thinking about other times at another hospital. But she pushed back images of Mama bandaged and broken, and stayed completely focused on Missy.

"They brought up a little gal up to the intensive care unit on the fourth floor a while ago," the receptionist said, popping her chewing gum between words. She answered without looking up the name on a computer screen.

To herself, Rachel cursed the small town hospital and hoped the medical care was more sophisticated than the clerical staff.

"The officer said her last name was Frank. Y'all, I'm real sorry. . . . "

While she was still in mid-sentence, Rachel and Michael sprinted toward the elevator, passing the gift shop windows lined with cheery teddy bears decorated with big bows. Rachel made a mental note to buy one with the orange and white ribbons for Missy in the morning. Michael nervously tapped the "up" button over and over like a Morse code for "panic."

He gripped his hand over Rachel's closed fist while they rode to the fourth floor. Her fingernails dug into her palm because he squeezed her hand so tightly. The doors rolled open, and he almost yanked her out of the elevator. The nurse's station loomed directly in front of them.

"Melissa Frank," he said frantically.

"Visiting hours are over."

"I don't give a tinker's damn about your visiting hours! Where is she?" Michael steamed, leaning into her face.

"Calm down, sir. That's no way to talk! I was going to say, that under the circumstances, we'll let y'all see her—five minutes, tops," the nurse said with an indignant look on her face.

"Let the attending doctor know we're here!" Michael's panic was palpable.

"Yessir. Follow me, but please keep your voices down. She's heavily sedated, but we don't want to disturb her, neither."

The nurse led them through a door with a small window at eye level. A bright ray from the hallway fluorescent fixtures flashed across the tilted hospital bed. Rachel spotted Missy's baseball cap on a metal chair beside the bed. The door shut behind them automatically, painting the room in a dim, ghostly green glow from the monitors and the small shaft of light streaming in from the observation window in the door. They nervously inched toward the bed with measured steps. Rachel squinted to trace the thin outline of Missy's body under the layers of bedding, rhythmically rising and sinking slowly to the beat of the machines. She moved closer to hear her angel's breath, to see her baby's face.

The last thing she remembered, Rachel let out a scream, "Oh my God! It's Jillian."

The room went black.

CHAPTER 10

RACHEL BARELY REMEMBERED how she landed in the backseat of P.J.'s car. She replayed in her mind a blurry picture of a nurse leading her to a private hospital room, lying on cold starched sheets, and being handed two little white pills and a paper cup of water to wash them down. The sedatives literally knocked her off her feet.

In the car, the dull ache washed over her in waves. She could still see Jillian's bruised face on the pillow. *Why couldn't it be Missy's?* No matter how hard she wished, it never would be.

Michael made all of the necessary calls, while Rachel was barely functioning mentally. Like seeing through a smudged lens, she watched him pull her address book out of her purse and thumb through the pages curled from wear. He called P.J. and Juan, asking them to pick her up and take her home to Dallas. Michael told Rachel it would be better if he stayed in Springland because he would probably be up all night dealing with the police. He had taken on the task of calling Rosy. Rachel heard him faintly speaking to her mother in slow, deliberate words, with his tears dripping onto the pages of Rachel's address book. Her heart ached that Mama was hearing the news while she was alone. She watched Michael trying to pull himself together enough to handle everything for the two of them.

Rachel felt it was a mixed blessing there was no need to notify Grandpa Izzy. In his deteriorated condition, he probably wasn't capable of remembering who Missy was. Rachel lolled back into her own state of semi-consciousness.

From the backseat, she occasionally saw the lights from oncoming vehicles flickering like strobes. She felt like they were traveling in slow motion but was sure Juan was speeding because they whizzed by other cars. It was close to two in the morning by the time they got back to Dallas. Rachel already regretted leaving Michael in Springland. She longed to hold him next to her.

P.J. unlocked the door with her own key to the Franks' house. Although she hadn't stayed with her friends on a regular basis for years since her father died, she still kept Rachel's key on her ring. Juan opened the car door to the backseat and bent toward Rachel. He held her arm firmly, guiding her out of the car. P.J. had turned on the lights in the house. Together, P.J. and Juan put their arms around her waist and helped her take the stairs one by one.

"Juan, let me get her settled into bed. Could you put on some tea for all of us?"

Settled? I'll never feel settled again, Rachel thought.

P.J. searched through Rachel's drawers for a nightgown. They could hear Juan rummaging around in the kitchen, the clatter of drawers closing and pots banging together. Rachel stripped down to her panties and bra and slid under the covers. P.J. finally found the nightgown, but Rachel lacked the strength to put it on. She felt her friend's impression on Michael's side of the bed and listened to P.J.'s responses during a phone conversation.

"Mrs. Miller, she's here, but that's about it. . . .   Okay, I'll put her on."

"Oh, Mama . . ." Rachel whispered into the receiver and broke down into choking sobs. Only those three syllables escaped from her mouth after remaining silent for hours.

"Honey bun, I'll take care of the details in the morning." Her voice sounded hoarse from crying. "First, I'll stop at Saltzman's to make the arrangements."

Rachel's mother tried to make things easier for her daughter by handling the funeral, since she had more experience in that area. The idea of browsing around to pick out a casket for Missy made Rachel's stomach jump. She swallowed her rising bile. "Thanks, Mama. What would I ever do without you?" The prospect of her mother's death one day made her sink lower, as if she were drowning in a bottomless well. The word "arrangements" that used to sound benign turned deadly.

"It's too soon to have the funeral tomorrow. I already spoke to Rabbi Sachs and he told me Jewish law says to bury as soon as possible, but it doesn't necessarily have to be the next day. Also, this way, we can get the announcement in the obits. Do you have a recent photo of Missy?" Mama asked.

"Just take one off the fridge. It's covered with shots of her."

Rachel knew most Jewish burials were held within twenty-four hours of passing. By rights, they could have held the service on Monday afternoon, but Missy's body wouldn't be returned to Dallas until late Monday morning and the schedule would be too tight.

In the hospital, Michael and Rachel had signed a medical document refusing an autopsy on religious grounds. Although Jewish law permits it for police investigations, Michael decided that the authorities could get all the clues they needed without it. He told them, with tears rolling down his cheeks, "Conduct your tests, and then give her back to us so we can bury our baby."

He wanted to do the right thing for his daughter—the last thing he would ever do for her. Michael insisted he should stay at the Springland Hotel overnight. He said he would try to remain near Missy as long as he could at the hospital morgue, since there was no religious *chevra kadisha* society in Springland to accompany her all night. There weren't any pious Jews who would wash her body and wrap her in a white linen burial shroud. He would be the one to watch over his daughter as he had tried to do so all of her life.

P.J. got up and walked over to the other side of the bed to turn off the light. Rachel reached up and grasped her arm. "Please stay with me tonight. I can't sleep alone."

Juan stood in silhouette at the threshold of the bedroom door, holding a steaming cup of tea. Motioning for him to enter, P.J. said, "Juan, I'm going to sleep in here with Rachel. Why don't you get yourself set up in the guest room, *mi amor?*"

He placed the cup of tea on Rachel's nightstand and bent down to give her a kiss on the cheek. He then kissed his wife goodnight and closed the door behind him.

"Just take a few sips," P.J. said. "It's chamomile—supposed to be soothing. It's about time to take another one of those pills." She held the mug up to her friend's chapped lips. Rachel took a few swallows that sent flames down her throat, and then she leaned back on the pillow. She couldn't muster the strength to get up to wash her face or brush her teeth. Mama had always warned her to never go to bed without removing her makeup because it causes wrinkles. Her tears had already washed away most of it.

P.J. changed out of her clothes and let them drop in a pile on the floor. She got into bed and flicked on the light on Michael's nightstand. The comforting sound of pages turning signaled to Rachel that she wasn't alone. She wept, thinking of poor Michael sitting by himself, watching over Missy in the stillness.

P.J. reached over and stroked her best friend's damp hair. "I'm here, Rach. I'm here."

The sun streamed in through the slats in the plantation shutters in the bedroom. Rachel awoke and saw only a jumbled sheet on the other side of the bed. She groggily made her way downstairs and found P.J. dressed neatly in slacks and a sweater, talking on the phone. Rachel's leather phonebook was open on the kitchen desk, like a gaping wound. Her closest friend had assumed the weighty task of notifying people about Missy's death, saving Rachel from having to recount the gruesome details.

The back door to the kitchen swung opened and Mama walked in. Rachel looked into her eyes, ringed with dark circles like targets, and dissolved into tears. The two women hugged and Rachel cried into the warmth of her mother's neck, as she had done so many times before.

Rosy took a seat at the kitchen table. "I called Saltzman's Funeral Home and the service will be at two o'clock tomorrow. The Temple sisterhood has been notified and Rabbi Sachs will do the eulogy. I've got to scoot over there to finalize the arrangements."

Another word Rachel began to hate: "finalize." *What could be more final than making funeral arrangements for my daughter?*

P.J. slipped Rachel a cup of coffee. She drank a sip and tried to get down a bite of toast but slid it back on the saucer. She dutifully swallowed the little round pill with a *V* stamped on it that her mother handed her. "Mama, I'll go with you. I won't make you do this alone."

Rosy drove them to Saltzman's. Rachel started to doze off and on during the ride, and her head felt like a bobble-head car toy. They pulled up front and parked in a spot marked "Family." As they entered the funeral parlor, soft Muzak piped in from hidden speakers. Rosy approached a man sitting behind a dark mahogany reception table. "We're here for Melissa Frank."

"Hello, ladies. My name is Frederick Jenkins. We've been expecting you." He looked up at Rachel and said, "So sorry . . . And you are?

"I'm the mother," Rachel said, just above a whisper.

"When will Melissa be arriving here?" he asked.

To Rachel, it sounded like Missy was a passenger on a late arrival flight.

"The Springland police promised they would be finished by noon today. My son-in-law will accompany the body back to Dallas," Mama replied.

Rachel sat silently. *All this talk—as if Missy would be late for the funeral.*

Her mother used to yell at Lenora when she wouldn't get ready for school on time, saying that one day she'd probably be late for her own funeral. Lenora's tardiness was her trademark. Missy was usually punctual, the way Rachel and Michael had taught her.

Mr. Jenkins moved slowly, stiffly holding his body in check. His arms hung at his sides and didn't swing as he made his way down the corridor. Rachel mechanically followed the back of his dark blue suit. The muted floral wallpaper blurred as they walked, causing her stomach to spasm into knots. She shuffled along, trailing behind Mama and Mr. Jenkins, who were a few paces ahead speaking in low voices. He grasped the calla lily-shaped brass handles and swung open a set of double doors. Rachel's knees loosened like rubber bands at the sight of a showroom full of rows of wooden and metal coffins.

"This beauty is our Royal Repose model," he said, stroking the fabric.

Rachel eyed the tufts of the creamy satin-lined interior, carefully arranged in pleats. *Just great! All this for someone who wouldn't know the difference between a plain wooden box and a hole in the ground.*

Mama said, "Mr. Jenkins, we'll stick more with the Jewish tradition, something plain and simple in pine."

"The Serenity is most appropriate. It has wooden pegs and no nails in the top, as many observant Jewish people prefer. We're required to use a full metal lining. Health laws, you know."

"I guess the Great State of Texas doesn't believe in dust to dust," Rachel muttered, thinking that Missy had always been like fairy dust. Then the smashed Mustang flashed before her eyes.

Mama shot Rachel a stern look.

"And what about the florals? It's really up to you if you want them, although it isn't really part of your tradition." Mr. Jenkins offered.

"No flowers," Mama answered quickly.

Words began to collect in Rachel's mouth. She stared at the casket for a few seconds until an image emerged in her mind. "Just one long stem yellow rose bud on the top of the coffin. Lay it there as if it were picked prematurely—before it had a chance to bloom."

On the day of the burial, a sheer curtain shielded Rachel and the immediate family from the rest of the chapel in the funeral parlor. She could barely make out the shape of the coffin with the spot of yellow on top. Her only clue the room was filling was when the low din of conversation rose to a steady buzz. Michael, Mama, and Rachel sat next to each other hidden from view.

Her sisters' families took their places on the front row of the sanctuary, accepting condolences from the other mourners. Rachel wanted P.J. to sit with her, but Michael thought it best if only her mother joined them in the private area behind the partition.

Rachel's eyes were swollen slits from the hours of nonstop crying. Michael held her hand tightly but said very little. Mama daubed her eyes with a handkerchief from time to time and placed it on her lap, like a wilted flower.

Rabbi Sachs walked slowly to the podium and began the service with sadness in his voice. "It seems like only yesterday when we gathered together for Melissa's baby naming."

Rachel's pain festered like an open wound. Her sobs escaped, defying her will, and she began to tremble. Michael pulled her head close to his chest and held her tightly. He cried softly, mixing their tears. The rabbi's words seemed hollow and failed to ease her sadness. All she could think was, *How could this happen, why?* Then she imagined little Missy dancing with abandon through the lawn sprinklers.

The rabbi noted the senselessness of Missy's death. "Once again we're faced with the eternal question of 'why do bad things happen to good people?'"

Missy twirled before Rachel in her ice blue prom dress, her hair piled in soft curls. Rachel let her mind wander, trying to escape to anywhere else. Mama reached over and squeezed her hand. Their fingers intertwined, warmed by each other's touch.

Missy marched through Rachel's memory in her short high school drill team uniform with crisp layers of net petticoats bursting into lacey bloom when she high-stepped. Then the girl faded and disappeared as Rachel caught more of the rabbi's words as they began to dig deeper into her heart.

At the end of the service, Rachel was relieved to be led out the back door to a black limousine with darkened windows that shielded her from the passing mourners. Taking a few turns along the winding lane in the funeral park, Michael, Mama and she were transported to the burial site marked by a small white tent erected above a freshly dug gash in the sod, draped with fabric. The sky looked gray and lifeless, like a "blue norther" was on the way.

They took their seats on the folding chairs that surrounded the coffin suspended from a small pulley. Rachel glanced up and spotted red-eyed sorority girls, Lynda Gayle Rutherford, and Mama's friend Irene in the crowd. Rachel's chin sank to her chest, listening to the monotone recitation of the prayers. By heart, Michael rattled off the Mourner's Kaddish in Hebrew—for his parents, and now for his daughter.

Rabbi Sachs pressed a button and the casket lowered automatically into the dark hole, the grinding gears interrupting the sad silence. Rachel couldn't bear to think of her baby girl being put into the ground, in perpetual darkness. The rabbi picked up a shovel with a black ribbon tied to the handle and scooped a clump of soft dirt, using the back of the tool. He tossed the earth onto the coffin and returned the shovel to the pile instead of handing it to the next person, to symbolize not passing along grief.

Michael scraped the mound and then scattered a few clods into the opening. Rachel's heart pounded in her chest, but not loudly enough to drown out the thuds of black soil hitting the lonely wooden box. She wore a torn black ribbon pinned over her heart as an emblem of grief.

Michael stood at her side and gave her wrist a loving squeeze when she picked up the shovel.

It became painfully clear to Rachel that scooping with the reverse side represented the reluctance to bury a loved one and say a final good-bye. Gently as possible, she sprinkled a few grains and then slowly dug the shovel back into the earth.

DEAD END

CHAPTER 11

AFTER THE FUNERAL, the Franks were spent and devastated as they pulled into the garage with an empty space where the Mustang would never be parked again. They opened the back door from the garage and were engulfed by a beehive of women swarming in the kitchen. Rachel's twenty-cup Party Perk bubbled shamelessly, filling the air with the welcoming scent of brewed coffee. The Temple sisterhood had retrieved her good silver trays out of their felt storage bags and had stocked them with cookies, chocolates, and miniature bagels. Rachel leaned against the kitchen counter to steady herself from the dizzying flurry of activity. Her head throbbed and she longed for the quiet and solitude of her room.

The house bulged with food everywhere she looked. The dining room table was laden with deli trays of stacks of cold cuts fanned in oddly festive displays. She ran her fingers along the finely tooled edges of the trays that held round foods—bagels and eggs, to symbolize the continuance of life—but couldn't reconcile the injustice that Missy's life had been cut short. The staggering abundance of food didn't make sense. She eyed a steaming pan of beef brisket on the stovetop, enough food for a week, but she had no appetite.

The sound of casual conversation diminished when Michael and Rachel arrived at the house. Lenora guided her to a seat in the dining room, and Hedy shoved a cup of steaming coffee under her nose. The mirror over the breakfront had been covered with a white damask tablecloth she hadn't used in years. P.J. hovered behind her chair, resting a hand on her shoulder.

People started speaking just above a whisper and then regained their normal pitch, overcoming the initial discomfort over dealing with the deeply bereaved. More began to arrive, slowly filing in to pay their respects. Michael sat quietly in a chair in the den, accepting warm pats on the back or kisses from friends who streamed into the room. Nephew Jack gave Rachel a hug and claimed Missy was like a little sister to him. Jenna, his real sister, nodded in silent agreement— awkward and unsure of what to say.

Amid the sadness, Rachel heard giggles from the corner of the den where Missy's friends were huddled on the couch. Her pain intensified because her daughter should have been sitting among them swapping stories, but she was in the cold, hard ground.

Missy's sorority sister Dena emerged from the group and ventured over to Rachel. Dena's fresh, smooth face was stained with sadness. "Mrs. Frank, I'm so sorry. How are you doing?"

"Shitty, just plain shitty."

Her eyes widened to bulging orbs at Rachel's response. Dena took a step back, plowing into P.J.'s chair.

"Honey, I'm sorry. It's just the pits. Thanks for coming." Then she whispered to P.J., "I just can't do this." Rachel pushed her chair away from the table and struggled to get up.

P.J. called for Michael, who rushed into the room to find out what was the matter. "Michael, she's about had it."

He put his arms around his wife and held her tightly. "Let P.J. take you up to our room. I'll stay down here with our guests. It's okay, dear. Just go rest."

P.J. held Rachel's hand and led her upstairs, like a child going for an afternoon nap.

Mama walked into the bedroom and wrapped her arms around Rachel's neck. She felt assaulted by the cloying scent of her mother's perfume.

"Honey bun, we've got to get through this. If we could only muster some of the strength we saw in Jackie when you were little. Remember how stoically she handled her grief?"

"You've got to be kidding. I don't give a damn about Jackie Kennedy!"

"I was just trying to . . . "

"I know, Mama. Sorry, but I can't be that strong. In fact, I can't stand the sight of people right now; my skin is crawling! Maybe I'll show up later for the prayers."

The sun finally set on the never-ending day. In the evening, several couples arrived. Michael came upstairs and sat close to Rachel on the bed. She hadn't left the room all afternoon.

"Rachel, the rabbi's ready to say Kaddish. We've got the ten men for the minyan, so we can start the service. Do you think you can come down now?" Michael asked gently.

She pulled the covers up to her chin. "Not now. Just let me stay here by myself." Rachel wanted to sleep away the pain and wake up to learn it was all a terrible nightmare, like in the bogus ending of the television show *Dallas*, but this time it wouldn't be a disappointment.

"Okay, but tomorrow you've got to eat something or you'll get too weak. I'll be up in a little while, hon."

"Tomorrow." Rachel rolled over and turned her back to Michael.

Over the next few days, she could barely go about the business of maintaining herself. Occasionally she managed to make an appearance in the living room for a few minutes when friends dropped by to pay their respects. Their stories made people brighten and find some joy in Missy's memory, but each word made Rachel's heart spasm in pain. The effort to brush her teeth, fix her hair, or put on makeup was beyond her reach. She cried incessantly—deciding it was of no use to deal with black streaks trailing down her face.

While P.J. was sharing remembrances of Missy, she mentioned that she treasured the drawings Missy had given her over the years. She had always encouraged Missy's artistic talents by giving her art supplies as presents, later supplying her with sophisticated computer drawing programs.

Michael periodically disappeared into his study to take calls from the Springland police. He felt frustrated that they were sorely lacking clues about the crime. No arrests had been made. From the sketchy reports gleaned from Jillian after she regained consciousness, and a few paint samples and skid marks, the authorities hypothesized that a pickup truck had forced the girls off the road. A lone man in a green truck had gunned them down at close range. Jillian had miraculously escaped death. Although their purses were stolen, none of their credit cards had been used. Michael fumed that there was no paper trail to track the murdering bastard.

The winding farm road into Springland had been quiet on the afternoon of the attack. Jillian was the only eyewitness. She had relieved her friend from driving because Missy hadn't slept much the night before and needed a break. She had borrowed Missy's baseball cap to shield her eyes from the late-day sun.

Jillian reported that she had never seen the man before—a complete stranger.

The police canvased gas stations to investigate if a green truck with scratches on the passenger side had been spotted. There were countless green pickups in the state, and the police were searching for a needle in a Texas-sized haystack.

The town sheriff reported the rumor that had spread around Springland with the speed of a prairie fire: An escapee from the State Correctional Facility committed the murder. But it proved false because all inmates had been accounted for right after the incident.

Background checks were performed on Missy and Jillian. Neither of them had any enemies—no stalkers or obsessive boyfriends at which to point a guilty finger. It was a totally motiveless crime without any provocation. The police labeled it an act of random violence. Rachel's anger mounted when she thought about the scum of the earth who had shot and robbed the precious girls, leaving them for dead in a ditch along a dusty road. He remained a free man. Free to do it again.

From Jillian's hospital bed, an officer gently probed her for details that slowly emerged from her brain fog caused by the shock and trauma. She groggily recalled that the driver was in his mid-twenties, medium build with greasy sandy-colored hair. His green truck slowly crossed the centerline and then rammed the Mustang, forcing it off the road, but she didn't catch the license plate number. The man slid out of the driver's cab holding a dark object in his hand. He raced over, carrying a pistol low to his hip, pointing it as he reached their car. Jillian frantically tried raise the top but remained completely vulnerable in the open convertible.

That's the last thing she could remember.

CHAPTER 12

T HE TOWN OF SPRINGLAND wasn't uncharted territory to Rachel's family. Her grandparents lived there, and she used to make stops between Dallas and the university in Austin.

In her day, getting ready for college wasn't as elaborate as when Missy went away to school. Her daughter required a laptop, fancy linens, and a new wardrobe.

In the early seventies, Rachel straddled the "fashion fence" when she was in college. She let her unruly hair explode around her face in wild red curls. Jeans were her fashion mainstay, but she stayed away from the total hippie look, refraining from tie-dyes and headbands.

Many students wore sandals because the weather was so blazing hot most of the year. There were some Decembers when Rachel went to school in cutoffs and then rushed back to her dorm to grab her coat in the afternoon when a "blue norther" rolled in and the temperature plummeted forty degrees in three hours. On those occasions, the weatherman usually chanted: "If you don't like the weather in Texas, just wait five minutes."

Over the passing of years, Rachel had also witnessed P.J.'s style change. At the beginning of their freshman year in college, she would spot P.J. on campus with her blonde tresses layered and feathered like the most famous alumna of her sorority, a sex kittenish television star. P.J. lived in one of the grandest sorority houses on campus, with imposing fluted white columns. She immersed herself in Greek life with a select handful of sororities and fraternities, virtually excluding Rachel from her social circle.

Rachel had packed for her college experience with the old light blue suitcase and a few cardboard boxes she carted to her dorm room full of dust bunnies and cracked linoleum. Mama had dropped her off at the dormitory, tears sliding down their faces as they hugged and said their good-byes.

Her mother whispered softly, "Honey bun, this is your chance to make something of yourself. Don't waste it. You're smart and you need choices in life. Education's the key that'll keep you free."

Rachel had heard this before, or some variation of it, for several years. Her voice quivered, "I will, Mama. I promise I'll make you proud."

"It's not for me. You need to do it for yourself."

The old Ford Fairlane pulled out of the loading zone at the dorm. Rachel watched the car disappear down Guadalupe Avenue.

Rosy made the trip home in record time without making any stops. She had gotten on the interstate and headed for Dallas, about two hundred miles away, bypassing the hamlet of Salado without taking a break at the Old Stage Coach Inn to have the best fried chicken in central Texas. She continued driving when she spotted the turnoff to Springland, Texas.

She had made the trip to Springland countless times before to see her in-laws, but there wasn't a reason to go there anymore.

By the time her husband's parents found out the full extent of what was going on in Rosy and Danny's marriage, it was too late to intervene. When they saw their daughter-in-law in the hospital bed with her broken bones and her beautiful face stitched from eye to jaw, they couldn't insist she stay married to their difficult son.

Over the years, Rachel wasn't eager to visit her grandparents in Springland, especially Grandma Marlena, but she occasionally made the trip to let Missy get to know them.

Rachel's paternal grandparents, Marlena and Israel Miller, had moved west from Philadelphia to Springland in the early 1940s and became the proprietors of a ladies' dress shop on the town square. In those days, there weren't many Jewish people in small towns in Texas, and the ones who were there usually worked as merchants. Many Jews progressed from peddling pushcarts in the East to owning their own stores in the West. The Miller family name had long been changed since Ellis Island when the clerk couldn't understand Russian and had Anglicized the surname.

Rachel's sisters used to visit the grandparents in mid-summer. While Rachel was at summer camp, Lenora and Hedy stayed in the stone house on Water Street with the shady porch covered by a light blue bead board overhang.

Every year, Marlena's Modes held a Fourth of July weekend sale. Rachel's grandfather tallied the receipts on an old brass cash register while her grandmother schmoozed the customers. Lenora and Hedy escorted the ladies into fitting rooms and re-hung the garments. Prices were slashed on racks of nautical boat neck jumpers and pastel Sunday-go-to-meeting dresses to make room for shipments of fall transitional cottons. The two sisters served iced tea and lemonade and provided customers with little mesh zippered hoods to hold their hairdos in place and keep makeup off the merchandise. Loyal clientele drove from Waco, thirty-five miles away, to take advantage of the discounts. Grandma Marlena also placed special orders for formal gowns selected in catalogs from the garment district of Elm and Ervay Streets in downtown Dallas.

Everyone thought Rachel was too young to help and would get in the way for the Fourth of July ritual. She felt as happy as a pig in mud to be shipped off to Camp Rio Bravo and never yearned to be under the thumbs of her older sisters. Even though it meant spending less time with her grandparents, she didn't feel very close to them, anyway.

At the turn of the century, Springland was an oasis for people seeking restoration of their health. Foul tasting mineral springs were discovered when the town's founding fathers were drilling for fresh artesian drinking water. The springs were considered to have curative powers, and people traveled from all over the Southwest to soak their polio-stricken, ravaged bodies in the mineral baths. An Eastern hotel magnate built the Grand Springs Hotel to accommodate the influx of tourists. But with the advent of modern medicines, Springland fell out of favor and became a backwater town. When the interstates were built, it remained on the outskirts of progress. Only a dusty state farm road led the occasional car or pickup to the town center.

When Rachel attended Grandpa Izzy's seventy-fifth birthday in Springland, he handed her a glass of cloudy iced tea. She inspected the murky drink and said, "This looks kinda funny. How long has it been sitting in the fridge?"

"Your grandma just fixed it to cool you off. Drink up, Rachie! *L'chaim!*"

She took a swig and barely made it to the sink to spit it out. "Grandpa, are you trying to poison me or something?"

"Nope, it's the only way I could get you to try the spring water— best stuff in the world. It keeps me going . . . keeps me regular. I never miss a bowel movement."

"Grandpa, you're grossing me out!"

"What?"

"It tastes like a glass of iced tea mixed with rotten eggs. Can I have a Dr. Pepper —quick, I'm gonna barf!"

"Ask you grandmother for a soda pop, but I never heard of anyone making a nice BM after drinking a Dr. Pepper. Go get your sisters; I want them to try it."

"Now you're talking, Grandpa Izzy!" She gave him a kiss on the top of his wispy "comb-over." She couldn't wait to watch her sisters drink the foul brew.

In the summers, Hedy and Lenora helped their grandparents in the shop until early afternoons, and then they roamed around Springland with their summer romances. Rachel found out about their escapades by reading Hedy's diary, written in her sister's barely legible chicken scratchings.

Hedy and Lenora had sneaked through the boarded windows with the crumbling gingerbread trim of the old Springland Bath House to neck and drink beer with their beaus on the cool tile benches near the cracked, drained pools.

By the time they explored the public rooms of the Grand Springs Hotel, the ballroom was dingy beige, no longer the buttercup yellow of better days. Swirls of plaster rosettes in the ceiling molding were chipped and weathered. The shriveled old desk clerk checked in an occasional railroad worker or relative of an inmate of the Texas State Correctional Facility that was down the road. Through the cataract clouds in his eyes, he watched Rachel's sisters' hazy silhouettes—a pair of girls sitting on the tattered wicker furniture or twirling around the ballroom, waltzing to the music in their heads.

Hedy and Lenora strolled with their guys in the shade behind the old hotel and kissed lustily in the July heat. It was one of the few secrets they shared and didn't tattle on each other because they were partners in crime.

Years later, when Hedy roasted Lenora at her fiftieth birthday luncheon at the posh restaurant at the Mansion in Turtle Creek in Dallas, she recounted the day when they were busted in Springland. Lenora, by then on her third husband, was already "three sheets to the wind" when Hedy began the tale. She did an uncanny imitation of the weather-beaten town sheriff, Carter Tompkins, who was as cocky as a tough old rooster.

Spilling the proverbial beans about how the lawman had caught them making out with the local boys, Hedy drawled, "Sons, we treat our young ladies in Springland with Respect—with a capital *R*! And gals, I wouldn't exactly refer to the two of you as 'young ladies.' Miss Marlena's gonna tan your hides when she hears what you've been up to."

Lenora, the center of attention at her birthday party, reached for the waiter's arm and pointed to her empty glass while she slurred, "And she did, believe you me."

"What a tempest in a handbag!" Hedy proceeded to inform the decked-out women at the luncheon that Lenora was shaking so badly that she almost peed in her pants in the back of the patrol car. She failed to mention it wasn't because she feared what Grandma and Grandpa would do—she was terrified Papa would find out.

Hedy ended her impromptu comedy act by quoting the old sheriff, lines that her family had repeated in jest for years: "Y'all might act that way up in Dallas, but our little ladies in Springland keep their knees glued together and their mouths shut tight, ya hear? When y'all are in my town, best remember that the Eyes of Texas are *always* upon you."

The grandparents did keep the two sisters under wraps for the next week. They weren't allowed to leave the shop until four o'clock every day, and then they had to march directly to the house on Water Street to start supper. After that summer, they weren't very eager to visit Springland, but Mama made them go anyway while Rachel was at camp.

When Hedy and Lenora got back to Dallas, they were grounded until school started. The first night home after dinner, Papa said, "Hedy, go get my belt!"

"No, why? I promise, we didn't do anything bad!"

"Lenora, get in here!"
Lenora entered the den and made a quick about-face.

"Get your little butt in here right now!"

She stood next to Hedy, ready to take her punishment, staring at Papa with eyes glazed over with hate.

Rachel edged away from her older sisters, trying to stay out of the line of fire.

"No daughters of mine are going to grow up to be sluts! I'll get the belt myself."

He returned from the bedroom with a look that frightened Rachel to the core. Her father took the strap of his wide leather belt and beat the backs of her sisters' legs until tracks of red welts erupted.

Rachel snuck away and huddled on the floor in the corner of the room she shared with Hedy, shrinking behind the closed door.

Lenora yelled, "Stop! Leave us alone!"

Mama pleaded, "Danny, you're going to ruin them! They're normal, good girls. Let them go!" She sobbed but the whippings continued.

"Rosy, we'll discuss this later, and if you don't leave me the hell alone, you're gonna be next!"

Away from the ruckus, Rachel turned the pages of Hedy's diary she had retrieved from under the twin bed. She soaked up the stories about the lazy afternoons in the bathhouse in Springland, against a backdrop of the beatings. She didn't heed the warning scribbled on the cover in thick marker, "Personal and Private—RACHEL KEEP OUT or I'll kill you!!!"

Her sisters' cries were a new chorus of pain in the household.

Hedy concluded her speech at Lenora's fiftieth birthday party by announcing that years after their summer escapades, Grandma Marlena mailed her a clipping from the *Springland Sentinel* about how Sheriff Tompkins had been picked up on a DUI for erratic driving on the highway between Waco and Springland.

Rachel figured he preferred to do his partying out of town, where the Eyes of Texas weren't upon him. She never liked being in his jurisdiction. The sheriff always gave her the evil eye, calling her one of 'those Miller girls,' even though she never had done anything wrong—always catching fallout from Hedy's and Lenora's mischief.

CAMP SONGS

CHAPTER 13

RACHEL PREFERRED TO SPEND her summers at camp instead of being underfoot in Springland, but she missed her best friend when she was away from Dallas. Seventh grade was the last school year Rachel and P.J. spent together in public school. The Rutherfords decided that a good private school was necessary for their daughter's education, and she attended Hartford Academy, an all-girls' school, from middle school through graduation.

In the summers P.J. headed for the cool, verdant forests of Maine, while Rachel went to a YWCA camp in the sweltering Texas heat. Many Jewish girls in Dallas attended the no-frills Christian camp because the emphasis was on sportsmanship and good values. Camp Rio Bravo was tucked among the sand, cactus, and mesquite of Big Bend, the part of Texas that curves around like a turkey wing. The Rio Grande River flowed nearby—in some places lazily and in others torrential—with its muddy banks lined with cavernous cliffs.

Local Indians believed that after the Great Spirit created the earth, the stars in the heaven, the fishes in the seas, and the birds in the skies, he took the pile of leftover materials and tossed them together to form Big Bend. The landscape is varied and majestic, with its "windows"— the space between the craggy mountains—and its winding waters and parched trails.

The camp was located right outside the official boundaries of the park. The cabins were built in 1908 and hadn't received a lick of renovation since. The rusted window screens and peeling wooden siding had been there for years, molting like snakes in the sunlight. On the long, tedious ride, Rachel thought of Mama and Papa and wondered how they'd get along without her.

They had hugged her before she boarded the chartered bus parked in front of the old red brick YWCA building on Elm Street in downtown. The dingy leather bus seat was cracked from age and mistreatment by countless other riders on their way to somewhere else. Rachel spotted her father leaning toward the slit in the streaked windowpane.

He called out, "Make sure you come home with some swimming medals this year! You've gotta get tough if you want to beat that asthma."

"Okay, Papa. I'll try out, but I don't think I'll be any good." Rachel knew she would never be as strong a swimmer as Hedy, but her father constantly goaded her to compete.

"That's horse pucky! Red, just remember—think medals!"

Mama blew her a kiss and let it fly into the steamy, thick air. As if it floated through the open window between them, Rachel snatched it in her fingers and closed them tightly. She tried to imprint her mother's beautiful face on her memory to last over the summer.

A hefty girl with Tootsie Roll curls sat next to her on the bus. Rachel jostled to one side to adjust for the girl's thighs that were invading her space. The bus lunged forward and expelled a dark cloud of noxious exhaust over her parents. With "CRB Chartered" on the header board, it chugged down the street and headed for the open highway.

Camp Rio Bravo was Rachel's safe haven in childhood. She longed for it during the school year. There was no Mama yelling at Lenora to get ready for school, no Hedy to torment her, and no Papa to tiptoe around.

The campers arrived in the evening and set up their bunks in the cabin, placing footlockers at the end of the beds. Toiletries were stowed on the cracked wooden shelves. Rachel sprawled out on her metal cot and looked at the underside of the shelf scratched with graffiti from campers of years past: "Susie Simms, Amarillo 1946, Apache Chief; Rio Bravo forever!" and "Jill, Comanche Firemaker, 1962"—ballpoint and magic marker artifacts from girls who once dreamed on the same spot.

Her counselor, nicknamed "Pecos," was lean and sinewy with an athletic body. "Girls, welcome to cabin nine—the best cabin to be in, and I'm glad to have you. When I read out your name, say *aquí,* for "here." We're so close to Mexico, you might as well learn some Spanish over the next few weeks," she said with a broad, toothy smile. The girls replied as she called out: "Judy, Rachel, Lottie, Adrian, Carmen, Sally Belle, Carolyn . . ."

"Call me Cricket!" a freckle-faced tomboy said.

"Okay, Cricket, and last we have Ang . . . Angenue."

When Pecos tripped over the final name—sounding out the letters slowly—the chestnut-skinned girl from Tyler, Texas, said, "My name's pronounced *on-gen-oo.* My mama heard it on the TV and liked the sound of it."

When a few of the cabin mates giggled softly, Angenue looked them in the eye and asked, "What's so funny?"

Cricket said, "Just a joke, but you wouldn't get it."

"Okay, y'all, make up your beds," Pecos gently intervened.

Rachel's seatmate from the bus, Adrian, selected the bunk next to hers. Adrian scattered her gear all over her bed, and it trailed unceremoniously onto the floor, encroaching on her neighbor's space. She reached over and grasped the long, thin gold charm on Rachel's necklace and asked, "Is that a skateboard at the end of your chain?"

"No, it's a Jewish *mezuzah.* It holds a little scroll of the Ten Commandments. Grandma Rosy gave it to me."

Sally Belle, a pixie from the little town of Carthage in East Texas on the Louisiana border, stared at Rachel's hair.

"Well, what? *What* are you looking at? Haven't you ever seen red hair before?" Rachel asked.

Sally Belle cocked her head to get a better look. "Don't you got horns? I can't see 'em."

"Oh my God, I can't believe this. You've never seen a Jew before, have you?" Rachel asked, her mouth agape.

"Reckon not."

Pecos stood up and said, "Y'all, let's get some things straight here. All creatures are blessed in God's eyes. Rachel's Jewish. Jews do not now nor have ever had horns. I won't tolerate discrimination of any kind in this cabin. If you have any questions about your differences or anything else, please come to me first, then we'll work it out as a group."

It was the first year the camp was integrated, and colored girls from all over the state attended Rio Bravo, some on fellowships. Many of the campers were in store for a new experience, with various levels of enthusiasm for the change.

The session began following timeworn traditions. The girls gathered to select tribes—competition teams—out of a hat in the old barn painted the color of dried blood, which had been converted into an assembly hall. One by one, the new campers reached into the moth-eaten felt cowboy hat with the rattlesnake band and picked out a tiny piece of folded notebook paper with either "Apache" or "Comanche" scrawled in red felt marker. Rachel considered her pick lucky because her two sisters were Apaches, and they would have tormented her if she had come home a Comanche. Hedy and Lenora had lasted only one season at camp before the lure of drive-in movie dates kept them from spending their summers with a bunch of girls at the edge of Texas.

Adrian picked from the old hat. Although trading was forbidden, she slyly snatched a crumpled piece of paper from a dark-skinned girl next to her, who wore a head full of braids secured by a rainbow of ribbons and a chartreuse "I love Jesus " barrette with a little heart where the word "love" should be. The little girl seemed afraid to make waves. Adrian's sister Roberta had been a Comanche, so Rachel figured Adrian must have picked the enemy out of the hat. Tribal rivalries ran as deep as political parties in Texas.

The next task at hand was to elect a slate of tribal officers. The older campers briefly campaigned for chief, stating their leadership qualifications. The second highest office was the medicine man, a sort of tribal vice president. The girls didn't say "medicine woman" because it never occurred to them to be sensitive to the gender of terms. There were two firemakers, and the low men on the totem pole were the four cheerleaders. Rachel marveled how Texas and cheerleaders always seemed to go hand in hand.

It felt good to escape from the cramped bus into the warm evening air that was accented with the faint flash of lightening bugs. Rachel decided to tryout for firemaker, a middle management position. She entered the circle of Apaches, all sitting cross-legged. Rachel was especially glad to see Cindy. Although Cindy was only four years older than Rachel, close to Lenora's age, she seemed like a mother to her, always watching her back.

Rachel began her election stumping, "Hi, I'm Rachel Miller." She had considered saying "how" but thought it might be dorky. "I've been coming to Camp Rio Bravo for the past two years. Even though I haven't been an officer yet, firemaker would be a real honor." Her throat felt as parched as the dusty raked path in front of her cabin. "Camp means everything to me, so please vote for me."

Pecos collected the ballots and announced Cindy as the new chief. "I'm happy to say my cabin has faired so well. Rachel and Sally Belle have been voted Apache firemakers, and Cricket and Angenue are cheerleaders," she said with a note of pride.

Rachel considered her win nothing short of a miracle, but Angenue's victory was even more spectacular because she was the first colored girl to be elected an officer at Rio Bravo.

"Tribal Games," the sports competition, commenced the following morning after players were selected for the various teams. Over the course of the two weeks, they competed in foot races, softball, volleyball, archery, tennis, and swimming. Rachel settled into the routine of sports classes, arts and crafts, competition, meals in the mess hall, and singing after each dinner.

On Sundays, white shorts and shirts were worn to the church services held in the old barn. Sometimes the Baptist hymnal felt like a hot potato in Rachel's hands. But when everyone sang "Shall We Gather at the River?" accompanied by an out of tune piano, she joined in full force because there was no explicit mention of Jesus—only peace, the throne of God, and the shining, beautiful river.

Once a session, the campers gathered for evening vespers along the banks of the river with a backdrop of jagged cliffs. Under a vow of silence forbidding conversation for the evening, they scuffled down the path single file singing, "We are climbing Jacob's Ladder, soldiers of the Cross."

Limestone altars were erected near the water's edge. Crosses made of post oaks sprinkled with gold glitter appeared as if on fire, illuminated by flickering rows of votive candles. The girls wore their pajamas and robes because they went straight to bed after the service.

The outstretched arms of saguaro cacti, silhouetted in the moonlight, pointed the way to the stone altar. Carrying her white pillowcase at her side, Rachel inched toward the altar lined with crosses that had made her feel out of place last year when she had declined to kneel before them. From her makeshift bag, she pulled out a pair of Popsicle stick triangles glued in opposite directions, covered with blue glitter. Her handcrafted Jewish stars glistened like the heavenly ones in the summer night that shown brightly without city lights dimming their radiance. One by one, the Jewish girls left their places in line and kneeled before the Stars of David. Pecos came over and sat by Rachel, giving her hand a warm squeeze. Then she, too, paid homage to the homemade, shining stars.

Rachel was proud to be a member of cabin nine. Pecos planned campouts with other cabins, where they stayed overnight near groves of bamboo and patches of prickly pear cacti. Rachel didn't mind her chores: keeping her cabin tidy for daily inspections of bunks made with military precision, footlockers all lined up, and dirt paths raked like Japanese gardens.

She showered in wooden stalls with rough concrete floors that they doused daily with harsh antiseptic cleaner that stung her nostrils. Rachel wore her flip-flops in the shower to avoid the residue of lye that never completely washed away. The toilet was in a private stall with the roll of paper impaled on the tip of a rusty horseshoe bracketed to the wall.

Rachel was late to volleyball practice because she was stuck on the Johnny past the time the triangle signaled the start of morning activities. A dull pain in her stomach persisted. It felt like a ripe watermelon, even though she was so thin she was called "Rachel the Reed" at school. Her panic rose as she walked toward the volleyball nets across the field of mowed bluebonnets, the flowers snipped to dried nubs. The worst thing she had feared for a long time was finally confirmed. She folded her arms over her aching stomach and grimaced from the pain that radiated in waves.

Cindy grabbed her by the shoulders after volleyball practice. "Rach, you've got to let me in on what's been bugging you. You're still my little sidekick, aren't you?" Her voice was warm and pleading.

"Cindy, I just can't. No way!"

"You can tell me *anything*. Is someone bullying you or have you heard bad news from home? Are you sick?"

"No, it's just that . . . I've got something awful to tell you," Rachel whispered.

Cindy sat down on a tattered lawn chair used by referees, to brace herself for the news. "Okay, just spill it, and we'll figure out how to fix things."

"I've got . . . cancer," Rachel confessed. Tears ran down her freckled, sunburned face.

Cindy looked like she had been smacked in the stomach by a softball. She stayed silent for a moment and then pulled Rachel close to her. "Oh my God, when did you find out?"

"This morning, for sure."

"What?" She held Rachel's face in her hands and looked into her eyes. "Now, tell me everything—from the top."

"Well, I went to pee after the volleyball match and there they were again—ugly dark brown streaks on my underwear. I know it's called discharge, and discharges are warning signs for cancer. I heard it on TV."

Cindy dropped her hands from her face and laughter spilled over her whole body. "Chile, you're about to become a woman. Didn't your mother ever tell ya? You don't have cancer; you've got the curse!"

"But it's not red like blood. Mama said I'd start bleeding one day and then I'd have to be careful not to get pregnant."

"Your mama needs a long lesson in communication. Sweetie, you're about to get your period," Cindy said, trying to stifle a laugh.

Rachel felt the air rush back into her lungs as the weight of "The Big C" flew off her shoulders. She could breathe again after holding the secret inside for weeks, not even writing about it to P.J.

To her amazement, her period officially came two days later. Unfortunately, it was the morning of the swim competition, so she had to withdraw because it was "that time of the month." She shuddered at what excuse to give Papa why she didn't swim, much less not garner a medal.

In the meantime, Rachel learned all about "being on the rag," having a "visit from her friend," and about guys who weren't afraid to "swim the Red River."

After lunch, she returned to her bunk for mail call. Pecos made a game of it. "I'll name a country-western singer, and you girls have to come up with the title of one of their hit songs," she explained. "Rachel, it's your turn. How about Johnny Cash?"

"That's easy . . . 'Oh, Lonesome Me.'"

Pecos sent a letter sailing through the air to her bunk. Postmarked from Maine, the pale blue envelope with scalloped edges on the flap landed on her khaki blanket—the first time Rachel had heard from her best friend in about a week. She wrote P.J. every other day, adding in tiny letters above her name, "*Oh How I* Miss P.J. Rutherford," telling her about the tribe, the contests, and even about the arrival of her "Aunt Flow."

Rachel loved P.J.'s tight, even script with each letter perfectly slanted and carefully formed.

Dear Rachel,

How are ya? Camp Lakewood is a blast!!! I've gotten pretty good at dressage, and we ride English here. No more Western for me!

I met the way coolest boy. His name is Timothy Ford Wallace III. His friends just call him Tripp for the third. Isn't that cute? I call him Timmy. My parents said that I could go to their home in East Hampton for a week after camp. They have their own yacht.

Daddy and Mother are going to visit me there for a few days. It is so nice and cool in the mountains here in Maine. No red dust storms like in Texas, ha, ha!

Just kidding. Have fun, and I'll see ya back in Big D.

Love ya lots,

P.J.

Rachel also received a small white envelope that Papa used to enclose checks when he paid the bills. Inside was a message written on a sheet from a plain white notepad.

Dear Red,

Hope you're enjoying camp. Your mother and I think you should stay for the next session.

Have fun,

Papa

Rachel stared at the letter as if it had arrived from the moon. Her father had never written to her before. Usually, she received fancy note cards bordered with roses, filled with loving messages written in Mama's looping, graceful letters she learned as a girl in penmanship class. Rachel could usually smell a hint of her powdery My Sin perfume. This time Papa wrote in his controlled, blocky, half-print-half-script that looked like the writing on maps she'd seen in the school library.

Mixing sadness and relief, Rachel was glad she wouldn't have to leave camp the next day but missed Mama and wanted to see her. She consoled herself that she wouldn't have to cry her eyes out at the Council Fire ceremony on the last night, knowing she wouldn't be at Camp Rio Bravo until another year passed.

The sunset on Tribal Council eve cast glowing embers over the Chisos Mountains. After the sun dropped behind the rugged peaks, the winner of the tribal competitions would be announced at the end of the ceremony.

Rachel and the other tribal leaders filed into the Council grounds, with egg tempera paint streaks slashed across their faces and feathers in their hair, signifying the various ranks. The chiefs donned full headdresses, complete with cascades of feathers adorned with trailing strips of ermine. Rachel wondered if it was genuine or just bleached jackrabbit.

"Help me with my feathers, will you?" she asked Angenue. "They won't stay put in my headband. I look more like a dead duck than a firemaker." As her friend poked the quills through the knotted turquoise felt, one pricked her scalp. "Yowee, I don't want them to fall out, but you're jabbing me like I'm a human pin cushion!" Angenue repositioned the two turkey feathers and then handed Rachel a single plume in turn.

With her costume adjusted, Rachel was ready to assume her role as firemaker: to carry the ceremonial torch to ignite a towering bonfire. From her window in cabin nine, she had watched the counselors earlier in the day stacking the logs higher than they stood. Her torch— a long, straight oak branch—was wrapped at the end with a feminine pad dipped in kerosene, but it wasn't apparent what it was when fully ablaze.

Her fellow campers bordered the pile of crisscrossed logs to form a circle. Apaches and Comanches stood side by side, linked hand in hand. The leaders surrounded the stack of logs in the middle of the circle. Cindy and the Comanche chief, Dianne, carried hatchets by the handles that were wrapped in beads. Walking in their Tandy moccasins, which they had stitched from kits in arts and crafts, they approached a thick tree stump.

Cindy said, "You've competed with valor, and now it's time to bury the hatchets. Only one tribe can be the champion of the session, but we have all won by the good sportsmanship and friendship that was shown during the past two weeks."

Each flung their hatchet into the log. The blades sank into the decaying wooden stump, signaling the end of the fighting, the Color Wars.

Rachel moved toward the pyre and shoved her flaming torch between a rung of logs. The blaze leapt higher as each firemaker added her fuel to the flame, sparks popping like swarms of fireflies, and then the searing heat made her retreat to where her fellow leaders were now sitting cross-legged on the straw-covered clearing.

They chanted "Kumbaya." When Rachel first learned it, Pecos had explained that its origins were unclear: some said it started as a Negro gospel song, "Come by Here, Lord," which had traveled to the West Indies where it was sung in Pidgin English as "Kumbaya." Finally, it returned to America as a folk song. Rachel sang out, "Someone's crying, Lord, Kumbaya, Oh Lord, Kumbaya."

Tum! Tum! Tum!—drumbeats tore through the night. A trio of counselors in full black Indian garb banged on hollow wooden logs stretched with rawhide skins. Out of the bushes, two warriors exploded through the darkness, with long, pointed spears gleaming in the firelight. One was dressed in a turquoise fringed loincloth with a beaded vest and the other wore deep rust. Black paint streaked across their faces, accented in ferocious patterns of either blue or rust. They circled around each other in a deadly dance. The drums pounded louder.

Rachel could tell from the taut muscles and nimble moves that the Apache in turquoise was Pecos. She darted around the other warrior dancer, jabbing at her enemy with her lance. The Comanche swirled around, sweeping the ground with her weapon. Pecos jumped it like a skip rope and lunged toward her foe. The drummers pounded the skins harder and their thumps grew deeper and faster. Rachel strained to watch the mock battle through the flickering firelight. Her eyes and throat burned from the thick campfire smoke, pushed in her direction by the shifting wind. Pecos jumped and hooted, tumbling in a summersault to avoid the attack. She stumbled on a rock as she attempted to regain her footing from a full flip. Through the smoke, Rachel tried to see if her counselor was wounded. The Comanche took advantage of Pecos's misfortunate fall and stood over her prone body, ready for the kill.

"Watch out, Mama!" Rachel shrieked. She hoped to God that no one heard her and prayed that the frantic drums and the gasps of other campers had drowned out her cry.

Suddenly, Pecos turned toward the Comanche and grabbed her leg. The Indian in rust hit the dry ground, and Pecos pounced, stomping her foot on her opponent's stomach in perfect simulation. With a yell that made Rachel's heart skip, Pecos shoved her rubber lance into the Comanche's side. Rachel stood stunned while the members of her tribe jumped up and down in jubilation. They had won the session. They were the victors!

The next morning, Rachel attempted to open her crusty eyes, swollen from the smoke and tears from the Council Fire. When she realized that most of her friends were going home, she felt like a truck was sitting on her chest. After a few squirts from the inhaler, her breathing returned to normal. News traveled that one camper was sent to the infirmary because the girl bordered on hysteria about leaving her buddies.

The cling-clang-cling of the triangle signaled it was time for breakfast in the mess hall. Rachel threw on her shorts and CRB t-shirt and swung open the screen door to the cabin.

"Let's sit together for our last meal," Angenue said.

"You make it sound like we're condemned prisoners, but I guess going home to the real world is a rough sentence." Rachel was glad hers was commuted for a few weeks.

"I doubt you know anything about prison, Rachel. You just don't want to know. Let's go get something to eat!" Angenue looked away but then regained her smile.

The two girls sprinted to breakfast. They slid into the long wooden bench at cabin nine's table. The camp cook, Lupe, placed platters of *migas*—scrambled eggs mixed with tortillas and chorizo sausages—at one end of the table. It was passed from girl to girl, the golden mound diminishing as it made its way down to Rachel's end of the table, followed by baskets of biscuits and pitchers of cold milk. The buses were already lined up along the circular road out front, so the campers had to eat quickly. They fortified themselves for the ride back to Dallas with homemade strawberry jam and biscuits as fluffy as white clouds.

After the meal, the singing commenced with "Michael Row Your Boat Ashore." Then Pecos started one of her favorites.

Grandma's in the cellar. You can surely smell her

making biscuits on her dirty ol' stove.

And the matter in her eye, keeps drip-ping in the batter

as she whistles while the . . . (sniff) runs down her nose.

Everyone giggled as one hundred and twenty girls snorted together like a herd of cattle with a bad case of the sniffles. The joke never got old.

Angenue started the next song. Her deep, clear voice sang out, "We shall overcome. We shall overcome." She and Rachel swayed together singing, "Deep in my heart, I do believe . . ."

Rachel had heard Joan Baez singing it before. Her duet with Angenue blossomed into a full chorus of female voices—rich and full, high and squeaky—singing together.

A mountain of duffel bags and footlockers flanked the bus. Its silvery sides were peeled open to reveal the cavernous baggage compartment. A muscular man with a black support brace around his middle tossed the luggage into the bus with the header board that read, "Dallas YWCA." Rachel's gear remained in cabin nine, where she would be spending the next two weeks. Angenue handed her an autograph book decorated with a hot pink dachshund on the cover.

"Sign it, girl. Let's stay in touch! We sing a *bad* duet," she said.

"You're the one with the bitchin' voice. I'm just the back-up guitar player," Rachel replied. Her Gibson guitar was neatly stowed under her bed in the cabin. "Angenue, I'm really gonna miss you. Promise to come see me in Dallas."

"Who knows? I might just do that. I'd better start saving up for the bus fare." The two friends hugged tightly and let their embrace last an extra beat.

Sally Belle grabbed Rachel's arm to get her attention. "Rach, sorry for that mess about the horns."

"And now I'll know a *mezuzah* when I see one," Adrian added. "Pretty lame, huh?"

"Not any dumber than me thinking I had cancer. How could I be so dense? Have a great trip, y'all. Don't take any wooden skateboards!"

Rachel faced the new two-week session with sorrow over her friends who went home and experienced trepidation about making new ones. She tried out for medicine man, but a four-year veteran defeated her.

As a last ditch effort to win a medal for her father, she entered the swim meet in the breaststroke form competition, even though the sound of it made her blush a little because she didn't have breasts that amounted to much yet. She and Jane, a younger camper, represented the Apaches.

They were required to swim the length of the Olympic pool, demonstrating the best stroke possible. Rachel strained to time her frog kicks so her legs would smoothly close and not scissor, a major deduction. Toward the shallow end at the finish, her feet slapped together, breaking the surface of the water. Members of her tribe clapped lightly as she climbed out of the ice-cold artesian pool water. *Maybe I didn't do too badly*, she calmed herself.

Her teammate Jane was the next competitor. "Good luck! Go kick some Comanche butt!" Rachel said, shivering from her swim, her goose bumps still stiff at attention.

"Yeah, but I'd better not make any splashes when I do!" Jane eased into the water. Although she was a year younger than Rachel, she made her way through the length of the pool without a ripple.

Then Heather and Gretchen swam for the Comanches, gliding more like swans than frogs with their strong kicks.

Rachel held her breath as she watched the judges mount the diving board to announce the winners. Sunny, who had played the dead warrior at the Council Fire last session, looked up from her clipboard and announced loudly, "Campers, we've scored the winners. Y'all, it's a bit unusual, but here goes: First place goes to the Apaches, with Jane doing a wonderful example of how the breaststroke should be done—flawlessly."

Rachel listened anxiously to hear her name.

"We have a tie for second place going to the Comanches with Heather and Gretchen. Good job, everyone!"

Rachel gasped for air as if she had swallowed a mouthful of pool water. *How am I going to explain this to Papa: coming in last and having three of the four girls medal. Maybe he won't ask—fat chance!* She thought it would be worse than telling him she had "the curse" during the first session swim meet.

With the exception of swimming, Rachel loved the rest of her activities at camp. She roasted marshmallow s'mores at the end of stretched-out coat hangers at the campouts under the big skies. Pecos pointed out Pleiades, the twinkling seven sisters. Rachel imagined that these sisters loved each other and wanted to spend an eternity together. She was glad to be away from her two siblings.

Pecos explained how they weren't really a constellation, but were part of Taurus the Bull. She scanned the sky to find the celestial group and explained how the Kiowa Indians had described the stars: "A long time ago, seven little Indian girls were playing so hard that they wandered away from their teepees. They came across huge bears that chased them. Unfortunately, they had strayed too far from home to get help."

Rachel lay in her bedroll listening to the tale, craning her neck to count the twinkling sisters.

 Pecos's voice rose dramatically, "They scrambled up the highest boulder they could find and began to pray for safety. Since they were good little sisters, the boulder answered their prayers and grew high enough to lift them into the heavens. The bears didn't give up and kept scratching and clawing at the rock to attack the sisters."

Rachel shifted to find a more comfortable position on the hard ground. *Even girls in myths aren't safe.*

By the light of the campfire, Pecos said, "But the rock lifted them to safety so the bears couldn't reach them. The little girls turned into stars, and the Kiowas named the craggy rock *Mateo Tipi*, known as Devil's Tower in Wyoming." A steady stream of smoke rose in the sky.

Rachel was consumed with worry. She would see her sisters in a few days, and she wasn't sure how they would treat her. She couldn't understand why Mama hadn't written in a long while. No word from P.J. either. Lately Rachel didn't have to recall many country-western songs at mail call. When Pecos asked her to name a Tammy Wynette tune in exchange for a small white envelope, she called out one of the singer's biggest hits, "D-I-V-O-R-C-E." Only the odd little notes from Papa arrived, about once a week.

The session flew by and Tribal Council approached with its customary solemnity. This time Rachel wept as she stood in the circle of campers surrounding the raging bonfire. She sang sad songs, hoping the warriors would stall a while before their final dance. She moved toward the searing embers, her braids glowing orange against the fiery backdrop.

Both chiefs bowed deeply to each other. Their rows of feathers and fur skirted the black dirt. As they straightened upright, the whoops and howls of the warriors crashed through the solemnity. This time, after a fierce battle, Pecos was sprawled out, still and broken in the dirt, in mock death after a Comanche lance felled her.

That night while Rachel lay in her bunk, thoughts of Pecos—beaten, lying lifeless on the ground—robbed her of a peaceful night's sleep. The images melded with the memory of Mama's old bruises, which crept up when she least expected it.

The next morning Rachel boarded the bus. During the ride, she passed the time by reading the autographs in her book, savoring the juicy messages from her pals. Addresses and jokes filled the pages lined with doodles in the margins.

The bus driver called back in a deep voice, "Campers, next stop is the Dallas YWCA. Welcome home, y'all."

Through the glare cast by the afternoon sun, Rachel looked out the window to see if she could catch a glimpse of Mama amid the crowds of parents huddled together, all awaiting the arrival of their daughters. She walked carefully down the wide steps of the bus, smack into the wall of July heat in Dallas.

"Red, over here!"

Rachel heard her father's voice from the pack of parents. It was Papa—alone. "Where's Mama?" she asked, frantically searching for her mother's beautiful face.

"She's not feeling so good right now. Just a little accident, but she's on the mend. We didn't say anything because we didn't want to worry you. She'll be just fine. So how many medals did you bring home?"

"Are Hedy and Lenora back from Springland yet?" Rachel asked, trying to change the subject.

"Your grandparents are dropping them off tomorrow afternoon."

Rachel was relieved he didn't resume his inquiries about the swim meet. She couldn't look at her father and desperately longed for her mother. Papa led her to the Chevy, and she sat hugging the door, staring ahead as they merged onto the expressway. They drove the whole way home in silence.

The next morning Papa and Rachel went to Parkland Hospital. He parked in a lot that seemed miles away from the front. The searing August heat beat down, doubling in intensity from the asphalt parking lot. His strong hand on her neck guided Rachel through the electronic doors at the entrance, where a blast of cold air from the stark lobby hit her.

Papa walked in front of his anxious daughter toward the elevator bank. He punched the button and they rode together in silence. The elevator doors peeled open and the pair stepped onto the third floor.

He stopped and turned toward Rachel, gripping her shoulders. "Red, Mom's had a terrible accident, but she's going to get better. Don't show how upset you are when you see her. Tell your mother she looks good. I promise we won't stay long."

Rachel nodded and wished she could escape on the elevator. They reached a door with a chart attached to a plastic bin; the name on the top line was written in blue ink—"Sharon Rosenshein Miller." Papa pushed on the metal bar to open the soundless door, and Rachel inched into the room, trailing behind him. Sunlight streamed in from the windows with parchment-colored shades in a roll at the top. A beam of light hit Mama's bandages on her face. One eye was closed and the other was wrapped in layers of gauze secured by wide white tape down to her chin. Her hand dangled from a sling around her arm. Mama's dark brown lashes of the closed eye began to flutter, and then tears leaked onto her pillow. "Honey bun, I'm so glad to see my little baby. How was camp?"

The blood seemed to drain from Rachel's head, and the room started to spin like a record on her turntable. Air wouldn't flow into her lungs. She thought she was breathing but emitted no sound. Papa caught her when her spindly knees buckled.

Through a haze she could hear Mama shouting, "Quick, get the nurse!"

GETTING OUT

CHAPTER 14

AFTER SEEING HER MOTHER lying broken and bandaged in the hospital, Rachel never liked to visit friends when they were laid up in medical facilities. Too many memories haunted her.

She also tried to erase the heart-stopping moment when she came upon Jillian lying in the hospital after the shooting—instead of Missy. The last time she saw her daughter alive was when she drove off to Austin, convertible top down, ponytail flying in the sun.

The house was filled with silence without Missy. Grasping for normalcy, Michael went back to work two days after the funeral. P.J. and Juan returned to Austin on Saturday, and soon after, the steady stream of visitors dwindled. Mama dropped over every day and tidied up and did some cooking—always remaining in a state of perpetual motion, flitting from room to room.

Rachel spent most of the time in her bedroom, occasionally venturing downstairs when her mother called to share a bite of lunch. Rachel dutifully sat at her desk and wrote thank-you cards for the many expressions of sympathy. Mama had ordered preprinted cards engraved with a simple line that was meant to succinctly express gratitude. Rachel merely had to sign her name, and if she felt the need, jot a personal note. Rosy had taught her that there's nothing worse than failing to acknowledge a gift or dinner at someone's home without promptly sending a thank-you note. She said it was considered ill-mannered to do otherwise and the same held true with condolences.

Michael came home from work, often to find his wife burrowed beneath her down comforter. He became adept at rifling through the pile of take-out menus in the kitchen drawer and ordering dinner for the two of them. Rachel gradually lost interest in her appearance and often wore a bathrobe or a loose-fitting denim shift and padded around the house in her slippers that cushioned her steps.

Cloistered in his study, Michael read or watched television until he was sufficiently tired or numb enough to sleep. A few nights after the funeral, he climbed into bed, molding his body against Rachel's plump back and hips. He whispered, "Honey, is this okay?" He kissed her ear and slowly began to press against her. "Just meet me a little," he pleaded like a hungry child.

She turned toward him, closing the space between their bodies. His kisses, moist and open, were the kind that usually ignited her passion, but she felt dead and brittle inside. But still she clung to Michael, hoping his warmth would revive her.

"Ready, babe?" he asked.

Rachel moaned softly in quiet whimpers. Without the usual response of her body, she felt like he ripped her flesh, pumping hard inside her.

During their lovemaking, she tried to push away the sense that Missy was hovering above their bed, wondering how her parents could find pleasure at a time when they should be grieving. Rachel tried to tell herself that maybe this would ease the excruciating pain. Then she realized Michael's movements had slowed and then he slipped out of her, limp and defeated. He stroked the dry strands of hair from her forehead and whispered, "Sorry, Rach, I guess I'm beat. We'll try again later if you want to."

I don't, she thought. "Okay, maybe later," she mumbled.

Rachel didn't notice the change of seasons. Suddenly, the trees were stripped bare and lawns had turned golden brown. The sun sank earlier in the sky, but the hours crawled by slowly.

Mama called one morning to suggest an outing. "Honey bun, it's time you got out of that house. I'm picking you up in an hour to take you to Ledbetter's."

"Not today. Maybe next week," Rachel begged off, still in bed at eleven o'clock.

"Just get dressed because I'm coming. And wash your hair . . . so let's make it twelve-thirty."

Rachel knew there was no sense arguing with her mother. She hung up and started to get ready, although Rachel had no appetite for her favorite burger. Instead of Seinfeld's "Soup Nazi," Dallas had the "Hamburger Heckler," Logan Ledbetter.

She stepped into the steaming shower and closed her eyes while she shampooed, remembering all the times she and Mama had been to that hamburger joint over the years since she was a kid. It required a fairly thick skin to eat at Ledbetter's because Logan took orders while flinging insults at customers, like Don Rickles on the main stage of a Las Vegas showroom.

They used to stop by for a quick bite before Cotillion when Mama didn't feel like cooking that night. Although she was still young and beautiful, Rosy would walk in the front door and Logan would ask, "What'll ya have, you old bag? Hurry up, I don't got all night, and you don't look like you've got much time left either."

Rachel shrank back from the counter, standing just out of his line of vision. Rosy knew she was good-looking, so his insults slid off her back.

He leaned to the side, fixing Rachel in his cool sights and asked, "What about you, pip-squeak? When are you going to clean those spots off your face, carrot top?" Logan instinctively honed in on her freckles that she hated and wasn't allowed to cover with makeup yet.

"She'll have the same as me: a rare BigBurger with no onions and extra pickles. We'll also split a brownie." Mama flashed her prettiest smile at Logan, expecting to disarm his tough guy act.

"And you, sweet cheeks, can wipe that grin off your lips. Take your seats, and I'll call ya when it's ready."

"Now Logan, you just behave yourself," Mama cajoled with a honey-coated twang.

"You just better watch it or you'll be eating your burgers in the gravel parking lot out back."

Undaunted, she paid in advance and grabbed a little table. Rachel looked into the sad black glassy eyes of a taxidermied head of a longhorn on the wall. Some friends from school rattled off their orders, cringing or giggling at Logan's insults about their acne, braces, or haircuts. Everyone put up with Logan's routine and hoped he would single out someone else to ridicule—the burgers were just that good.

Over the years, Rachel figured it must have been in his training manual that it was against the rules to be friendly to customers. Logan probably taught his cooks how to sling burgers without cracking a smile. The brownies were as rich as fudge, topped with powdered sugar that made Rachel cough at the first bite, spreading a white film over her lap. On Cotillion night, she covered herself in extra napkins and kept a stick of Juicy Fruit gum in her purse.

For years, a red hand-lettered sign appeared above the wood grill, declaring the right to refuse to serve anyone. That included Rachel's high school and college dates with long hair, who had grown up wolfing down Ledbetter burgers. Hippies, suspected red Commies, and just about anyone who displeased Logan were turned away. In the early sixties, he erected in his parking lot a statue of the Soviet Premier Nikita Khrushchev holding his shoe between two sesame buns. The inscription engraved on the pedestal proclaimed, "Hey, Hoss, Eat This!"

Following her family tradition, Rachel took Missy there occasionally, although her daughter's burger of choice was from a commercial chain. Rachel couldn't understand how Missy didn't fully appreciate the joy of eating a patty with real crisscross grill marks and juice that dripped into the paper wrapping, amid the insults. Logan still barked at everyone from behind the dingy counter, but Missy was fearless. She stood at Rachel's side when they placed their orders.

"So, you brought the little carrot top with you this time. How you doing, you old bag?" he asked Rachel.

She wanted to tell Logan that if anyone were old, it was he, because his greased-back hair had dwindled to a glossy dome. Rachel mustered her courage and said, "Now, Logan, you act nice. I know you want to smile, but your face has gotten frozen in a frown after all these years."

Missy ordered her burgers, rattling off, "Two rare BigBurgers, no onions, extra pickles, and two Dr. Peppers," flashing a big grin at the end. Logan's piercing blue eyes settled on Missy, then he turned and bantered with his rotund cook standing near the searing wood fire, "These two gals are really pushing their luck, don't ya think, Slim?"

Slim gave Rachel the required scowl, wrinkling his sweaty brow, and then flashed a quick wink at Missy when Logan turned his back to pour their soft drinks.

Two short beeps of Mama's car in the driveway signaled her arrival. Rachel's hair was still damp. Ignoring her mother's life-long warning that she would catch her death if she went out with wet hair, Rachel set the burglar alarm and ran out the front door. Leaning across the seat, she gave Mama a quick peck. Rachel suspected that her mother drew back a little, but she wasn't sure.

"Honey bun, did you brush your teeth this morning?" Mama asked.

"I guess so," Rachel muttered, running her tongue across the sticky surface of her front teeth, trying to remember.

"And that wet head of hair . . ."

"Don't start on me, Mama. Let's skip Ledbetter's today. I don't know if I can handle Logan's tough guy act right now."

Mama dug into her purse and pulled out a silver tube. "Here, put on a little lipstick. It'll do you a world of good, Rachel." Mama continued driving in the same direction. "Once you're set on eating something, it's hard to change horses mid-stream. Ledbetter's, here we come, ready or not!"

Miraculously, as they pulled up in front of the restaurant, a car backed out from a spot near the front door next to Khrushchev. Mama always had good parking karma.

The hinges of the front door squealed when they entered, and Rachel thought the stuffed longhorn gave her an accusatory stare. Logan turned around from the grill to size up his next prey that had entered his lair. He wiped his brow with his sleeve and called out, "Hey, Rachel, what'll ya have, darlin'?"

She was surprised at the first nice thing Logan had ever said to her. Rachel surmised he must have heard the tragic news about Missy.

THE SECRET

CHAPTER 15

FOR THE LIFE OF HER, Rachel couldn't figure out why Michael's touch chilled her to the bone. His caress made her feel dead inside. She used to love his scent, the way he rested his hand on her hip while he slept, but now he left her cold. She decided to look at old photos to try to find something that would rekindle the feelings of love she once felt for him.

Rachel climbed the stairs to the attic to find the footlocker she had used at Camp Rio Bravo, shuffling the stacks of old newspapers and magazines off the top of the scratched and dented lid. She had saved issues of *Life Magazine* and editions of the two competing local news dailies encased in plastic bags. In *The Dallas Morning News*, yellowed headlines announced, "Kennedy Slain on Dallas Street" and "Club Owner Kills Oswald." Jack Ruby's .38-caliber pistol was pointed at Lee Harvey Oswald a moment before he fired in the police station in the basement of the Dallas Municipal Building. The *Times Herald* captured the full horror of the next split second when Oswald flinched from Ruby's single fatal bullet severing his major abdominal blood vessels.

Rachel gingerly opened the brittle newspaper to read the inside article reporting that Oswald had died from cardiac arrest about an hour and a half after he was wheeled into the same hospital trauma unit where President Kennedy had been pronounced dead two days earlier. A little rip skittered across the center gutter of the paper when she opened the spread.   She didn't dare remove the plastic bag protecting the "Warren Report" issue of *Life Magazine* with freeze frames of the Zapruder film on the cover. She carefully replaced it in the trunk.   These papers that celebrated death—violent times in the nation—were part of her history, along with the unrest in her home.

Rachel sniffled from handling the musty relics of her past. Her chest constricted slightly from inhaling the dust particles from her memories: old loose photos, dried corsages, and her wedding album. She started to flip though the pages.

Years before when shown the trunk of keepsakes, twelve-year-old Missy said impishly, "Mom, you probably keep this stuff to remind you of when you were a *wild and crazy girl*."

Rachel doubted ever being really wild. She and P.J. were never in any serious trouble when they were youngsters.

"Why in the heck do I hold onto these old textbooks and class notes? They're still in the same boxes your Grandma Rosy gave me when your dad and I bought our own house. I can't seem to get rid of these college linguistics books and assignments from my elementary students at East Austin," Rachel said, sorting through the trunk.

When Rosy moved into a high-rise in an enclosed development of apartments and condos near Northwest Highway, she had handed over most of the childhood clutter, saying it was time for Rachel and her sisters to be responsible for safekeeping their own pasts.

Missy sat on the floor next to Rachel and rifled through her mother's memorabilia, retrieving a tarnished silver chain with a huge peace sign hanging at the end. Dangling it in front of Rachel, she asked, "Mom, when did you ever wear this thing?"

"At the Texas International Pop Festival in the summer before I went to college. The Who played."

"How should I know who played?"

"Yeah, they were great!"

"Well, if you don't remember who was the band," Missy sassed.

"I just said that The Who played. It killed me every time Peter Townsend smashed his guitar. Since you don't seem to know, The Who was the coolest rock band ever. This is beginning to sound like an Abbott and Costello routine," Rachel said, fingering the silver amulet.

"Who?"

"For God's sakes, never mind!" Rachel tossed the peace sign back into the pile.

Missy reached into the trunk again and pulled out a yellow-tinged wedding invitation. "Okay, tell me again how you and Dad met."

"Oh, honey, you know the story." Rachel began the sanitized version she had always told her daughter: "Your father was a gifted young architect who was in Austin for a conference, and he met me at a party. We hit it off right away. He always says I stalked him all night, but every time I looked up, he was checking *me* out. We started dating long distance, and then when I finished my master's degree, we got married and I moved back to Dallas."

Missy seemed satisfied and was soon lost in examining her parents' wedding guest book and piles of old snapshots.

The weekend Rachel and Michael met, he had flown to Austin for an urban development conference. On the first night of the three-day symposium, renowned local architect Julian Miers hosted a reception at his townhouse. A trailblazer, he renovated a crumbling historic building on Travis Street downtown amid the juke joints and dingy bars where men drank in the half-light and played forty-two, a Texas-style version of dominoes. Jules and his wife, Alicia, occupied their oasis of comfort and style securely locked behind a decorative wrought iron gate that served as a protective barrier against the seedy street life. Electronic controls to open the gate and remote cameras were discretely hidden from view. Only a modest, engraved brass nameplate, "J. & A. Miers–Private

Residence," nestled in the beige limestone façade, gave a hint as to what lay within.

Alicia and Rachel met at an antique shop in Buda, a small town about twenty miles from downtown Austin. Rachel was working on an eponymy field study for her linguistics class to research the derivation of the name Buda, incongruent for a hamlet in central Texas. Sarah Lambert, a long-time resident and owner of Lambert's Antiques and Nonesuch, informed her that the name "Buda" was a bastardization of a Spanish word. A Mexican widow once owned a large spread in the late nineteenth century. Eventually the Texans transformed the Spanish word for "widow," *viuda*, to "Buda," because *V*s and *B*s sound alike in Spanish.

A woman with wiry salt and pepper hair and smiling eyes who was browsing through the frayed Navajo blankets said, "I always thought it was because a Hindu sect once lived here. These days it's such an art colony—with all of the potters and woodworkers—and the hippies who run the Chinese Restaurant."

"No, it's from people messing up a Spanish word. But come to think of it, pretty wild to have a Chinese Restaurant way out here in the middle of the sticks. But don't they make the best bubble iced tea?" Rachel said.

"I'm crazy about pearl milk tea! But I bet the food probably comes straight out of a can, because how could they get all of those exotic ingredients out here?" The woman extended her hand. "Hi, I'm Alicia Miers. Sounds like we should go out to dinner together sometime. Are you married?"

Rachel gently pulled her hand away and then stroked the scratchy weave of the blanket. "No. I'm Rachel . . . Rachel Miller. I'm a graduate student at UT."

"Rachel, happily married women are as unrelenting as Hari Krishnas—always trying to bring others into the marriage fold. It's kind of a game. My husband, Jules, and I are throwing a party tomorrow night—a reception for TLC. I hope you'll try to make it."

Rachel began to feel like she was being recruiting by a dating service. But Alicia seemed so genuine that she pursued it a bit further. "What's TLC?"

"The Texas Leadership Coalition. We spearhead the urban council that revitalizes downtowns in Texas while still preserving their original character. There will be lots of young architects from Austin, Dallas, and Houston—a very fertile hunting ground."

"Sounds hard to resist. I'll really try, but I'm not sure about what's happening without my calendar," Rachel vaguely agreed to attend.

Later she considered the idea overnight and figured she had little to lose by going, other than a few hours of studying.

The next evening at seven sharp, she stood outside the iron gate, speaking loudly into an invisible microphone to a disembodied voice from inside the townhouse.

"Alicia, it's Rachel Miller—from the antique store in Buda."

"Hi, Alicia. It's Michael, too," a voice echoed from behind her.

The buzzer sizzled through the crisp November night and the lock automatically clicked open. "You first," he said.

The pair entered the warmth and light of the architect's home—a mixture of Southwestern and Bauhaus. The clean lines and white walls were punctuated with hand-hewn knotty pine beams, and a cantilevered staircase led to a landing draped with kaleidoscopic, patterned Navajo blankets. Clusters of candles and statues of saints were grouped on a pile of architecture books that served as an end table.

A middle-aged man holding a carved pipe emerged from a group. He reached to put his arm around Michael's back and gave him a warm hug.

"Jules, with all that security, I'm surprised you're not issuing guns," Michael jibed.

"Very funny. Michael, glad you could make it. Who's your date?"

"She's from an antique store in Buda. I don't know her yet, but hopefully that'll change."

Alicia rushed over to them in a swish of suede fringe on her shawl. "Rachel, so glad you could make it. Meet Michael Frank from Dallas. Michael, this is Rachel Miller."

They smiled and nodded to each other.

"Why don't y'all grab something to drink? The sangria's in the kitchen," she said, disappearing into a group of guests.

"Rachel, so you're into antiques? Good thing you're not another architect, so we don't have to talk shop all evening," Michael said, his warm eyes sparkling.

"No, I don't have anything to do with antiques. Alicia and I just met yesterday in a funky shop in Buda. I'm working on my master's degree in Romance linguistics while teaching Spanish at East Austin Elementary."

The ping-pong exchange of information when two people meet began. They asked about hometowns and siblings. Rachel confessed that at times it felt like she had two too many. Michael said he was an only child. *Probably spoiled*, Rachel thought.

Michael confided he hoped to have a lot of children because he always felt so alone as a kid. His statement made Rachel regret her snap judgment. Never before had she heard a man volunteer that he was interested in having a family. Usually the guys she knew were only up for the fun that comes without making babies.

Michael had lost both of his parents to different cancers within two years of each other while he was in graduate school. Rachel awkwardly stuttered a few words of sympathy and failed to tell him that in a way, she, too, had lost her father.

The conversation drifted toward their professions. As if Jules had radar when he heard an architectural term, he walked over to Michael and asked, "Did you hear that the contract for the new arena is up for bids?"

Rachel took this as her cue to move along and mingle. "I'm going to check out the nachos." She walked across the room to where Alicia was standing. Michael was deep in conversation with Jules, but his eyes followed her.

Interesting-looking people filled the room, like a Southwestern version of eclectic cocktail parties Rachel had seen in movies like *Auntie Mame*. A famous local potter and his adoring female apprentice cuddled in a corner near a massive R.C. Gorman vase decorated with a bevy of Indian maidens. Rachel collected snippets of conversation as she wove in and out admiring the artifacts. Kevin, the owner of a nearby restaurant, was talking to friends about expanding to a second location across from the campus. A professor of anthropology from the university gesticulated wildly while expounding on the rituals of body language at social gatherings.

Rachel overheard a silver coiffed TLC board member responding to a young woman who had admired the doyenne's diamond rose broach that was as enormous as a Texas cockroach. The older woman said, "Darlin', I've got a lot more in the safe at home that are better than this ol' thang. I married well—but divorced much better!"

Richard Roberts, a Houston architect with slicked back hair, stopped Rachel and bragged about how he used to own a mansion in River Oaks, the swankiest part of Houston, but his ex-wife got it. *Why do guys always try to impress you with their money right off the bat?* Rachel wondered. When he was complaining about the enormous settlement his third wife stole from him, Rachel desperately looked around the room, hoping to find a reason to escape.

Out of the corner of her eye, she spotted Michael chatting with an attractive, slim blonde. He was laughing and they seemed to be hitting it off. Then he glanced over and caught Rachel watching him. She quickly turned her attention to "Mr. Moneybags" and then excused herself to go to the little girls' room. Up the stairs, which seemed to float in the space by hidden suspension supports, she found her way to a guest bath. In the mirror, she looked at what a man like Michael might see in her. *Not too bad,* she assessed herself. Her red hair always caught people's attention. The purple cut velvet dress set off her figure and coloring well. She decided if he had any interest, he'd stop her before she left the party.

Heading toward the stairs, she saw Michael leaning against the railing on the landing. "Oh, great, you're still here!" he said. "I wanted to get back to you, but Alicia's sister-in-law and I had a chance to catch up with each other. She and her husband live in New Orleans. Ever been there?"

Rachel hoped he hadn't noticed her sigh of relief and berated herself for being so uncool. She felt surprised that so quickly after they met, the prickly green thorns of jealousy had sprouted.

"Not yet, but I've heard Mardi Gras is a zoo." He was close enough that Rachel could smell his cologne.

"You should see the *real* New Orleans. I think you'd love it."

They went downstairs and sat on a sofa in an alcove lined with shelves of neatly arranged pre-Columbian pots: mothers crouching in childbirth, three-legged vessels shaped like bulbous mammaries, and various feathered serpents coiled as if ready to strike. Michael described his passion for commercial urban structures, envisioning skyscrapers on a more humanistic scale—not the gleaming, reflective glass and steel rectangles that were sprouting up all over the Southwest.

Alicia glided by and slipped a glass of sangria into Rachel's hand. Slices of oranges and peaches bobbed on the surface. "We call our little downtown hideaway, *La Sorpresa,* 'surprise' in Spanish. But, Rachel, you probably already know this since you're a linguist. People are always surprised by what's behind our gate out front. We love living downtown instead of in the lily-white suburbs." She clinked their glasses and then left to circulate.

"Urban planning needs more multiculturalism. White flight's killing our inner-cities," Michael said.

"Glad to hear you have a social conscience. I figured you were a good ol' boy, with that crack you made about totin' guns," Rachel teased.

"I'm good—but not so old." His eyes sparkled, and she decided his flirting didn't seem rehearsed. "And what about you, 'Miss Politically Correct'?" he sparred.

"I teach in a racially mixed school while I'm getting my master's. I'm hooked on the structure of language, but with Romance linguistics, there isn't much chance of doing anything with it unless I teach on the college level."

"Romance linguistics, that's a new one."

"It's all about how languages are built—the bricks and mortar of communication. I study how Vulgar Latin metamorphosed into Spanish, French, and Italian. My minor's Spanish, but you need written command of all of those languages to trace the verbal evolution. I hope I'm not making your eyes cross with all this."

"No, we both work with building blocks, of a sort. How about getting out of here to check out Sixth Street?"

The sangria began to kick in and her cheeks suddenly felt flushed. Michael intrigued her. She decided he wasn't slick like that awful Richard from Houston. "I'll go find Alicia to tell her we're taking off."

"Don't worry, we'll catch her when we get back."

Rachel grabbed her purse. Michael draped her coat around her shoulders, brushing his hand against her neck as he smoothed the collar. Surprise!—a current sizzled through her. Alicia smiled from the doorway in the kitchen and waved to the newly formed couple while Willie Nelson softly wailed in the background about being crazy and lonely.

The pair left behind the tinkle of glasses and swells of conversation as the gate clanged shut. Stepping into the cool night air, Michael held her elbow to steady Rachel as they ambled over the sidewalk that was a jigsaw puzzle of cracks. The noise from the bars blasted the stillness, and then a man staggered out of the Rusty Bucket Saloon, almost plowing into them.

After a few more steps, Michael took Rachel's hand. Their palms molded to each other and his smooth, artistic fingers warmed hers.

They talked about Willie Nelson's beat-up guitar named Trigger, architect/designer Michael Graves, linguist Noam Chomsky, and the constellations. Even with the city lights, the stars winked clearly above Austin. Rachel looked for Pleiades and pointed it out. Michael said he used to attend Boy Scout camp and had earned a merit badge naming the constellations. He ran through about six before she made him quit, laughing that she was getting a crick in her neck from looking up.

They ambled past the historic Driskill Hotel, beyond its prime like a grande dame whose youth and beauty had faded. Michael said it was sorely in need of restoration and pointed out remnants of its former elegance. They continued walking and turned right on South Congress Avenue toward the pink granite State Capitol Building with the statue of the Goddess of Liberty glowing atop the dome like a crown jewel on the skyline.

"It's made of sunset red granite from Marble Falls," he said.

"Who'd guess that they'd pick pink for the color of the Texas Capitol?" Rachel suddenly regretted her remark, hoping Michael didn't think it was insipid or homophobic. She began to shiver in the moist night air and leaned toward his warm body.

They walked with his arm around her for a few blocks. "It's cooling off. Want to head back?" he asked.

"I'm sure Alicia's congratulating herself that we skipped out together. But if you're ready, so am I." On the return lap, she asked, "What have you been working on lately?"

"I've put in a bid for a neighborhood branch of the library in South Dallas. Hopefully, it'll double as a community learning center as well. The rooms fan out in a pentagon."

"Bad choice of words these days," Rachel kidded.

"Yeah, but the space works. The plans are in my room in the Driskill, if you want to see them?"

The couple was standing in front of the stolid pillars of the hotel entrance. "I've heard of guys trying to show their etchings, but coming up to see blueprints is a new twist!" Rachel said, putting her hands on her hips in mock anger.

"No, honestly, I didn't mean it to sound like a pick-up line," he laughed.

"Okay, let's have a look." She felt like a teenager sneaking into the hotel. Rachel gazed up at the stained glass domed ceiling in the lobby's grand hall and then guiltily studied the patterns in the deep cut carpet while Michael asked the desk clerk for the room key. The filigreed elevator chugged upstairs and stopped with a gentle bounce on the fourth floor. They headed down the hall, passing by paintings of cattle grazing in torrid Texas sunsets.

Michael slid the oversized brass key into the lock and pushed open the heavily carved door. An electric gas-lamp bathed the room in a honeyed glow. Rachel tossed her coat on the tufted chintz chair and surveyed the room. The bed, with the burgundy fringed velvet spread, had already been turned back with two bedside chocolates wrapped in gold foil on the pillows. She checked to see if they were her favorites, Austin-made Lammes chocolate turtles called Longhorns, but they weren't.

Michael went to the desk and pulled a set of blueprints from a leather tube. He rolled them out on the desk, securing the curled pages with the lamp base on one end and Rachel's purse on the other. Their heads drew close together when he pointed out the features of the library. "The card catalogs are bleached white oak, and the stacks . . ."

They moved toward each other for a kiss that seemed inevitable, and he lifted her chin with his long fingers. He was still talking when their lips first met, and then their mouths found each other. An explosion went through Rachel's mind and body when he kissed her. His probing intensity made her quiver and feel moist in the right places.

They moved around the room, wrapped in kisses, caught in the privacy of the old hotel room with the bed looming everywhere. When they came up for air, Michael said, "Rachel, I really didn't bring you up here to get you in the sack. I'm not that smooth."

"I'm not like that either," she said, pulling him closer.

Somehow, Rachel knew that their chemistry had happened spontaneously—that they were connected in some inexplicable way. *Maybe I just like the way he looks or how he kisses, but it's more than that,* she thought. Something about him moved her. She wanted to be with him.

Their hands moved over each other's bodies. Then with increasing speed, arms flailed to remove errant buttons and release zippers.

"Michael, I don't just jump into bed with just anyone," Rachel said, fumbling with his belt.

"Me neither. Just promise you'll respect me in the morning!"

They laughed and kissed. Rachel felt transported to another world, in the hotel room from another era. Couples had made love and fought in that room for a century. When the last of their clothes were piled on the floor, Michael guided them to the high four-poster. Up the step stool, she reached for his neck as she perched on the bed. "Just lean back, Rachel," he whispered and kneeled on the Persian rug. His hungry mouth made his way down from her lips to her breasts. "Let me teach you a thing or two about Romance linguistics," he whispered.

They woke up the next morning and knew it was the beginning of something powerful.

Michael said, "Let's not tell our kids about this."

"What's with you and children?" She looked into his sleepy, dark eyes.

His words planted the seed for their future. Rachel never imagined she would meet and bed her *bashert*, Yiddish for "soul mate," at that party.

Rachel and Michael never told Melissa everything about the night they met. Some things were meant to be private, especially from their daughter. They had to bribe "Uncle Jules" and "Aunt Alicia" with a Navajo chief blanket to keep their mouths shut.

Rachel lost track of time, sorting through stacks of old photos from her honeymoon in New Orleans. She examined a snapshot of Michael and her enjoying brunch at Commander's Palace in the Garden District. They beamed with love and the expectation of happiness.

Rachel closed the lid of the trunk. *Is he still my bashert?* She blew her nose and climbed down the stairs from the dusty attic.

CHAPTER 16

RACHEL BELIEVED THAT her best friend also had the good fortune of finding her soul mate. P.J. met Juan when they were art students at The University of Texas. The two girls' friendship easily expanded to three, once P.J. and Juan were an official couple—and eventually Michael completed the foursome.

One day while shopping on the Drag near the campus bookstore, Rachel spotted P.J.'s silky, straight blonde hair.

"P.J., wait up. What's happenin'?"

"Everything's cool. I've just been up to my ears in alligators lately. We've been trying to get my pots fired before the end of the semester. My critique's coming up soon."

"Hey, what's this *we*? Aren't you still dating 'Mr. No-neck'?"

P.J.'s alabaster skin was tinged with pink. "No, I've been seeing a new guy. He's into sculpture."

"How'd you meet him?" Rachel asked, surprised she was left out of the loop.

"In my ceramics class. His amazing hands were what I first noticed—so strong and expressive, like Michelangelo's *David*." Her face relaxed as if she were envisioning them as she spoke.

"Only his hands?"

She smoothed back her hair and laughed. "Well, let's just say at first."

"Is he from Dallas?"

"No, El Paso. He's so talented that he got into UT without the grades or SATs. He's on 'sco-pro' for the year until he proves himself or they'll kick him out. Juan's incredible!   He'll make it out of scholastic probation, I'm dead sure. He wanted to study sculpture with Professor Larson, the best in the state. What's up with you?"

"Just dating around. I go through guys at breakneck speed. Nobody special right now."

P.J. glanced at the clock on campus tower to figure out if there was enough time to make it all the way across campus to the art building for her class that met on the hour. "Gotta run. I'm late. I'll call you tonight to give you the full scoop," she promised.

Rachel watched her cross Guadalupe Street and then disappear into the sea of students scurrying into buildings. The searing rays of the sun assaulted her eyes as she peered up at the observation deck on the twenty-sixth floor above the clock face.

Access to the open area had been off limits for the past several years, ever since a sniper with an arsenal, Charles Whitman, took the tower by force and killed fifteen people and wounded thirty-one others in less than a half hour from his perch above the campus. Rachel was reminded of the gunfire whenever she saw the tower. She stored a collection of violent episodes in her memory, which she couldn't seem to erase.

Rachel knew the details of Whitman's crimes. Before he began his killing spree of picking off unsuspecting strangers from as far as two blocks away, the clean-cut architectural student viciously stabbed to death his mother and wife in their homes. He then drove to school and boarded the tower elevator with a footlocker filled with guns, rifles, and ammo—taking it as high as he could go. He lugged the trunk on a dolly he brought with him for the last five short flights of steps that led to the open platform.

Rachel had learned about the horrible news while she was at Camp Rio Bravo in the scorching August of 1966. It hadn't even been a month after she was reeling from the accounts on the radio about Richard Speck murdering eight nursing students in Chicago. She couldn't believe that another madman had gone on a rampage. It was the first time Rachel ever heard the term "mass murderer." Violence loomed large everywhere.

The news commentators had painted a picture of Whitman's background that seemed as normal as "the boy next door." He had been the youngest Eagle Scout ever, but he grew up at the hands of an abusive father who beat him and his mother. The reports made Rachel shudder when she thought about the way Papa had treated Mama, and it frightened her to hear the details about how Whitman battered his wife and claimed in a note that he killed her to spare her the misery of living in an unjust world. Rachel worried about what drove him over the edge of sanity to commit murder.

Ramiro Martinez, an off-duty policeman who dashed from his home to the tower, put an end to Whitman's troubled life with six well-placed bullets fired at close range. In his autopsy, doctors discovered a walnut-sized tumor on his brain stem, opening speculation about the source of his uncontrollable rage. Whitman's note had also explained that he had killed his mother so she wouldn't have to endure his father's abuse any more.

Rachel wondered if Papa had little a little acorn of hate sprouting in his brain, too.

In the aftermath of the worst mass killing in U.S. history at that time, Governor John Connally finally pledged to re-examine the state's gun laws—this after he himself had been shot three years earlier when President Kennedy was assassinated in Dallas.

To most people, the tower symbolized triumph, but to Rachel, it represented terror. Although it always blazed orange when the university's sports teams were victorious, she imagined it bathed in crimson from the blood of innocent people who were senselessly picked off while they were walking down the street or riding their bikes, even four blocks away.

After her friend left for class that afternoon, Rachel ducked into the bookstore, out of range of the tower.

Later that evening, P.J. called to talk about Juan. She giggled when she described how they made-out between classes on the grass under the wisteria arbor outside the art building.   P.J. loved Juan's eyes, which she described as dark as chocolate mole sauce. A few weeks after she met him, she dropped her jock boyfriend. She and Juan became inseparable, staying late in the ceramics lab to fire their pots until the sun came up, watching the temperature cones melt when it was time to shut off the gas.

"We're getting ready for our Spring Social. What's happening at your sorority?" Rachel asked.

"My sorority big sister is such an asshole," the curse word rolled easily off P.J.'s tongue. "Puddin said she thought it was gross I was dating a Mexican. For one thing, there's nothing wrong with Mexicans, but he's Mexican-American. His parents were born in the good old US-of-A."

"How can you stand being around a bigot? She's the one who's gross!"

"I can't. I'm thinking about dropping out of the house, even though the rest of the girls are pretty nice. Puddin's bullshit is really starting to get to me. Juan told me that when he was a kid, he couldn't drink out of water fountains marked 'for whites only.' He's been called a 'spic,' a 'wetback,' the 'Frito Bandito,' and a bunch of other stuff I don't even want to repeat." The pitch in her voice steadily rose with each epithet. "Rachel, you've even heard Mother say some of those things before."

"Yeah, but never from your dad."

"I know Mother would have a cow if she knew that I was dating Juan, but somehow I don't think that Daddy would mind."

A few days later, P.J. and Juan were in the Student Union, sitting at a battered wooden table, playing hearts with two other students. Her striped poncho skirted the gray linoleum floor, and her knee, as pale as bisque, poked out of her jeans. P.J.'s huarache sandal dangled from her foot tucked under her leg. In contrast, Juan's easy good looks were set off by his university polo, pressed jeans, and high-tops.

Rachel called out to him, *"Hola, ¿qué tal? ¿Estás jugando con el corazón de mi amiga? ¡Ten cuidado!"*

"Rachel, my folks didn't teach me Spanish. I know a few cuss words, but that's about it—like *chinga* and *puta,* pardon my Spanish."

"I just said to be careful playing hearts with my friend," Rachel replied.

"My parents never wanted me to speak Spanish. It was always 'Juanito, *e-speak* English!' They used Spanish like a secret code to keep things from us kids."

"I know what you mean. My mama and grandparents used to speak Yiddish in front of us. All I ever could figure out was *oy ve* and *hoc me a chinuck*—something about how my sisters and I were driving them bonkers."

The afternoons floated by, one after another, as they drank enormous red plastic tumblers of iced tea, whether it was hot or cold outside. The three friends started hanging out together. They went to the Smoothie Shop on San Antonio Street or to a sub sandwich shop, where P.J. and Juan critiqued the mural on the wall—yellow roses blossoming on thorny, trailing vines along with armadillos, the unofficial mascot of Austin.

They spent the weekend evenings at the Armadillo World Headquarters, a National Guard Armory that had been converted into a concert hall. Through wafts of sweet and pungent smoke, they listened to Johnny Rodriguez singing, strutting onstage in his tight jeans. Many of his songs were in Spanish, and some in English were getting airtime on the country stations. Rachel and P.J. were pale spots in a sea of brown faces.

She called Rachel the day after the concert, her voice cracked and nasal.

"Hey, what's the matter?" Rachel asked. Tension sizzled through the wires.

"My mother is from another century. She heard about Juan and me, and she threatened to yank me out of school if I don't stop dating him."

"I'm so freaked. She's just bluffing, isn't she?" Rachel put down her textbook and listened to her friend.

"No, Mother said she and Daddy didn't give a huge endowment to the art department so I could end up with one of 'those people.' When I told her that Juan and I were serious about each other, she said it would be 'over her dead body.' So much for a big church wedding, huh?"

"Wedding, you didn't tell me the two of you were *that* serious. I'm so stoked!" Rachel squealed, forgetting to feel slighted.

"I hope you'll be at the ceremony, whatever it is."

I dreamed of the day, even back when we played with our Barbies. Nothing could keep me from your wedding," Rachel vowed.

"You'll never guess what Daddy did." She just kept talking, not waiting for her friend's response. "He called Juan and asked him to 'slow things down to a trot.' I'll tell you more about it at the Student Union tomorrow."

The next day they encamped at their favorite table near the iced tea dispenser. Juan slouched back in his chair, waving one hand in front of him, his fingers forming a V holding an invisible cigar. In a slow, deep drawl, he mimicked Russell Rutherford, "Juan, ya know, if the day of the week ends with a Y, then Lynda Gayle's gonna have her feathers ruffled over this here wedding. Why don't y'all just put things on the back burner and let 'em simmer for a while, Patty-cake?"

P.J. and Rachel laughed at his dead-on imitation.

Fresh from taking psychology 101, Rachel added, "P.J., I think your dad avoids intimacy with all those folksy sayings."

P.J. frowned and sat straighter in her seat. "He just likes to be colorful. It's his way of being funny. Now, Mother's a horse of a different color, all together."

Juan's eyes met Rachel's for a split second, but they stifled their smiles.

"No, come to think of it, Mother's more like a herd of wild mustangs! She called all her friends and forbade them to give any parties in honor of my engagement or marriage. Elena overhead her shrieking on the phone. Then Mother called me last weekend to say she wasn't going to attend the wedding."

"How can she act this way? What'd your father say?" Rachel asked.

P.J. shifted in her chair, the wooden legs squeaking on the dull linoleum. "I haven't spoken to him lately. He's been involved with some big business deals. Now listen, then she phoned me two days later and offered me a new T-bird and a trip to Europe if I'd call off the whole thing."

"Who'd think I'd be like one of the doors on *Let's Make a Deal?* Behind door number one . . . a brand new car, door number two . . . a fabulous cruise, or door number three . . . a Chicano husband!"

"Not to worry, Juan. You're the only door I'm walking through." She leaned over and kissed him.

"As long as you didn't say 'walking on,' we're in good shape." He poked his finger through the kneehole in her jeans.

Months went by and P.J. didn't hear much from her parents. She moved out of the sorority house and settled into a makeshift unit in a dilapidated mansion north of campus that had been subdivided into apartments. It was known as "hippie haven" because of the frequent pot busts that occurred there. The rent was cheap and it was within walking distance to the university. P.J. and Rachel didn't discuss the Rutherfords during their calls that were almost nightly before bedtime—back to their old habit of ending the day together.

Rachel went downstairs to the mailroom of the dorm, where rows of bins had names taped to them. A large beige envelope poked out from the slot marked "R. Miller." She ripped open an envelope and pulled out a card with a cutout of a bride and groom assembled from a collage of construction paper, silver doilies, dried flowers, and raffia. The groom resembled a gingerbread man in burlap overalls with a sunflower on his lapel. Her hand trembled as she held the invitation for P.J. and Juan's wedding at Zilcher Park in South Austin.

In the late summer of 1974, Patricia Jane Rutherford and Juan Miguel Siguieros were married during a tequila gold sunset in an open field. Rachel walked down the bike path toward a group of people gathered in a clearing. A dog leapt in front of her, snatching a red spinning saucer out of the air with pinpoint accuracy. The smell of links and burgers from the public barbecue pits hung in the evening haze. In their multi-colored tie-dyes and flowing gauzy skirts, a gang of students from the UT art department resembled a band of gypsies. The bridal couple eschewed the tradition of official attendants in matching taffeta gowns. Rachel was grateful P.J. hadn't asked her to wear some horrid bridesmaid dress in granny apple green or fuchsia, unflattering hues that would make the bridesmaids look awful so the bride would be stunning.

P.J. looked around, hoping to see the hulking silhouette of her father against the setting sun. A dog barked and ran back and forth with the circular prize in its mouth. No one was going to give the bride away because her parents had stuck by their guns and didn't show up for the wedding.

When the sun was beginning to drop low enough to touch the hills, Rachel pulled P.J. aside, disengaging her from her pottery friends. They walked a few steps over to the unlit party pavilion draped in lush vines and exuberant sunflowers. In the sun-streaked shadows, Rachel said, "P.J., we've only got a few more minutes together before the wedding. I know it's old-fashioned, but I brought you 'something old' and 'something borrowed.' You've already got the 'something blue' in the blue bonnets in your bouquet."

"What'd you get me? You're such a hoot." She eyed the tissue-wrapped package in her hands. Carefully, she unknotted the ribbon and unfolded the filmy paper, slowly revealing an aged linen doily with a faint green stain in the center near a pair of Rs embroidered in red.

"It's from that first time I went with you to the ranch. I snatched it and I've meant to give it back to you all of these years. I spit out my artichoke in it," Rachel confessed.

"Yeah, I know. I saw you stuff that whole leaf in your mouth," she said, laughing. Tears collected on the corners of her eyes. "I remember how Daddy's rattlesnake boots scared the holy crap out of you." When she fingered the embroidered letters on the cloth, her face clouded over like the sun engulfed by a thunderhead. "Oh, Rachel, why didn't he come? I'll bet Mother made him stay away." A torrent of tears poured down her face. Her body started to shake and then she was silent.

Why'd I give P.J. that stupid doily that made her think about her parents? Rachel reached up and rubbed her friend's damp neck. "I'm so sorry I ruined your day. I wouldn't do anything to hurt you. You're the only real sister I have."

P.J.'s frail body heaved against her. "Thanks, Rach. You're my family, too—especially so today." She tucked the piece of stained linen into the white ribbon sash of her wedding dress—the "something new" now had "something old" to go with it.

"Prove to me that marriage can be great," Rachel said.

Juan walked over and put his arms around their shoulders. "Hey, this isn't a private party. Don't worry, the two of you will still have each other. Rachel, you're not losing a best friend, you're gaining *un amigo*."

Juan and P.J. introduced Rachel to his parents and cousins, who were dressed in their Sunday best. His mother's peacock blue heels sank into the grass.

Rachel was glad to see Elena and Maddy there. She thought he looked the same, with just a light layer of snow on his slicked down hair, while Elena had put on a few pounds, probably from eating her own good cooking, but she was pretty in a yellow dress, free of her starched white apron. They had the weekend off and had driven to Austin together in the old blue Caddy.

The rest of the guests were P.J. and Juan's classmates. At the request of the female reverend, everyone formed a circle around bridal couple. Rachel held Susan's hand, a girl from P.J.'s raku pottery class who smelled a little smoky, like pots that are cured in smoldering leaves.

The lovers faced the glowing orb in the western sky and exchanged their vows. Juan smiled into her eyes: "Patty, you're the only woman for me. I promise to always be there for you and never to want anyone else. We'll share our love for each other and for art . . . and will have a great life together."

She clutched her bouquet of white roses and bluebonnets. The petals shook slightly as if caught in a gentle breeze. "Juan, when you came into my life, my happiness began. You're my true love, my soul mate." Her voice started to crack with emotion. "In front of our friends, and your family members, who have embraced me—I come to you on my own. No one has to give me away. I'm free to choose my life and I choose to be with you forever."

The sun slipped out of the sky. The minister flicked her bangs to one side and bowed her head for a final prayer. The crowd whooped and clapped when she announced, "Everyone, let's give it up for P.J. and Juan Siguieros!"

They kissed passionately, wrapped in each other's arms. Rachel cheered and hugged smoky Susan. The dog barked and leapt in the air, crash-landing into the backs of Juan's mother's knees, sending a run snaking up her stockings. Teetering in her heels while laughing, she asked, "Who invited him?"

The scent of steaming *cabrito* wafted from the reception area where the ceramics students had roasted a goat in the salt kiln. Paper luminaries lit by glowing candles dotted the freshly mowed grass, and the sounds of Mariachi trumpets and whirring blenders filled the park's party pavilion. Fireflies and fat brown June bugs swarmed in the warm night air. An occasional bat from under the bridge at Town Lake flew by to devour an unlucky insect.

P.J. appeared illuminated from within. Her light blonde hair fell softly on her shoulders beneath a wreath of daisies and baby's breath. Traces of brown earth bordered her white cotton Mexican wedding dress laced with satin ribbons. Juan's dark coloring contrasted with his light linen pants and open-neck guayabera shirt.

Rachel hugged the newlyweds tightly after the ceremony. P.J. plucked a white rose from her loosely tied bouquet and presented it to her. The single women mingled and danced, not bothering to gather to catch the bouquet—considering it too bourgeois and sexist. Rachel figured if P.J. had on a lacey wedding garter, it wouldn't be flung into the crowd, either.

Mr. Siguieros stepped forward and held his glass aloft: *"¡Salud, dinero y amor! Y el poder para disfrutar los."*

Rachel seconded his toast that called for health, money and love. She raised her frosted goblet and shouted, *"L'chaim! To life!"*

She was in between boyfriends, so she didn't expect to dance much. After her toast, Rachel returned to a gray weather-stripped picnic bench under the starry skies and ran her tongue around the salty rim of her glass. She nursed her drink, concentrating on its contrasting tart and sweet flavors. But a gnawing feeling at the pit of her stomach wouldn't subside. The music pulsated around her while she watched her best friend with her new husband twirling and spinning on the park lawn.

Popular music blared over the speakers when the band took a *cerveza* break. A strong, sinewy hand and one as fine as porcelain pulled her up from the bench and into the mass of dancers. P.J., Juan, and

Rachel jumped and spun around together until they were too dizzy to continue.

The live band returned and Rachel boogied with most of the art students—male and female. She coaxed Maddy to frug with her. Afterward, the rough post of the party pavilion supported her while she struggled to catch her breath.

In the distance, a small dot of light moved toward the celebration, like a shooting star that had plunged to earth. The pinpoint grew steadily larger. Finally, Rachel could make out that it was a figure on a bicycle on the path that led to the pavilion. A park official in khaki shorts dismounted and stood on the edge of the dance floor. He motioned for Juan to come over to him, leaving P.J. and Rachel to prance and swing together to the music. The two men moved closer until their silhouettes merged, and then the ranger patted Juan on the back. He mounted his bike and headed back down the path. Juan studied the ground as he returned to the two perplexed women.

"Did he have a message from Daddy?" P.J.'s face lit up with hope.

"Yes, love, but it's not the one you were hoping for." Her smile melted like wedding cake frosting in the Austin heat. Juan took his new wife's hands and softly said, "Patty, it's your dad . . . . "

"What, is he okay? What's the matter?"

"He's had a massive stroke. He's still alive, but in bad shape," he explained slowly, as if he were speaking to someone who couldn't comprehend English.

P.J. seemed to dissolve, unable to stand. Juan led her, like a blind person, over to a bench. A couple of dogs yelped, and then the members of the blaring Mariachi players fizzled one by one.

Rachel couldn't hold back her emotions. She hugged Maddy for support and her tears stained his good jacket. Elena kept pacing around repeating, "¡Ay Dios mío!"

Maddy said, "Rachel darlin', I'll drop you where you stay, and then Elena and I better head on back to Dallas."

Guests collected in small groups, whispering. Juan attempted to put on a friendly face and called out, "Thank you so much for coming. Ya'll, please stay and enjoy the music and margaritas. Hey, everything's already paid for!"

People milled around, not knowing what to do, while P.J. and Juan slowly walked arm in arm across the grass toward the blacktop parking lot into the darkness.

Lynda Gayle Rutherford had vowed that her daughter's marriage to Juan would occur 'over her dead body.' Instead, it was over her husband's oxygen-starved brain. The ranger had informed Juan that P.J.'s father had suffered a massive stroke. He had heard from the paramedics that Lynda Gayle had discovered Big Russ slumped in his leather chair when she got home from shopping until closing time at Neiman Marcus.

She had passed by the den and caught a glimpse of him with the phone receiver in his lap and a half-smoked cigar smoldering on the Persian rug.

Rachel imagined the shopping bags hitting the floor and Lynda Gayle not knowing whether to stomp out the little fire on the expensive carpet or to first check on her husband.

Dropping In

CHAPTER 17

J UAN AND P.J. postponed their Riverwalk honeymoon in a suite in San
Antonio overlooking the twinkling lights of the restaurants, bars, and
shops along the Paseo del Rio—the stone-lined waterway of ditches or
acequias originally built to supply water to the five nearby Spanish
missions. The newlyweds would have to remember the Alamo some
other time. P.J. wanted to be near her father during his valiant battle
for life.

Once he was stabilized, Lynda Gayle deposited him in an assisted
living facility a few miles from her home. Over the years, P.J.
frequently traveled to Dallas to visit her deteriorating father. She
avoided her parents' cool gray house, and preferred to bunk with
Michael and Rachel after they moved to Dallas. She had her own key
to their house, like a member of the family. Occasionally, Juan came,
too.

One day, Rachel left for work at the usual time to make it to South
Dallas Elementary. Students were absent because it was a Teacher
Administration Day. She was pleased with the stroke of good luck
when the conference ended early. Rachel was expecting P.J. to arrive
from Austin around suppertime, but when she cleared her driveway
gates, her friend's car was parked in front. She clicked the garage door
opener and was also surprised to see Michael's car at home in
the afternoon.

She ran her hand across the hood, cool and dust-free. He always prided himself on keeping an immaculate car. She noted that hers always lost its new car smell within a few miles of the showroom.

Rachel rummaged for her keys in her purse and unlocked the door to the house from the garage. She entered and stashed her satchel on the kitchen table. The downstairs was quiet. She called out, "Michael, is P.J. here?"

No answer.

A wad of blue fabric in the living room caught her eye. On the armchair, a light blue blouse was crumbed in a pile along with a pair of jeans. She moved closer and stumbled on a small tennis shoe. Rachel wore size nine, so she knew it wasn't hers. Then she remembered how P.J. never was required to be tidy as a kid; either Elena or Maddy would follow her around, picking up her belongings and hanging them up in her walk-in closet.

Where the heck are Michael and P.J.? At first, she giggled at her foolishness to even consider they might be upstairs having illicit sex. *P.J.'s my best friend and the last person I would expect to do something like that. What a dumb thought!*

Michael had always been her rock and had never given her any reason for jealousy. But she found herself looking at her best friend's clothes strewn around the living room. *Evidence!* The pounding in her chest expanded into her ears. She tried to dispel the thought of an affair, but a wave of nausea forced her to collapse on the chair, further crushing P.J.'s garments.

Rachel's head began to explode and her eyes could barely focus. She looked toward the landing that led to the master bedroom and dragged herself upstairs. Then she picked up speed, bolting up the last four steps. The closed door to the bedroom loomed in front of her like a monolith. Rachel sucked in a breath and flung it wide open. Michael's suit was laid out neatly on the bed and his wallet rested in its spot on the nightstand.

Her chest tightened, and she struggled to breathe. Rachel sank onto the bedspread without caring if it wrinkled. She clutched her head in her hands, admonishing herself for being ridiculous to have suspected them.

The front door slammed and she almost literally levitated from the bed. From upstairs, Rachel could hear P.J.'s cool laughter mixed with Michael's deep, warm voice. She raced to the bedroom door and peered down at them. Water dripped from the pair onto the living room carpet. Their wet bodies were draped with towels decorated with a trio of Dancing Raisins with large white gloves and broad smiles.

Michael looked up at his frantic wife. "You look like you just saw the Texas Chainsaw murderer. What's up?"

"P.J., I didn't expect you this early. And what are you doing home, Michael?"

"My office had a power failure, so I figured I could make calls from the house instead of sitting in that hot box. The heat was insufferable. Remind me to design windows that actually open in my next high rise!"

"Michael came home right after I got here. I guess I looked so beat from the trip that he suggested we go for a dip."

"You won't believe what I thought when I came home," Rachel confessed. "It looked like the two of you tore off each other's clothes on the way upstairs—not that I want to give you any ideas."

The three of them looked around the room. Michael's tie was draped limply on the armchair. P.J.'s incriminating other sneaker was lodged under the coffee table. They burst out laughing.

"It does look like a sex scene, but I swear I'm innocent!" Michael protested.

"I brought my bag in from the car and didn't feel like going to the upstairs guest room. I just changed in the powder room and tossed my stuff on the chair. I figured I'd take it to my room later. You know what a slob I am. It's not like you just met me," P.J. said.

Rachel giggled nervously. "I thought the two of you were upstairs together. At first I was crazed you were having an affair. But even though I love the two of you more than anything, I *would* have taken a chainsaw to the both of you!"

"Rachel, you're not being funny now. When we heard you pull up, we got out of the pool to find out why you were home so early and see if anything was the matter," Michael said.

"Nothing—just a flight of temporary insanity!" Rachel replied.

"I'm going to change into dry clothes now and make my calls. P.J., hanging out with you today has gotten me into way too much trouble. Rachel, why don't you put on your suit and go cool off for a while. I'm getting out of here while I still can."

She changed out of her clothes and grabbed a towel. She rocketed into the deep end and sank to the bottom of the pool to touch the drain. When she came up for air, P.J. was wading in the shallow end. The sunlight danced on her glistening hair. Rachel couldn't resist the urge and called out, "Marco!"

P.J. darted under the water and swam toward her. She surfaced near her friend and shouted, "Polo!"

Rachel occasionally went with P.J. to the hospital when Big Russ had a crisis, but the mixture of antiseptic and urine clung in the air. She thought he looked small in the miniature jail— in his railed hospital bed. His girth had dwindled from days of bland food and an endless array of pills that kept him floating on the topside of life.

Rachel hated being there and only went when P.J. needed a shoulder to lean on when she visited him. He was usually hooked up to tubes, breathing with the aid of oxygen strapped to his nostrils. The speckled linoleum floors reminded Rachel of her mother's hospital stay after the camp session. She closed her eyes and tried to doze, to push away the memories of Mama's broken body and spirit.

Rachel was startled when she heard a phone ring. A female voice answered, "Baylor Hospital sixth floor. May we help you?"

In a far away voice, P.J. was calling her name, "Rachel, are you all right?"

Rachel tried to put up a front and said, "Yes, I'm sorry. Was I spacing out?" She was sorry to realize she was in the waiting room, in an uncomfortable chair next to P.J.

"As a matter of fact, you were."

Three years after his first stroke, Russell Rutherford suffered another attack and had been in a coma for two weeks. His health was touch-and-go.

P.J. asked the duty nurse, "How's he doing today?"

"About the same, but y'all can go in now."

P.J. pushed open the door to her father's room. Rachel followed her and heard the beeps of the heart monitor. His thick, wavy black hair was scattered about his head, with shocks of gray. The smell of his foul breath lingered in the air. Rachel hung back near the door while P.J. moved in to get a closer look. His eyes were tightly shut in a deep slumber.

Leaning close to his stubbly cheek she asked, "Daddy, can you hear me? It's Patty-cake. Please wake up."

The staccato of clicks on the heart monitor were the only response. His once robust body was sunken beneath the drab hospital sheets and light waffle-weave blanket that covered him. Two weeks and no response.

Rachel settled in the metal chair to watch television, resigned to show P.J. her support. She flipped channels and *General Hospital* appeared on the screen.

"That's the last thing I want to watch!" P.J. shouted, losing her usual reserve.

Rachel continued channel surfing. Then a familiar tune and the satin heart opening credits from a rerun of *I Love Lucy* caught her attention. Ricky Ricardo flung open the front door to his apartment and called out in singsong, "*¡Ay caramba!*" He feigned anger at his redheaded bride. Lucy and Ethel, her faithful sidekick, sat on the couch, looking innocent with their eyes as large as saucers. Rachel waited for P.J.'s approval of the new program choice but only heard the soft rustle of starchy sheets. She turned quickly to witness Mr. Rutherford's mouth open wide.

P.J. bolted from her chair and hung on the bars that surrounded his bed. He clinched his teeth and then relaxed his jaw, subtle signs of movement. She yelled excitedly, "Nurse, come here. I think he's waking up!"

No one came to the door. P.J. fumbled for the call button on the end of the chord that was behind the back of the bed, among the tangle of wires that fed the multitude of contraptions that kept him alive. The TV suddenly blared—wrong button. She grabbed the other cord and continued to stare into her father's face.

"Daddy, can you hear me? It's P.J. Please wake up."

Rachel's heart ached for her friend. Only his eyelids answered in little ticks and twitches.

"If you can hear me, move a finger," P.J. pleaded, uncovering his pale hand from beneath the sheets. He raised his pinky slightly above the thin mattress. "Move your finger again if you hear me."

The nurse walked in. "Everything all right here?"

"I think he's waking up." P.J. didn't take her eyes off his finger.

Then his wrinkled lids revealed the deep blue eyes that had been masked in the depths of a coma for the past fourteen days.

The nurse spoke up, "Mr. Rutherford, do you know where you are?"

No answer, but his eyes scanned the room.

"Mr. Rutherford, do you remember your first name?" The electronic sputtering continued. Lucy and Ethel mugged for the camera, and then the nurse clicked off the television.

P.J. edged close to his ear and asked, "Daddy, do you know my name?"

He glanced sideways at her and the edges of his mouth turned up slightly. "Do you think I'm about as dumb as a post? Of course I know your name. It's Patty-cake." His eyes rolled back and then the lids half shut. He was gone again.

Rachel looked at P.J.'s father and wondered if her own dad was tan from lying on a California beach or if he was as pale as the gray walls of a hospital corridor. He had moved out of the house after Mama was released from Parkland Hospital, only a few days after Rachel saw her after "the accident."

He never told Rachel good-bye or said he loved her.

Years later, when Rachel finished college, she lost track of him. He completely abandoned his girls.

THE GIFT

CHAPTER 18

AFTER THE MURDER, Rachel suffered remorse that she had lost the chance to tell her daughter how much she loved her before Missy headed back to Austin. She imagined all the things she would have said. The regrets piled up, and soon they buried her, like the stacks of catalogs on her desk in the kitchen that signaled the onslaught of the holidays.

She considered ordering by mail or online but was afraid of being a victim of stolen identity. The thought of walking into a shopping mall was as inviting as a visit to dentist for a tooth extraction.

Rachel used to shop for weeks on end to find the perfect presents for Missy and Michael. Although they had a family tradition that eliminated the guesswork by providing wish lists, she searched for just the right thing. Sometimes Missy would cut out pages from catalogs, showing the exact color and cut of the clothes she wanted.

Rachel's list usually remained the same each year: a cashmere sweater, scented padded hangers, and decorative candles. She secretly hoped Michael would surprise her with a piece of jewelry, and sometimes he did. She was a firm believer of the saying: Good things come in small packages.

Hedy, Lenora, and Rachel stopped exchanging presents years ago. Locked in perpetual sibling rivalry, they still competed in the annual gift-giving contest of who would give Mama the thing she would favor the most.

She hoped Michael would be understanding that she hadn't shopped for presents this year. Celebrating didn't feel right, and she decided her mother really didn't need anything, anyway.

From time to time, Rosy tugged at her face and whined she wanted a facelift. She swore she could still detect the faint scar down the right side of her face through her layers of pancake, along with the usual crow's-feet that come from just being alive. In the next breath, she warned Rachel to get a grip on herself and stop crying because it was going to ruin her eyes.

Every morning Rachel awoke to the reality that Missy was gone, and the thought encased her heart. Her tears pooled the minute the veil of sleep lifted and didn't stop until she finally got out of bed. Michael had long gone to work before she began to face the day, and he usually came home to find her glued in front of the set watching nature documentaries or cooking programs, although she seldom made meals anymore. She steered away from the legal or cop shows, anything with guns, but even the nature shows occasionally aired survival of the fittest scenes that she had to switch off.

On the first evening of Chanukah, Rachel rummaged through the bottom shelf of the hutch under the gray felt bags that held silver trays and pulled out the menorah. A box with a few small twisted candles in primary colors smelled waxy and stale. She needed enough to light the flames for each of the eight days of the festival and the helper candle, the *Shamus*, to light the others each night. The half dozen leftovers from last year were more than enough to get started, and she figured Michael could pick up a fresh box during the week. She crammed the white *Shamus* and a blue candle into the holder, hoping they wouldn't teeter. *I'll worry about the other nights tomorrow*, she thought as she placed the menorah on the counter.

Double-checking for more remnants in candle boxes, Rachel shuffled through a drawer in the hutch. A tattered drawing of a reindeer peeked out from under recipes she had cut out of *Texas Today Magazine* but had never bothered to make. She forgot that she had stored it with a pile of baby announcements and helpful hints from the newspaper about how to get wine stains out of tablecloths with club soda and peanut butter to remove chewing gum from hair.

As she unfolded the artwork, the loopy colored shapes blurred together. Her tears dripped onto the paper and glistened where the crayon was thickest. Rachel had kept the best of the drawings Missy had brought home, and this one particularly touched her heart: a reindeer with teardrops that splattered a stack of presents.

She and Michael had gone to parent-teacher night around the holidays when Missy was in the second grade. The teacher, Miss Samples, produced a large sheet of paper with the sad reindeer Missy had sketched in crayon. "Your daughter shows real talent. Have you considered giving her private lessons?"

"Thanks, she's taking ballet right now, but we'll keep it in mind. My friend who's an artist encourages her," Rachel said.

"The way she approached the Christmas assignment was very unique—shows imagination."

"Did you ask Missy why she drew the tears? We're not talking Rudolph with a red nose here," Rachel asked.

"No, I just thought it was cute," she answered with a puzzled look.

"Cute, I think it's a clear sign that something was bothering Missy."

"Hon, we'll handle it ourselves at home," Michael intervened.

"I thought it was precious. Y'all, thanks for coming. We need more parents like you who are involved." Miss Samples hurried to meet with the next parent.

Rachel was disturbed that her daughter had a warped view of the holidays. She wished for Missy's world to be joyous.

In the evening, Missy bounced into the kitchen to get a snack and wrapped her arms around her mother as she peeled the potatoes for *latkes*. Missy loved the potato pancakes that Rachel seldom made from scratch except at Chanukah.

"I saw your artwork at school today, the one you haven't brought home yet. I liked the reindeer, but why's he so sad?"

Missy bit her lower lip and looked down at the kitchen tiles.

"It's okay. You can say. What was on your mind when you were drawing?" Rachel asked.

Missy's big green eyes were tinged with sorrow. "Mommy, the reindeer was crying because he's Jewish and he felt funny about having to deliver all of the Christmas presents on Santa's sleigh."

Rachel stroked her little chin. "The next time you feel funny about something, think about what's the right thing to do. Tell the teacher and come up with something else—like drawing a beautiful menorah with all of the colorful Chanukah candles." She fumed that Miss Samples hadn't picked up on her child's consternation about the assignment.

Rachel remembered back to when her stomach tightened when she had to sing Christmas carols in elementary school. As she stood in her kitchen with her seven-year-old daughter, she thoroughly understood the predicament.

And now it was another holiday season, more than a decade after Missy sketched the reindeer. Rachel unfolded the tattered drawing when Michael walked into the kitchen. He peered over her shoulder to look at the sheet of paper in her hand. His smile dissolved and his upper lip quivered as he refolded the artwork along the crease lines worn into the paper. "Rachel, she's everywhere. Even when we put things away, Missy still turns up unexpectedly. She's still part of our lives and we've got to try to get past this limbo of not knowing how to think about her right now."

Missy's face, shaded by the UT baseball cap, smiled at them from the photo under a magnet on the refrigerator door. She had loved that cap they had given her, and it was her trademark that ironically had given them a ray of hope on the night of her death. Neither one of them had wanted to strip the house completely of her presence. A family portrait of the three of them was still anchored in its place, reflecting on the black gleaming top of the piano. Rachel had shut the door to Missy's room and opened it only so the maid could dust. She planned on calling the Salvation Army or a children's shelter to pick up the clothes—eventually. She vowed to donate the menagerie of stuffed animals to a children's hospital—someday.

Michael cleared his throat. "Uh, come here, Rach. Let me hold you." He put his hands on her shoulders to pull her close. "Poor baby, you're tight as a drum."

"You know I always keep my tension in my shoulders. Thanks, honey, I'm really okay." She disengaged herself and bent down to pick up the menorah, anything to keep from crying together in the kitchen. She attempted to change the subject. "Mama called to tell me it's the first night of Chanukah. Want to light the candles?"

His eyes seemed to brighten at the suggestion. "All right, but you say the blessing. I can never remember it."

Michael set the menorah on a glass dish on the kitchen counter to catch the melting wax and lit the lone blue candle.

Rachel recited, "*Baruch atah Adonai . . .*" The golden light flickered across Michael's face, highlighting deep grooves and folds she hadn't noticed before.

"Wait right here. Don't move!" he said. She heard the den pocket door slide on its track, and then he reappeared carrying a powder blue box with a white satin ribbon.

"Michael, I didn't do any shopping this year, so I don't have anything for you." A cold wave of guilt washed over Rachel.

He handed her the box. "It doesn't matter, Rach. I just want you to be happy again."

"I don't feel like celebrating anything right now. Please don't be upset, but I want to save it for later—not just now. It'll give me something to look forward to."

Michael quickly retreated, sliding the doors closed. Rachel sat at her desk in the kitchen and stared at the flickering candlelight, the reflections dancing on the granite counters. After about an hour, the candles dripped down to tiny flames peeping out of the holder. One by one, they disappeared, leaving little smoke trails. She retreated upstairs and stowed the little blue box in the top dresser drawer beneath a pile of cashmere sweaters.

The next morning the doorbell awoke Rachel at eleven. She struggled into her faded robe while walking down the stairs. The chenille felt soft against her skin. Her other clothes seemed to chafe and ride up, constricting her.

"Who's there?" she called through the closed door. Rachel peeked through the sidelights, and she saw a shipping box on the welcome mat. The driver was sprinting back to his truck. She opened the front door and the cool, damp air stung her face. She hadn't even realized the temperature had dropped, since she hadn't left the house in weeks.

The courier called out, "Merry Christmas, ma'am."

She picked up the package and brought it into the kitchen and checked the return address. *What has P.J. sent me now?* Rachel was touched that her friend constantly mailed her cheery greeting cards and cute Ziggy cartoons she cut out from the funny pages of the *Austin American-Statesman.*

Rachel tugged at the sealed end, finally ripping open the box, breaking her one remaining fingernail. Wrapped in blue paper with little Stars of David was a flat, rectangular object she deduced was a book. In no mood to read, she tossed the wrapped package on top of the magazine pile on her kitchen desk.

Michael started spending more nights at the office working late on the final touches on the Rutherford Plaza. He usually grabbed a bite at the deli in the lower level of his office building before coming home.

From their bedroom, Rachel could hear him enter the house when the alarm beeped when a door was opened. He usually headed directly for his study before closing the doors behind him to check details for the February construction deadline.

He made his follow-up calls to the Springland police department from work. They still hadn't uncovered any leads on a trail that was getting as cold as the hard ground in December. Michael's latest brainstorm was to put up a billboard on the highway near the exit to Springland, offering a reward for information about the unsolved shooting. He said the outdoor company was going to donate the space *pro bono*. Michael had been going over layouts, but Rachel couldn't bear to look at them.

He provided the graphic designer with one of Missy's photos from a silver frame that had been in the living room. He agonized over whether the poster should be all type or incorporate the photograph. Rachel hoped she'd never lay eyes on the road sign. She always considered Missy to be pretty enough to be on a billboard but never in a million years imagined under these circumstances. Michael hoped to garner at least one viable lead, but all Rachel could think about was that they'd never get their daughter back.

The holiday season passed slowly and they declined invitations to any parties. Rachel was ready to embrace the saying, "Out with the old year, in with the new." She was ready for the year to end, but in some ways knew it would never actually be over. The rest of her life would be marked by the milestone: before or after Missy's murder. She didn't want to be awake at the stroke of midnight.

Michael ordered Chinese delivery food. Rachel ate right out of the carton without offering to share. He quietly downed his spicy Kung Pao chicken while she concentrated on her sweet and sour chicken, scraping the last tangy morsel from the corners of the white box. She brushed Michael's lips with a goodnight kiss and headed to bed. He remained downstairs to watch the big ball drop on Times Square on television. From the bedroom, she could hear the music and the shouts of the revelers.

The Franks were alone that year. In the past, they often rang in the New Year with P.J. and Juan, who decided to stay in Austin to celebrate with his family. She promised they'd get to Dallas after the first of the year.

At the end of January, P.J. came for a weekend visit. She said she'd get an early start and would arrive by noon. Rachel forgot to set the alarm and woke after eleven. She needed a glass of water to soothe her lips that were chapped from the central heat in the house, but the doorbell rang before she had a chance to get one. She threw on a robe and ran down the stairs to let in her friend.

They hugged tightly in the foyer, and then P.J. stepped back to look at her. "Nice of you to dress for the occasion," she noted with a bit of sarcasm.

"Yeah, this is my formal robe. Nothing's too good for my best pal. How about a cup of tea to warm you up?"

"I'm beat from the drive. Tea sounds great. What flavor do you want?" P.J. asked and went to the pantry to help herself.

"You decide. Anything."

"What kind do *you* want?" she repeated.

"Whatever you're having," Rachel said. The water from the faucet spilled out of the kettle into the sink.

"For God's sakes, Rachel, make some effort!"

"You know, if you're going to dish out this shit, then maybe this isn't a good time for you to be here."

"I came to help you. Michael told me you barely get out of bed these days and you hardly ever swim. And this back-to-nature, no bathing nonsense has got to stop. Only a friend will tell you, and I'm surprised your husband or your mother hasn't had the guts to say that you stink!"

"Well, you stink, too, with your holier-than-thou attitude! You didn't lose a child, so you don't have a clue about what I'm going through!" Rachel shrieked.

"Not lose a child? What the fuck do you think my whole life has been? I couldn't get pregnant and you know that. Mother took doses of DES to keep from miscarrying, and I've paid the consequences my whole life. Because of it, my uterus is so tipped that it's like a ski jump for embryos. Missy was as close to a child as I'll ever have. I wish she were here, too, but you don't see me walking around like a zombie. How dare you talk to me about children! And by the way, open your damn present! It's still sitting right there on that shit pile on your desk."

"Thanks for snooping!" Rachel yelled.

"You could have at least had the decency to put it away so I wouldn't see it, but that would take some effort." P.J. threw the box of tea on the counter. "You know, Rachel, you could really use what's in that book I gave you."

"And what the hell were you and Michael doing talking about me behind my back? Some friend you are—probably telling him all of my deep, dark secrets."

P.J.'s porcelain face turned splotchy. She wiped her eyes with the back of her fist and stormed out, leaving the front door ajar. Rachel slammed it, rattling the cut-glass transoms.

The steady whistle of the kettle reminded her that the pot was at full boil. She walked back into the kitchen toward the cloud of steam, but her knees buckled beneath her. Like a rag doll, she sank to the floor in front of the stove, doubled over. Gasping, her airways were tight as a pencil. Rachel's head was spinning from anguish, and her eyes and nose stung from the flood of tears. She rolled her cheeks against the cool tiles, rocking back and forth. Finally, the air slid easily into her lungs, but her back ached from lying on the floor. She pulled herself up by grabbing the chair, and then extinguished the flame beneath the whistling teapot.

From the kitchen, the den sofa seemed so far away. She staggered like a drunk to the couch and collapsed, too weak to go to bed.

Lost in the haze of sleep, Rachel heard the garage door close and then Michael flipped on the kitchen light. It spilled into the den, cutting into her sleep like a serrated edge.   He passed the couch on the way to his study.

"What time is it?" she asked, lying on the cushions.

"Whoa," he exclaimed, laughing at being startled. "What are you doing in here, Rachel? I didn't see you there. Where's P.J.?"

"I guess she went home. I really don't give a fig where she went."

"Okay, what's going on? You two never fight. What the hell happened?"

"First of all, I don't appreciate your conspiring against me. She told me you sent out an SOS about me. Thanks a lot!"

He nudged her legs off the cushion and sat beside her. "I thought you might need someone to talk to. You certainly don't want to talk to me anymore."

"Well, we didn't have a chance because she came in here loaded for bear. She was pissed because I hadn't opened her stupid present. I haven't even opened the one you gave me, and you haven't said a word about it. She really ticked me off."

Michael went to the kitchen and retrieved P.J.'s gift. He ripped open the wrapping and tossed Rachel the volume with the cover photo of an overweight woman in cowboy boots embellished with yellow roses, stretched out on a bed that was covered with flowers and pillows. It was titled in satiny crimson letters, *Make Your Own Bed of Roses* by Rosemary Williams. She sat upright and flipped to the tightly penned inscription by P.J.

Dear Rachel,

I think Rosemary is truly amazing. She lives near Dallas in Oak Cliff. If you met her, she could change your life.

Love as always,

P.J.

Rachel tossed the book to the other end of the couch. *This Rosemary person can't even get her own weight under control. How's she going to help me get my life together?*

A Big Reception

CHAPTER 19

"RACHEL, I'm leaving now. Time to get up!" Michael said. The citrus scent of his after-shave smelled both sweet and tangy. It lingered in the air when he wasn't around. Rachel seldom saw him in the morning anymore.

"Okay, I'm up," she mumbled and turned on her other side, drawing her knees up to her chest.

"I'm leaving now and I'll call you later. Rachel, the limo's coming to get you at seven tonight, so please be on time. I'll meet you at the reception so we'll only have one car afterward."

She grunted and pulled the covers up to her chin.

"Rach, leave enough time to get ready. Why don't you wear that black beaded suit that looks so good on you? A lot of bigwigs will be there, and I want everyone to meet you. Call you later." He opened the plantation shutters in the bedroom, wrapping ribbons of light around the room.

"Okay, I'll be ready," she slurred, drifting back to the comfort of sleep.

Rachel heard his footsteps bolting down the stairs at a lively clip. It was an important day for Michael—the grand opening of the Rutherford Plaza—which marked his firm's biggest project to date, and he was a bundle of nerve endings. Usually nothing ruffled him, but lately he was absorbed in the completion of the office tower. Rachel fretted that he was logging hundreds of hours at the office, spending more time with Susan Lovett, his executive assistant, than he had with her over the past four months.

At noon the nagging ringing of the phone awoke her. "Yes, Michael, I'm up," she lied, feigning her daytime voice. "I'll be ready, I promise." She reached for the bottle of pills near the phone. *Calm. I need to be calm to face all of those people,* she thought, wondering what they would say to her. She feared someone would ask about Missy or look at her with eyes full of pity? *Two pills should be about right.* She washed them down with tepid water in a paper cup that had softened on her nightstand overnight.

At 6:45 p.m. a car pulled up in the driveway. Rachel peeked out the shutters and saw a shiny black limo parked out front. She panicked. *Oh my God, I haven't even fixed my hair!* She pulled it into a wad twisted with a clip that fanned the hair upward, called the "New York fashion editor's updo," hoping she had successfully tamed her tangled mass of red hair. Squeezing into a knit skirt, she checked her profile in the full-length mirror. It hugged her curves tighter than the last time she had worn it and the fabric stretched into a ridge that pulled across her backside. Rachel prayed the jacket would hide it, but the double-breasted rhinestone buttons seemed farther apart than she remembered. She thought she looked like an overstuffed sequined sausage but decided it was too late to change—and nothing else in her closet would fit any better.

At seven sharp the doorbell rang. She shouted into the intercom, "I'll be right there!" Rachel shuffled through the boxes in her closet to find her good pumps, and her heart raced as the clock flipped to 7:05. Her wedding ring caught on her only pair of black stockings. "Damn it!" she swore to herself out loud, considering forgoing the hose, even though it was forty-five degrees outside. She ran her hand against the bristly stubble on her legs and hoped the light would be dim enough in the room to get away with it. She selected her everyday purse because it was black and there wasn't enough time to sort through it to decide what to put in a fancy little cocktail bag that would barely hold her reading glasses. She downed two more little pills to take off the edge. *Ready or not, here I come!* Rachel was out the door at 7:20.

The driver pulled in front of the Rutherford Plaza and cut the engine. Rachel rubbed her bare wrist. "What time have you got?" she asked as he offered his hand to help her out of the backseat of the stretch limo.

"7:45, ma'am. I got you here as fast as humanly possible."

"Don't worry, you did just fine." She ran through the revolving glass doors and entered the cavernous lobby of the new Rutherford Plaza, finding the elevator marked "P.H.," the express one to the penthouse. She tried not to look at herself in the mirror in the elevator because it was too late to make any corrections to her appearance. The spikes of her hairstyle looked more like the unruly topknot feathers of the rockhopper penguins she had seen at Sea World in San Antonio than a chic fashion editor in New York. Surprisingly, her ears didn't pop on the smooth ride to the thirty-second floor. The doors opened and a tuxedoed waiter with a gleaming silver tray of champagne glasses approached. He whispered, "Welcome, the festivities are underway. Care for a glass of champagne?"

Her heel caught on the back of his shoe and they did a slow motion dance to regain her balance while he frantically tried to control the avalanche of sliding champagne glasses. Rachel grabbed one of the slender stems before it toppled and kept walking toward the reception area in the direction of the reverberating voices. The tinkle of shattered glass on the marble floor echoed behind her. She spotted Michael midway through a microphone handoff to Lynda Gayle. "Oh, hell. I missed his speech," she mumbled, downing the last fizzy drop. She was relieved Michael hadn't noticed her. She wondered if she should pretend to have heard his speech from the back of the room, because she still remembered some of the text from his practice run at home. Rachel caught the eye of another server who handed her a fresh glass of bubbly.

Lynda Gayle drew the portable microphone close to her bejeweled bust and began to speak, but only high-pitched squeals and a few muffled words ripped through the air. Michael lifted her hand to bring the mic to her lips. She started over. "Thank you, Michael. You're a very talented speaker *and* architect! You talk almost as well as you design!"

He acknowledged her compliment with an unctuous smile and a nod.

"This project was the dream of my late husband, Russell Rutherford. I've had to try to step into his size-thirteen boots and keep that dream alive. I consider all of us here at Rutherford Enterprises as one big happy family. Big Russ would have liked it that way. I first met Michael through my daughter, P.J., and it's been a rewarding relationship ever since the git-go." She paused to take a sip of water from a crystal glass that spread a prism of light across the faces in the room.

Rachel thought it could have been the reflections from the diamond rock she wore on her bony, manicured finger. A shiver ran through Rachel as she glanced around the room and P.J. wasn't there to see the realization of her father's goal of a multi-media empire. She stepped forward, steadying herself on the back of a folding chair. Her mouth opened and suddenly she yelled, "Bullshit!" The words simply leapt out, propelled by their own force. "You don't know the first thing about being family. Anyone who treats her only daughter like you do ought to be ignored instead of kowtowed to."

Michael's mouth formed a dark oval, and then he sprang into action toward his out-of-control wife. Susan Lovett reached for his arm to stop him.

Rachel slurred loudly, "And you can keep your grabby little hands off my husband, Susan!"

Michael snatched the empty glass out of her hand and slammed it down, splattering the contents. Like a parent reprimanding an errant child who has run amuck, he almost dragged her by the elbow to the foyer. He stared at the closed elevator, waiting for it to arrive, without another word or look at anyone. When the door slid open, he pulled Rachel inside the cold metal box that silently headed down to the lobby.

He waved his valet ticket in the air without letting go of her. Within a few minutes the tires of the Mercedes screeched to a halt. Michael drove the car, clutching the wheel, never looking over at her. His silence spoke more than if he had yelled. Rachel whimpered quietly, slouched in the seat next to him. Her legs were cold, but she didn't dare complain. Soon she felt numb, and in the darkness, she faded into sleep.

"Rachel, you've got to help me get you to bed. Lean on me." Michael said.

She was surprised to have been somehow transported to their garage. The car door was open on her side and Michael was trying to maneuver her out of the vehicle. *Have my legs dissolved?* She felt like she was walking on rubber when finally entering the warmth of the house. She struggled to hold onto his shoulder while he clutched her thick waist, almost dragging her through the kitchen like a dead weight. They made it as far as the den couch before he had to catch his breath. She slid out of his grasp, landing onto the down cushions and curled up as best she could without her rear end hanging out. Michael tossed her the crocheted throw Mama had made as a housewarming gift. Rachel struggled to find a comfortable position because something pointy was jabbing her leg. She reached between the cushions at the end of the couch and pulled out the book P.J. had given her. Then she let it drop to the floor and dozed off, dead to the world.

TRIALS AND TRIBULATIONS

CHAPTER 20

THE HOUSE WAS STILL as a grave when Rachel awoke. She sighed with relief that Michael had already left for the office, so she wouldn't have to face him. She also tried to push away from her spongy brain the memory of yelling "bullshit" at the reception. *What is wrong with me? More sleep is the only thing that could possibly help.* She dragged herself upstairs to her bed and closed her eyes to shut out the light. The phone shattered the silence, but Rachel didn't move. The machine finally picked up after four annoying rings.

A familiar, dulcet voice emanated from her recording machine, "Rachel, *shalom*. This is Rabbi Sachs. I'd like to drop by today at one o'clock. Just a quick chat, so don't go to any fuss. Unless I hear otherwise, I'll see you this afternoon."

She stared at the telephone, figuring Michael had arranged the call. She fumed that P.J. and Michael were on some sort of misguided mission to save her.

She vowed the rabbi wasn't going to be met at the door with a nice *glezel* of tea and a plate of warm rugalach to munch on. *He invited himself, for God's sakes. If Mama starts to interfere, I swear I'll down the whole damn bottle of pills!* Rachel was thankful that she rarely heard from her two sisters—claiming their indifference beat interference.

Then another phone call. This time, she decided to pick it up because the persistent ringing made her brain beat against the inside of her skull. "Hello," she croaked.

"Rachel, it's Rosemary Williams. You don't know me, but I'm a friend of P.J.'s. She asked me to give ya a shout. Gosh, she's awfully concerned about ya."

First the rabbi and now this self-help guru. Rachel mustered the tone she used when trying brush off telemarketers, "Well, Miss Williams, now's not really a good time for me."

"Yes, I know. That's why I'm calling. Can I call ya Rachel?"

"You already did, but that's fine. What can I do for you?" she asked matter-of-factly.

"I know from P.J. that you and your husband have suffered a mighty loss. All I ask is that you come visit me one afternoon. I'm in Oak Cliff. It's really just a hop and a skip from where y'all live in North Dallas."

"I really can't right now. Thanks for taking the time to call me, and I'm sure you're a busy person with many more important things to do than to see me." Rachel hoped flattery would derail the caller's train of thought.

"I'll make you an offer: When we have a warm spell, come and set a while with me on my back porch. That's all I ask. If we meet each other and you never want to lay eyes on me again or you don't like my rockers or cups of tea, I'll leave it at that. Fair 'nuff?"

Rachel wondered if Rosemary smelled of patchouli oil or fertilizer—either a new age sage or a cowgirl. She was friendly and inviting, but Rachel still resisted. "I'll give it some thought. Thanks for calling, but I've got to run now."

Like a man who can't be late to a funeral, Rabbi Sachs rang the doorbell punctually at five minutes to one. Rachel had dressed quickly without showering and dabbed on the dregs from the bottom of a bottle of Joy, the only scent that didn't make her nose run or her eyes water in an allergic reaction. Her denim shift still fit and wasn't too badly wrinkled.   She sniffed the armholes before putting it on and deemed it passable.

Rachel ushered in the rabbi, who was casually dressed in a corduroy jacket and khakis, looking more like a college professor than a man of the cloth. The closest room to the front door was the seldom-used formal living room, so she thought it would be a suitable place to have their talk. No one ever sat on the expansive three-sided white couch, except at Missy's shiva when the house overflowed with people.

Rachel sat in an armchair across from the couch, separated from the Rabbi by the wrought iron coffee table with a large silk flower arrangement. She twisted a leafy stalk of the life-like bromeliad to clear a line of sight.

His face almost brushed against a leaf when he leaned foward to speak. "Rachel, you probably figured it out by now that Michael's very worried about you. He loves you very, very much," he uttered as solemnly as a prayer.

I wish people would love me less and leave me the hell alone. Rachel looked at the arrangement, not meeting the Rabbi's eyes and stammered, "Uh huh. So he says." She wondered if she had spoken aloud "leave me the hell alone" that she had been thinking. The line between thought and speech was increasingly blurred.

He continued, so she surmised the insult had remained silent. "I came here today to talk to you about a biblical verse, a type of poem."

Rachel hoped her eyes hadn't rolled when he said "poem," like the boys in high school used to do when faced with serious literature. She struggled to remain motionless.

"Rachel, do you remember the story of Job?"

With eyes riveted to the dried Spanish moss at the base of the arrangement, she replied as if in Sunday school, "Oh, something about the trials and tribulations of Job. Those two words always seem to go hand in hand. Do I get a gold star? A Star of David, of course."

He chuckled softly. "Rachel, this isn't a pop quiz. I want to give you some perspective on what's going on in your spiritual life and to let you know I'm here for you if you need me. Even over three thousand years ago, the righteous suffered. Satan convinced God to test Job's faith, a man of utmost piety, by removing all of his pleasures in life. As you recall, God smote his herd, burned his house, covered him in noxious boils, and worst of all, killed his children to find out if he still was as devoted to God when things got tough."

"Excuse me, are you going to sit there and tell me I'm supposed to feel better about some son-of-a-bitch who murdered my daughter because a man in the Bible lost everything except for his wife and kept his faith?"

"Yes, Rachel, I am. His wife even suggested suicide as the answer to end the suffering, but he kept his faith and proved his steadfast love of God in the face of evil and adversity."

Her cheeks felt warm, but her hands were cold and scaly. She pushed away the flowers to look at the rabbi's face. "Well, maybe *she* was the one who should have prevailed. A mother feels the loss of a child the deepest. A man crumbles if he's unjustly fired or if his reputation suffers, but it's the woman who cares about the family. Mrs. Job only got very little mention in the whole book of Job, so it's no wonder that no one listened to her." Tears rolled down Rachel's face and she sat with her arms tightly crossed across her chest. "And by the way, Job was rewarded for keeping the faith by having ten more children. What's my heavenly reward?"

"Rachel, I came here to comfort you, not to upset you. I often talk about Job's trials to demonstrate an unwavering belief in God amid untold suffering. I'm surprised by your knowledge of the story."

"Rabbi, for one thing, I studied linguistics in college, and we looked at the language of various cultures, including ancient Hebrew poetry. Yeah, I know a lot about Job—how its text doesn't use rhyme as in most Western poems; how allegory, alliteration, and metaphor separate it from prose. So if you don't mind, I'm really tired and I need to go upstairs now." Her stomach growled loudly, a reminder she'd forgotten to eat lunch.

Rachel followed him to the door, keeping her distance a few steps behind. Rabbi Sachs reached for the doorknob and said, "You're a very intelligent person and I'm sure you'll find a way to get past this. If you don't choose call on *me*, I beseech you to find some help through this difficult time of bereavement. *Shalom*, Rachel." The golden afternoon sun shone into the foyer like a ray of light from God, illuminating the dust mites swirling in the air.

When Michael got home, he never mentioned Rabbi Sachs. Rachel figured the rabbi had called her husband to give him a full report. Michael felt the need to take action, but she needed to be still. The rabbi's visit hadn't made her feel more settled, and he would need the patience of Job before she would call on him for help.

After a few weeks, Rachel left the house to go to the market. Mundane chores were all that was occasionally required of her. Rachel put on jeans and a sweatshirt and headed for the Simon David grocery. If she had to do the shopping, she preferred a small, manageable store. She couldn't bear the thought of the endless aisles at the A&P.

She carefully pulled onto the heavy traffic on Royal Lane and made a right on Inwood, passing streets of beautifully designed houses with manicured lawns. At the intersection at Northwest Highway, a billboard caught her attention with its headline, "Celebrate Do Unto Others Week. February 12–18." The caption beneath a photo of Rosemary Williams, tipping her red cowboy hat with a yellow rose on the brim, proclaimed, "Be a good neighbor to all neighborhoods." Although not particularly metaphysical, she wondered if it was an omen that she spotted that billboard during one of her infrequent outings.

It also reminded her that Missy's highway outdoor sign hadn't yielded many leads. A tipster had called in a sighting of a dark green pickup with suspicious scratch marks and a broken taillight leaving Fort Hood, an army base not far from Springland. When the police investigated the vehicle, they discovered that the man's mother had accidentally backed the truck smack into one of the biggest live oak trees in the state of Texas that was located on the grounds of the trailer park. The suspect, their mentally challenged grown son, had been at work pushing a broom on the maintenance crew at the base when the crime was committed. The father had been declared legally blind years before, so he couldn't have driven the truck, even if he had wanted to.

All the clues were dead ends. Missy's death was declared an act of random violence. Rachel was tormented by the thought that some demented guy got his rocks off by shooting two young girls in broad daylight. The billboard, which she considered another of Michael's bad ideas, failed to yield even a tiny piece of the macabre puzzle.

With renewed hope, she stared at Rosemary's outdoor board on the corner of Northwest Highway, wishing it were a sign—a burning bush. *What would it hurt to talk to that outrageous woman waving the red cowboy hat on the massive poster? Besides, it would be a good way to mend some fences with P.J.* A cool silence had hung over the friends for the three months since P.J. stormed out of her home, flinging the self-help book at Rachel.

Mama called one morning and made Rachel promise to get out and leave the house for a spell. Rachel drove down Preston Road toward Highland Park, an elegant neighborhood, to witness firsthand the evidence of an early spring. Red bud trees splashed across the yards of Dallas and banks of lipstick pink and cotton white azaleas adorned Turtle Creek with garlands of flowers. The sun warmed her face through the windshield. Rachel turned on the car air conditioner, but the musty smell from a winter of nonuse assaulted her lungs. She quickly shut it off and opened the sunroof. The weather reporter declared a "blue norther" was on the way and temperatures might plummet thirty degrees by four o'clock. Nonetheless, she decided it was getting to be time to find out what sitting and rocking on Rosemary's deck was all about.

Rachel snaked along Lakeside Drive, caught in a parade of cars taking in the display of color. She could barely glance to her side for fear of rear-ending someone. A bumper sticker in front of her warned,

"Don't mess with Texas." The path along the road was clogged with joggers, and people everywhere were stretching and running. Her fingers coiled tightly around the steering wheel, and then her vision began to blur from the tears that pooled and spilled onto her lap. She squinted into the glaring sun. There was no sign of the predicted dark clouds from Canada when she turned toward home.

Locating the book P.J. had given her wasn't an easy task. A pile of note cards from friends, magazines, and catalogs on her kitchen desk began to resemble the ancient strata of an archeological dig. A fine layer of dust had collected on a few of the precariously balanced stacks, probably untouched by her housekeeper for fear they would collapse if disturbed.

Toward the top the lowest pile, she spotted the garish red book jacket. She thumbed through the pages to find the inscription with Rosemary's contact information. Rachel dialed the first nine numbers and sucked in a deep breath before punching the last digit. The line rang three times, and then a voice drowned out the thuds in her chest.

"Hey there, it's Rosemary. . . ."

She listened for the rest of the recorded message. Dead air.

"*Hello-o-o*, this is Rosemary. Is anybody on this line or am I just yanking my own chain?"

"Sorry, it's Rachel Frank—P.J. Rutherford's friend."

"Of course . . . Hi there, I was 'spectin' to hear from ya sooner or later. It must have been hard for you to actually pick up the phone and call. That rocker I told you about is as empty as a campaign promise after an election. So when are ya stoppin' by?"

Rachel was amazed that Rosemary remembered her. She stammered like a schoolgirl being asked on a first date by a boy she doesn't want to be seen with. "Maybe in a few weeks. I'll give you a call after I check my schedule."

Rosemary's voice crackled with laughter. "It's just for tea—not a proposal of marriage. Why don't ya come over after lunch tomorrow at around one? Despite what the weather clowns say, I think this warm spell's gonna hold. It'll be a good day to catch some rays on the porch."

"Well, okay. See you tomorrow," Rachel said, twirling the telephone cord around her wrists.

"Then I'd better tell ya where I live: 2840 Sycamore Street. Dress casual," she snorted with a deep laugh. "See ya then, Rachel."

"Okay, unless something comes up. I might have to cancel at the last minute, but I'll let you know."

"*Hasta mañana.*" Rosemary hung up.

Rachel's appointment with Rosemary was a secret she didn't want to share with Michael. If it went well, she might let him know; if not, he wouldn't have the opportunity to talk to P.J. behind her back, scheming about the next step.

Rachel picked up the volume of *Make Your Own Bed of Roses* and scanned chapter headings in the table of contents: "Picking Strange Bedfellows," "Bedtime Stories," "No More Bed Sores," "On the Deathbed," and "Bed, Bath and Beyond." The chapter about nurturing was titled "Tending your Flower Beds." The book fell open to the first page of "No More Bed Sores." A large capital *P* dominated the paragraph:

> "Pain is part of all of our lives. Everyone has experienced pain of one sort or another. I think people are like onions: When you peel back the layers, it's enough to make you cry. All of us have suffered, but the difference lies in how we handle our pain—which layers are helpful and which need to be exposed to the air, even though they might make us weep."

Rachel feared she wouldn't show up at Rosemary's if she read any further. She took the book upstairs and stashed it in her nightstand drawer.

While clearing phone messages, a familiar voice spoke after the machine clicked and whirred. "Rachel, I won't be home until after dinner. Don't wait for me."

She reached back into the drawer and grabbed Rosemary's book.

CHAPTER 21

THE SUN STREAKED ACROSS Rachel's bed, painting white lines across the down comforter. She willed her sleep-encrusted eyes to focus on the clock on Michael's nightstand. Eleven thirty-two flipped to eleven thirty-three. Her head sank back into the pillow, thinking she had plenty of time to rest a little longer and still make it to Rosemary's by one o'clock. But she couldn't fall back to sleep, so she decided to get ready.

Rachel knew that Rosemary had been joking about dressing casual, but she wondered what to wear. She picked up her jeans from the chair next to her bed and battled with her bulging thighs. *If I keep the button open and unzip them about an inch, they'll work if I wear a sweater long enough to hide a multitude of sins.* She laughed at herself, looking in the mirror. *Who am I trying to impress? A celebrity guru whose credentials probably aren't any better than the baggers at the Simon David?*

She went downstairs and defrosted a few rock hard pieces of rugalach from a plastic zip bag in the freezer. There were still several mystery packages in silver foil that had been put there by well-meaning friends the week of the funeral. Rachel thought it funny that Jewish women get a moratorium from cooking if there is a death in the immediate family. In the last few years, she was living proof of the old joke that the only thing she wanted to make for dinner was reservations, seldom cooking for Michael, once Missy went away to school.

Rachel popped a few of the fruit-filled pastries into her mouth and ate on the run. There wasn't enough time for lunch and still arrive at Oak Cliff on time, and if she wanted to grab a quick burger, she only frequented Ledbetter's, out of misguided loyalty.

She paused at the door, realizing she didn't know where to go. The address Rosemary had dictated was still on the magnetic pad stuck to the fridge. Rachel ripped off the sheet, stuffed it into her pocket, and headed for Sycamore Street.

As she approached her destination, the Trinity River meandered below the overpass—little more than a muddy gully in South Dallas. She shoved a Willie Nelson tape into the player and drove past streets with hulking live oaks with roots that burst through the sidewalk, like gnarled fingers reaching up from the ground. The houses had the haphazard look of a neighborhood in transition. Some were fastidiously restored, while others bore the vestiges of generations of families living and dying in them. The odd numbers climbed on the left side until finally 2840 swirled across the side of a red lacquered mailbox in front of a rambling Tudor. Chocolate brown beams framed the cream-colored façade, punctuated with a Chinese red door. A pair of spiraling cypresses in carved stoneware planters flanked the riotous entry.

Rachel parked in front of the house, hoping to hear Willie Nelson sing the end of "Like a Bridge Over Troubled Water," but it was getting late. His voice wavered on the refrain, matching the twang of his guitar. Willie always made her laugh or reduced her to tears, so if she sat any longer, she thought she might lose the nerve to leave the car.

Slowly, Rachel walked up the flagstone path to the front door that swung open before she even had the chance to knock.

She stood face to face with Rosemary, who smiled warmly. "I saw you sitting out there in your car. Glad you decided to take a leap off the high board," she said in a deep drawl.

"No, really, I was just listening to one of my favorite songs. I'm a huge Willie Nelson fan."

Rosemary ushered her into the house. "Me, too. He ought to be declared a national treasure. My first husband and I once saw him in concert at the Armadillo World Headquarters, and I passed my favorite hat up to him to sign while he was onstage. Heck, he was autographing gym socks and girls' underwear in the middle of his set. One old woman hobbled up there to get a kiss in the middle of "Good-hearted Woman," and I swear that after she got it, she threw down her crutches and was healed!"

"It was probably more from a couple of Shiner Bock beers." Rachel laughed, breathing a little easier, feeling that Rosemary's metaphorical diving board just lowered a bit closer to earth.

"Well, come on in. Shame on me letting you stand out here in the hall. I haven't properly welcomed you. Rachel, it's mighty good to finally meet you." Rosemary squeezed her wrist and led her into the living room. They passed a hall tree near the front door, sprouting cowboy hats from every branch: straw ones in a rainbow of colors adorned with jaunty feathers and ribbons, and at the top, a red felt Stetson with yellow roses exquisitely stitched in silk thread.

They wove their way past a red undulating contemporary sofa covered with a bouquet of floral needlework pillows. "People send 'em to me all the time, with crewelwork roses and the like, because my last book cover for *Bed of Roses* had me sitting with a pile of embroidered pillows and flowers. I donate most of them to women's shelters, but I've kept some of my favorites."

Other collections dotted the room. Pottery teetered on the edges of bookshelves and plants trailed along the walls and furniture. Above the limestone mantel, a framed montage of four images of Rosemary smiled with full lips, and her violet eyes flashed. Her signature cowboy hat morphed from red to green, yellow, and magenta, in otherwise identical panels. Rachel didn't need to read the black scrawled signature of the artist that danced across the lower right hand corner of the silk screen.

"Andy gave it to me when we lived in New York. He took the image from a clipping of me in *Rolling Stone* while I was partying at Studio 54, but that's another story. How about some tea? Come pick a mug."

Through an archway, they entered the kitchen—a magnificent jumble of textures, aromas, and colors. Dishes weren't stacked in neat piles behind closed cabinets; instead, open shelves bulged with handmade platters, teapots, and mugs shuffled together in miraculous harmony. Rosemary picked up an oversized dinner plate, stroking its wide, richly glazed rim. "This deep color is called oxblood. Not too appetizing a name, but it's actually from copper. An Austin potter Enrique Hidalgo made these plates. They're heavy as hell, but they're so beautiful that no one cares what kind of food I serve on them."

Rachel ran her finger across the deep red glassy surface. "Get a mug, and we'll go out on the back porch and set a spell."

Rachel stared at what seemed like about fifty cups nestled inside one another. She was terrified that if she pulled one out from the middle, the whole stack might come crashing down. Picking a bottom one was unthinkable. Rosemary was busy slicing something at the cutting board. Finally, Rachel liberated a satiny white cup toward the top of one of the piles.

"Good choice!" Rosemary said. "That's a Ruth Duckworth. She's a slip of an Englishwoman who either makes massive vessels or the most delicate porcelain works in organic shapes. Great choice. One of my favorites."

Rachel silently said a prayer of thanks that she wasn't asked to select a flavor of tea. Decisions didn't come easily. Rosemary deposited several scoops of loose leaves into a stoneware pot with a clay handle that swirled like a ribbon. Her guest picked up the tea box and examined the contents on the artsy label: rose hips, hibiscus blossoms and raspberries. The idea of rose hips always made Rachel wonder what part of the plant they came from.

On a black lacquer tray that reflected the empty cups, Rosemary placed the steaming teapot and a platter of domino-sized cheese slices the color of peanut butter. "It's called gjetost—from Norway. To me, it tastes slightly sweet, a lot like the caramel flavor of *dulce de leche*."

Rachel felt like she was attending a modern-day version of the Mad Hatter's tea party and had fallen down the rabbit hole the minute she stepped through the red door. Everything was familiar, yet slightly off kilter. She noted that a half hour had passed since she arrived, and they still hadn't started to talk about anything of substance.

"Grab the door, darlin', and let's go out back on the screen porch," Rosemary said, nodding toward to rear of the kitchen. She deposited the tray on a wide wicker ottoman surrounded by six rockers. The deck wrapped around like an outdoor living room. A stacked stone fireplace clung to the side of the house, and a stag horn chandelier dangled above a bent twig table and chairs in the corner. In the backyard, planted terraces were carved out of deep slopes that led to a creek lined with jutting limestone boulders.

"It's gorgeous out here," Rachel said. "You must really have a green thumb."

Rosemary arranged a faded needlepoint pillow that was wedged into the worn wooden frame of her rocker. "You should see the terraces in about a month. They're almost all perennials, so I don't have to worry from year to year about replanting annuals." She pointed to the chair next to her and said, "Take a seat and rest your bones. The garden dies back over the winter, but it's like a resurrection each spring when it warms up."

Rachel struggled to remember if there had been any religious undertones in the self-help book. With her faith shaken after Missy's death, she really wasn't up to any attempts at being converted.

"I feel like I get a gift from the garden each spring. In fact, I've heard it said that each day is a gift. That's why it is called the present," Rosemary said.

Rachel flashed to the Ziggy newspaper cartoon attached with a magnet on her refrigerator, captioned with same sentiment.

"Rachel, green spaces are very important for the spirit. In fact, there's a discipline called ecopsychology that teaches us that many of the problems we face today are due to our disconnect from nature."

Rachel rocked and surveyed the patchwork of colors on the porch. Miniature oranges clung to delicate branches, and purple pansies with yellow monkey faces spilled out of planters. On the twig table, several glass vases held sprouting bamboo stalks in beds of crystal pebbles.

"Did you ever read a memoir of a Plains medicine man?"

Rachel sipped her tea and tried to push away the memories of sitting on Missy's bed, reading to her until it was time to turn out the light and kiss her goodnight. "No, I don't think so."

Rosemary poured more tea and Rachel deeply inhaled the fragrant herbs, drawing the moist warm air into her lungs. The scent of the orange trees mixed luxuriously with the steeping liquid. In her favorite chair, Rosemary leaned back and set the rocker in motion, making the deck rhythmically creak to her to-and-fro sway. She spoke in a cadence that rose and fell like the chair. "It's the story of an Indian shaman who looked for the source of life and peace and the mystery of growing. He erected a sacred teepee and gathered six elks and four virgins. He'd have a heck of a time finding any today!" She snorted and took a sip of tea. "The virgins represented the life of the nation, and the six men, painted black and yellow, symbolized seeds that sprout from the ground. You still with me?"

"Yes, Indian lore reminds me a lot of my childhood at summer camp."

"Well, good, because I'm fixin' to tell you more."

While she described the flowering sticks the women carried, Rachel thought about Missy as a girl of six confronting a large hole in the front yard. She had found a stick and shoved it down the opening. When she pulled it out, a black fuzzy tarantula flailed helplessly impaled on the end. She ran screaming into the house, waving the huge spider, never thinking to drop it. Although they lived in the city, the country vermin didn't always know it. Occasionally field mice gathered beneath the bird feeder, and scorpions made their way up the drains in the bathroom.

Rosemary's rich voice made the vision of Missy evaporate like the steam from Rachel's teacup. She wove the story while the two women sat in a circle of chairs, like the clasped hands of young girls around a campfire. Her tale evoked the sounds of little critters scurrying and June bugs dive-bombing the glowing embers of the Council Fire at summer camp.

Then the creaking of the floor stopped. Rosemary leaned forward and rested her elbows on her knees. "The ancient peoples knew the healing power of nature for the body and soul. I had to go to Southern California to get my Ph.D. to find that out for myself."

"Where are you originally from, Rosemary?" Rachel asked, since the door to her background had opened a crack.

"I was born in Kansas, but my parents moved to San Francisco when I was eight."

Rachel was confused when she discovered Rosemary was a citified scholar and not the homespun sage she appeared to be. *She's as bad as trained painters with master's degrees who try to pass themselves off as self-taught folk artists,* she thought. It annoyed her that Rosemary was pulling the wool over the public and wasn't exactly how she presented herself.

Rachel turned her attention to the crimson cardinal that landed on the railing across from her chair, noisily clicking until the dull-coated female appeared. Her mate swooped down, grabbed a few grains from the feeder, and then flew to a nearby branch. His clicking chirps taunted his mate.

"Tell me how you and P.J. met," Rosemary inquired.

Rachel turned from bird-watching and faced her. In the afternoon sun, she looked younger and prettier than in the photos on her book jackets. Her sparkling eyes shifted from navy to violet, depending on how the light caught her full face.

"Oh, we've been best friends since grade school. Always a team. But we've hit a rough patch right now." She shifted in her chair. "I'm not sure she'll ever want to speak to me again after the way I treated her. Sometimes I just want to pick up the phone, but she's probably sick to death of my whining. In fact, I know she is because she told me so."

"You sure think relationships are as fragile as glass, don't you? Well, Rachel, glass is surprisingly strong and can even withstand harsh elements. For Chris-sakes, Dale Chihuly makes massive glass sculptures for the garden that cost hundreds of thousands of dollars. When I met him at the Boathouse—his residence and studio in Seattle—he told me he's got boundless faith that they're more durable than they look. I guess his trusting and well-heeled clients do, too."

Warhol and now Chihuly. What is she, an art groupie? Rachel's skepticism was increasing. She tested the waters, "You certainly know a lot about art."

"Yep, I guess I do. I met P.J. while I was getting my master's degree in Austin. I was involved with art therapy and loaded up on art history courses. Somehow I discovered my passion for studying and collecting art. While in my program, P.J. helped me with some of my fieldwork."

"I was at UT, too. The campus is huge, but I'm surprised we never met."

Rosemary downed the last few sips of tea. "I was really Juan's friend at first. I used to go out with him before he dated P.J. Initially she and I didn't click, but over the years our connection grew."

"I must have been married and living in Dallas by then. Small world, huh?" Rachel marveled at one more surprise from this woman who seemed to have nine lives. She figured Rosemary picked up her drawl and folksy speech while living in central Texas. Rachel had previously noted that she sometimes said "you" and sometimes said "ya" but had passed it off as her own obsession with linguistics and the intricacies of language.

"Rachel, I've got cut this short to go meet with my agent about my next book. She's in town from New York. I hope you'll stop by again. How about next Tuesday, same time?"

"Let me check my schedule. My calendar's at home, so I'll have to give you a call. Thanks, I hope I didn't overstay my welcome." She wondered if the invitation stemmed from an obligation.

Rosemary collected the cup, brushing against Rachel's fingers. "I think we're going to get to know each other much better. Why don't you take home a piece of this lucky bamboo? It's so hardy you can't really kill it. Even if you don't believe in Feng Shui, it's just something lovely and green for your house. The Chinese use it to attract positive energy and promote health, happiness, and prosperity."

"That's a tall order for such a small plant," Rachel murmured.

Ignoring the remark, she said, "I'll just put a couple of stalks in a little vase."

"No, really, I couldn't."

Rosemary was already a blur of motion in the kitchen, reaching high on the shelf for a paper-thin white porcelain container. She pressed a delicate vessel into Rachel's hand.

All the way home Rachel balanced a ceramic vase between her legs and listened to Willie Nelson singing his heart out.

Birthday Wishes

CHAPTER 22

Rachel cancelled her visit with Rosemary the next week, thinking, *I can't, for the life of me, figure out why she'd want to see me.* She left a painfully transparent message on the answering machine begging off, promising to reschedule.

Generally, she stayed close to home. Friends occasionally called to go for lunch, but she rarely accepted. An ornate invitation to a forty-fifth birthday lunch for her old school chum Carrie Anne arrived in the mail.

Rachel had kept in touch with Carrie Anne over the years, seeing her at PTA meetings, the summer musicals at Fair Park, and an occasional lunch date for old time's sake. Reminiscing about playground incidents and what they wore to Cotillion had made them cackle like schoolgirls, but Rachel was in no mood right now for a trip down memory lane.

The invitation landed on top of the pile on her kitchen desk and stayed there for a few weeks. Finally, she dialed the number on the RSVP, hoping to get her machine, but Carrie Anne picked up.

"Hi, it's Rachel."

"After thirty-something years of phone calls, I can certainly recognize your voice."

"I've got to pass on the party. I'm tied up that day," Rachel said softly.

"Well, you just better untie yourself because you've got to show up. No ifs, ands or buts. I'll come get you, so that's that. I won't take no. Bye now." She hung up before Rachel could protest further.

The party was set at the Zodiac Room at Northpark Mall—the suburban branch of Neiman Marcus. Rachel finally decided that the prospect of seeing the old gang might not be all that bad. At eleven-thirty sharp Carrie Anne arrived in her silver Jag and did most of the talking on the way to Neiman's. Rachel was thankful she only had to utter an occasional "uh huh" to maintain her end of the conversation. They pulled up to the front entrance, and a valet in khaki Bermuda shorts and a polo shirt hopped into the car.

"Cute glutes!" Carrie Anne said in a stage whisper. The valet winked at her as he tore off in her car.

They entered the store, breezing past the St. John boutique on their way upstairs to the restaurant. Three saleswomen in the exquisitely tailored knitwear called to Carrie Anne as the two women ascended the escalator, climbing toward a shimmering mobile of feather butterflies and mirrored disks suspended from the ceiling.

Carrie Anne giggled and shouted down to them, "Put aside a few things for me, y'all. I'll be back downstairs to try them on after my birthday luncheon's over."

The dim lights in the restaurant cast a subtle glow on the sophisticated taupe palate. A long table in the center of the room was set for eleven: five on each side, and one at the end—the seat of honor for the birthday girl. A small flat box—wrapped in diaphanous Japanese rice paper trimmed with loopy bows of gold and celadon organza ribbon—decorated each place setting. One of the guests had already opened her box, revealing a lacey white linen handkerchief with her initial embroidered in gold silk. Next to the oversized charger plates, filigreed silver picture frames served as place cards. Rachel picked up her frame and stared at herself as a teenager with a face full of freckles and a curly patch of bangs hovering above her eyebrows. Mama always managed to cut her bangs too short right before it was time to pose for school photos. In the frame on her right, she glanced at a faded photo of a reedy girl with corn silk hair and a Mona Lisa smile.

A voice from behind her said, "Isn't there a famous slogan about not getting older but getting better instead? I hope to God it applies to us!"

Rachel turned around and saw P.J. Instantly tears welled up and streamed down her face. She grabbed her old friend in a tight hug, dripping mascara on P.J.'s lacey white top. "I'm so sorry," she cried.

"That's what dry cleaners are for," P.J. replied, wiping the moisture from her eyes.

"No, not your blouse. I'm plain sorry about everything," Rachel said between sniffles. "I could really use a handkerchief right now, but it's wrapped up in that frilly box that would take a rocket scientist to open."

Carrie Anne shouted out, "Okay, you two, break it up! This is my birthday party, and unless you girls have some earth-shattering announcement about how y'all are finally coming out of the closet, all the love at this table needs to be headed my way."

The waiter scooted Carrie Anne's chair, and she settled in like a mother hen on a roost. She commanded him to bring on the wine. Although the Zodiac Room had expanded its menu over the years to include nouvelle and spa cuisine, Carrie Anne informed the group that she had pre-ordered her all-time favorite lunch: chicken salad nestled in a ring of frozen orange gelatin soufflé.

Rachel thought the demitasse of clear chicken broth that arrived at each of their plates was much more refined than the murky chicken soup she made at home for the Jewish holidays. Then the waiter delivered massive crusty popovers, which she cracked open and slathered with strawberry preserves and honey butter. Rachel's popover was perfectly cooked and steaming—her favorite part of the meal.

Christie slyly pointed to her ring finger. She whispered to Rachel, "Carrie Anne says her emerald cut is six carats, but it doesn't look very white to me. Oh, did I show you what Bradford gave me for Christmas?" She shoved a massive, blindingly pristine diamond in front of Rachel's face.

P.J. leaned over and said, "Now we know whom to call if one of our headlights ever goes out!" She asked the group, "Has anyone been to the new restaurant, Tierra, on Lower Greenville? I heard it's great."

Carrie Anne's eyes lit up. "Tiara, now that sounds interesting! What kind of food do they serve?"

"No, it's *'Ti-er-ra,'* not 'Tiara.'" P.J. trilled her *R*s in exaggeration. "It's not a hangout for old homecoming queens, it's a new Southwestern restaurant."

Carrie Anne glanced conspiratorially at Christie. "Heavens knows that between the two of us, we've got enough of our own tiaras to crown everyone at this whole friggin' table!"

"I haven't laughed this hard in a long time. If this keeps up, I'm going to need a box of Depends," Rachel joined in.

"I'm sure 'the birthday girl' will lend you hers," P.J. quipped.

Carrie Anne raised one eyebrow into a pointed triangle and then smiled, showing too many sparkling white teeth.

The main course arrived and everyone remarked how the food was still as good as ever. Rachel prayed that Carrie Anne, in her perpetual quest for youth, hadn't selected the dessert that had delighted Rachel as a kid: an ice cream clown made of a single scoop embellished with candy eyes and nose, wearing a sugar cone hat—too many calories for grown women to consume. She had eaten her first clown at P.J.'s sweet sixteenth birthday at the downtown Zodiac Room.

Instead, a cadre of waiters rolled a teacart with a sheet cake iced with a spray of yellow roses and one lone candle. Carrie Anne said, "Who needs reminders of how old we are? I told them to just give me one big candle, so I could blow on it hard and make a wish that's bound to come true." She closed her lids with lashes that resembled two little furry tarantulas and puckered her artificially plump lips. And then she blew.

Carrie Anne opened her eyes and announced to her guests, "I want to play a game, since it's a birthday party. Everyone must say what they wished would happen by the time they were grown. Me first! I always dreamed I'd be married and wouldn't have to work. I hoped my body would still be good enough to enjoy whatever I wanted to do." A faint blush rose through her makeup. She caught herself, "Of course, I mean to play tennis and golf."

Christie shouted out, "Don't you mean to *do* tennis and golf . . . pros?"

"Very funny. And how's your pool man these days? Next victim! "

Rachel looked at all the made-up faces painted with the satisfied expressions of lives in order and wondered what she would say when it was her turn.

Carrie Anne's cousin Sara confided she had wanted to become a partner in a law firm. A graduate of Harvard, she had achieved it by age thirty. Now she longed to ease up, but she made the women swear collectively not to tell anyone at the firm. They held up their right hands and Carrie Anne placed hers on the wine list while everyone swore to guard the confession.

Suddenly, Rachel felt like the thermostat had been cranked up. She dreaded that her turn was fast approaching and began to furiously fan herself with the menu.

Christie leaned over and whispered, "Try Premarin. I swear by it."

P.J. was next in line, and she toyed with her new embroidered handkerchief, the only one with two initials. "I wanted to be an established artist by now. I made the right career choice and am happy to say I've managed to spend as much joyful energy on my marriage to Juan as I do on my artwork." There was light applause from the table. "I think the old adage about how opposites attract is a total crock. Juan and I are very much alike in our values and interests, and that's what works for us."

Carrie Anne said, "Well, Joe Bob and I are like oil and water. He's found most of the oil in Texas, and I'm just swimming in jewelry. Now it's your turn, Rachel. You can't look down at your lap like when we were in school when you didn't want Mr. 'Sharp' Spears to call on you."

"Hey, I was the one who always knew all the answers. That's probably where you got your nice long neck—from copying my papers." The group giggled and hooted, causing Carrie Anne's face to drop for a second, and then she regained her beauty queen smile.

The dazzling grin expanded into a full shriek of joy when out from behind a large palm at the entrance of the room, Carrie Anne's twin daughters, Madison and Taylor, ran over and draped their arms around their mother's swan-like neck. The perfectly coifed and made-up hostess was reduced to a blubbering mess. She stood up, smoothed her wrinkled lap, and introduced her daughters.

"Everyone, y'all know the twins. They came all the way from Austin to surprise me." She turned to them and wrinkled her brow in a parody of disdain. "Does Daddy know y'all skipped school?"

They chattered their response, finishing each other's sentences, saying their father had sent them plane tickets and a limousine to deliver them to the luncheon as a surprise.

Carrie Anne laughed and instructed her daughters, "Now, you take your daddy's charge card and have a little fun downstairs in honor of Mommy's birthday. Make sure to tell the salesgirls to give you the Butterfly bonus points for the InCircle program. I've just about got enough for a free trip to Paris."

Madison and Taylor chirped in unison, "Happy birthday, Mommy. You rule!" They were on their way to the escalators faster than Rachel figured they had ever tried to make it to class on time.

Then all eyes seemed directed at Rachel, making her painfully aware it was still her turn. Carrie Anne picked up her wineglass and declared, "That's enough of Fabulous Fillies Truth or Dare. Let's finish my cake before my next birthday rolls around!"

Rachel started to stand and the waiter dashed to pull out her chair. Looking at no one in particular, over the heads of everyone across from her, she took a deep breath and stammered, "I would never have guessed . . . that at this age, I would be amazed if I could get out of bed to attend an old friend's luncheon. My plans were much different. I imagined being able to see my daughter at Parents' Weekend, take her shopping, and watch her try on what I bought her. I never thought my marriage would be torn to shreds by her death and that I would be so fat and ugly. Never in my wildest dreams did I imagine I would ruin someone's birthday party like this. I'm so sorry, everyone. I never should have come. Big mistake!"

Rachel didn't sit down. She turned and ran toward the escalator, blinded by the thousands of glittery, suspended feather butterflies that swarmed around her. Without stopping to chat with the St. John ladies near the entrance, she burst out of the revolving glass door into the fresh air. Then all motion stopped when the crashing truth hit her: She hadn't driven her own car. She covered her face in her hands and shook in heaving sobs. The jingle of metal caused her to peek between her fingers—P.J. was dangling her car keys in front of her face.

"Let's get you home, pal."

They didn't say much on the drive home and just listened to oldies on the radio, occasionally picking up the harmonies they used to sing together as kids. Rachel was anxious to get back to her room and her bed. In the driveway at last, she gave her friend a quick hug and opened the car door. "P.J., you don't have to say a thing. My behavior was unspeakable, and I promise I'm going to give Rosemary a call tomorrow."

P.J. smiled and then backed into the street and was gone before Rachel entered the house.

CHAPTER 23

TWO DAYS LATER, Rachel walked down the stone path to the red lacquer door. Branches poked out of the spiraled cypresses on the porch. Sorely in need of pruning, the trees looked like they were struggling to reestablish their natural shapes. Rosemary met her at the door, wearing a large grin and a massive silver and turquoise belt. She saw Rachel staring at the intricate geometric patterns and said, "This piece won the grand prize at the Indian Festival at Gallup, New Mexico, two years ago. I had just received my advance on *Rose Garden*, so I didn't bat an eye before I grabbed it. It's Zuni and the work's really extraordinary."

"Never seen anything quite like it—amazing!" Rachel said. The large silver disks inlaid with turquoise, purple sugilite, and coral captured the afternoon light.

"In that neck of the woods, they refer to turquoise as 'Southwestern diamonds.' Enough about my jewels—let's talk about you. First, let me make you some tea."

Rachel was ready this time. She announced with conviction, "I'd like some ginger tea. Do you have any?" She followed her host into the kitchen and grabbed a cup that was displayed on a small wooden pedestal.

"That's a Gertrude and Otto Natzler—potters who immigrated to the U.S. during the late thirties from Austria. She threw the forms and he formulated the glazes. Excellent choice! It's one of my most valuable cups, and some people would say I'm crazy to actually use it. In this case, I say function should follow form." Running her fingers across the smooth porcelain, she said, "Aren't the crystalline stars in the surface of the glaze just magical? Yes, I do have ginger tea."

"No gjetost for me today. I'm going to start cutting back on snacks."

"Sounds like you're ready to make some changes, Rachel. What's been going on?"

"Rosemary, I think I'm completely losing it. I can't seem to go out in public without creating a disaster. I embarrassed my husband at one of the most important events of his career, and a few days ago I turned an old friend's birthday party into a wake."

Rosemary leaned against the kitchen counter and put down the teapot. "It sounds like you've hit a rough spell. Let's sit in the living room and talk about it. Go on in there and I'll be there lickety-split, soon as the tea brews."

Rachel cleared a spot on the curvy red couch, tossing aside some of the needlepoint pillows. She amused herself by surveying the collections scattered throughout the room while Rosemary clattered around in the kitchen. A desktop in the corner was checkered with photographs, and from across the room Rachel could make out the white shock of hair on Andy Warhol's head in the center of a frame.

Rosemary entered the room and sank into an overstuffed chair that faced the couch. She set down a wooden tray with the steaming pot and mugs on the coffee table. With the solemnity of a Japanese tea ceremony, she poured the steaming, fragrant liquid and passed her guest a cup. Rachel admired the iridescent glazed starbursts and then took a sip.

Rosemary picked up a remote control and switched on soothing melodies of ancient woodwinds harmonized by the sounds of trickling streams. She locked eyes with Rachel and asked, "What's causing all of your pain? Just tell me what you feel."

"Not much of anything these days. All I keep doing is losing control and making a fool of myself. I probably haven't said three words to my husband in the last five months." Her words poured out to Rosemary, who drank tea and leaned back in her chair. "I can't look at Michael without thinking about Missy. I don't know why I feel so angry when I see him going about his business as if nothing has changed in our lives. He goes to work and comes home late. I don't have a clue about what he's doing half of the time."

Rosemary learned forward. Her violet eyes turned into dark pools in the low light. "Think he's having an affair?"

"I wouldn't blame him if he were, but I've never found any evidence yet. He's got plenty of opportunity and motive, and he's never around. Hey, I'm not sure of anything these days."

"How has the loss of your daughter put a strain on your marriage?" Rosemary glanced over at the desk and then fixed her gaze on Rachel.

"What do you think? How can we possibly be happy without her?"

The sound of trickling water and the warm tea made Rachel feel the urge to pee. She stood up and was about to excuse herself when she heard a sharp click from something on the desk. Walking over to investigate, she distractedly picked up the Warhol photo to get a closer look. Hidden behind the frame was a miniature tape recorder sitting on the desk. "What's this?" she asked.

Rosemary answered with an innocent smile, "Oh, that's a tape recorder."

"I know it's a tape recorder. What the hell are you doing taping our conversation without my permission?" The blood rushed to her head and she temporarily forgot about her full bladder.

"I always record conversations of this nature," Rosemary replied evenly.

Rachel looked down at the desktop again and spotted a mock-up of a book jacket with a photo of Rosemary holding a steaming cup of tea. She picked it up and read the title aloud, *Women are Like Tea Bags.*

"Yeah. 'Women are like tea bags; the more hot water they get into, the stronger they get.' It's a variation on a quote by Eleanor Roosevelt. Think I should be dangling the bag or should it be swimming in the cup? We shot it both ways."

Rachel boiled with rage. "You've got a lot of nerve faking interest in me just to research your new book. I didn't agree to be one of your case studies."

"Don't get your panties in a panic! I never use real names in my books. The examples are based on composites of actual situations. That makes them relevant to a larger segment of my audience."

Rachel headed for the door, turning around to shout, "You couldn't pay me enough to be in your book."

"Well, darlin', you're too cheap to shell out for my help. Ya didn't seem to mind it when you thought you were getting free therapy. Better learn lesson number one in life: Ya can't get somethin' for nothin'."

"I can't wait to tell P.J. what a fraud you are—you with your fake Texas accent. You can't even keep your *ya*s and *you*s straight." Rachel opened the door and stumbled onto the front porch, scratching her arm on a loose branch.

She ran down the stone path. Rosemary followed close behind and said in a slow drawl, "What makes you think she'd really want you as a friend? P.J. and Juan have told me enough about how they feel about you to make me wonder why they still hang on."

Rachel jumped into the car and unrolled the window. Flipping Rosemary the bird, she screamed, "I don't believe you ever set foot in Studio 54 or ever met Andy Warhol! And if you did, you probably would have been too stoned to even remember it!"

CAMP STORIES

CHAPTER 24

MORNINGS BECAME AFTERNOONS. Afternoons melded into evenings, and eventually the summer went by unnoticed. The peach-colored walls of Rachel's bedroom lulled her into a sense of security against the outside world. The occasional intrusion was a pharmacy delivery of the little pills that took the edge off day and eased her into night.

Mama called frequently to check up on her. Usually, she let the phone ring until the answering machine picked up.

Her mother's voice penetrated the quiet, "Rachel, I know you're in there, because where else would you be these days?"

Rachel made a mental note to next time select a machine with a limited incoming message tape.

Mama continued as if her daughter were listening to every word, "This nonsense has got to stop. I want to see for myself how you are. I'm coming over later with Irene. My car's in the shop, so she's going to pick me up." Rachel listened for the click that signaled the end of the message, but her mother just kept talking. "We'll be over around two-ish. Honey bun, get yourself into the shower before we arrive. Fix yourself up. You'll feel much better."

Her mother never could resist doling out advice. Rachel was upset that Mama had invited someone else to join them, and although she had known Irene since birth, she wasn't up for company.

Irene and Rosy used to be inseparable until they had a falling out at their weekly mah jongg game. Rachel used to watch them briskly clack the tiles on the table when they made their moves. The two women must have sounded like magpies although the shuffle of the game pieces is said to mimic the birds chirping in the reeds in China.

Rosy groused how Irene had let their opponent beat them by losing track of the game play. She had carelessly discarded a seven-bam tile that Sylvia needed to complete her hand. Irene could have foiled her attempts to get a mah jongg, a win, by throwing Sylvia a dragon tile instead. Rosy admitted she must have muttered in exasperation, "She's a *meshugenah*." She hadn't realized that she had spoken her thoughts aloud.

Insulted at being called crazy, Irene scattered her tiles and yelled back, "*Gai kakhen afenyam.* I'm sick of your *farshtinkeneh* attitude!"

After being told to go crap in the ocean, Rosy didn't speak to Irene for two years. In Yiddish, telling someone to go jump in the lake has a sharper bite than in English.

After that incident, Irene could be heard at the synagogue making comments about her best friend's outfits. Her gravelly voice carried loudly over the din of conversation before the services began.

When Irene's husband Joel died suddenly of a stroke, Rosy swallowed her pride and offered the olive branch. She arrived at the shiva condolence call with enough of her homemade mandel bread to feed the whole congregation of Beth Israel. While the mourners were gathered in the living room for the minyan to recite the Kaddish, Irene's white standard poodle with a round, fluffy tail, Matzo Ball, apparently lost control due to grief over her master's absence and devoured most of the unattended cookies.

Matzo Ball was known for her legendary reserve when it came to food. When Rachel was little, Joel and Irene always entertained her by showing off their pet's most impressive trick. They would argue over who would get to demonstrate the poodle's brilliance. One of them would dangle a treat directly in front of the dog's eager chops, and she would greedily grab it—only after Irene proclaimed it to be kosher. If her master declared that the food was the opposite, *trayf*, the dog would spit out the biscuit like her mouth was on fire. Irene would stroke her and sing her praises, "Such a gifted and pretty girl." Rachel couldn't even imagine what type of training methods were employed to make Matzo Ball possibly the world's only dog that willingly observed the dietary laws of *kashrut*.

After Joel's passing, Rosy and Irene gradually gravitated back to each other. They met for lunch every Wednesday, often followed by shopping. In the years after Rosy's divorce, Irene had shunned her. She was dropped from the social circle. Most of the Jewish community didn't believe that divorce, alcoholism, or abuse existed among the Chosen People. Rachel's mother had the dubious distinction of being the first in her crowd to leave an ill-suited mate. Rosy always thought Irene held her nose a little too high because her marriage was intact. The history of the two women's friendship was like Rosy's famous meatballs—sweet and sour.

Rachel's doorbell rang at two-fifteen. Rosy and Irene were both dressed in crisp polyester slacks with floral short-sleeved blouses. They were competitive shoppers, often selecting the same outfit, trying to beat the other to the cash register first. Rachel decided that their similar outfits could be classified as copycat dressing. One of them had probably spotted the ensemble first and then the other bought something virtually identical.

Mama breezed into the entry hall, extending her cheek for her daughter to plant a kiss as a sign of contrition.

Irene grabbed Rachel's hands and squeezed them tightly, digging rock-hard, frosted talons into her palms. She pumped their joined hands and her charm bracelets tinkled like wind chimes. "Rachel, when are you coming to see my new puppy, Bissel?"

Rachel loosened her grasp and replied, "Oh, Irene, I haven't gotten out much lately, but I promise I will."

"How about a cup of coffee, Irene?" Rosy offered.

"I didn't make any, Mama. I'm all out of fresh roast, but there's some instant in the pantry," Rachel said.

Her mother walked toward the kitchen calling back, "Instant, *shminstant*. I'll find some grounds and make you a nice cup."

Rachel glanced over to Irene, who had already seated herself on the couch. Her stumpy legs barely touched the floor. "I'm so sorry, Irene. I haven't been to the store lately."

"Not to worry, *dahlink*. I like mine as black as a *schwartze*."

The word Rachel considered horrid, *schwartze*, made her temples pulsate. She bristled that it translates literally as "black" in Yiddish, and Jews who use it usually claim there's no negative connotation. *It's funny, but they hardly ever call blacks 'schwartzes' to their faces,* she thought. She swallowed deeply and decided to fight that battle another time. The pills seemed to have taken the edge off her will to confront, even though she shuddered at the thought of anyone calling Maddy a *shwartze*.

Irene grabbed her hand, this time stroking it as if she were petting her prized poodle. The old woman's veins protruded like a road map of her life, leading to a series of blue-black stenciled numbers on her inner forearm. She usually kept them hidden with long sleeves, except when she was among life-long friends. Rachel had never seen them so clearly, indelibly branded on Irene's leathery skin.

She ran her fingers over Rachel's hand while she spoke with a heavy Czech accent tinged with a bit of a Texas twang. "Your mama tells me you have been having a rough time of it. *Dahlink*, she is worried sick about you and she loves you."

Rachel mused that when someone said they loved her, it was usually right before they offered unwanted and unsolicited advice. She forced herself to let Irene continue uninterrupted.

"Sweetheart, you might not know that my late husband, Joel, was not my first great loss. Life has not been so easy for me, but I am grateful for each day God gives me on earth. I wake up and tell myself that I can choose whether I am going to have a good day or a bad day." She rubbed her arm and continued, "It was not always so easy to think this way. Rachel, I got these numbers in Auschwitz. I was there for a brief time before the war ended. My family was picked up in Prague in '42, and we were sent to live in a concentration camp in a fortress town called Theresienstadt—you might know it as Terezin."

"No, I don't. You don't have to tell me this." Rachel started to get up.

Irene looked at her with warm, fixed eyes. "Sit still. You need to hear this."

Rachel leaned back and tucked her feet beneath her like when she was a child.

"My parents stayed crammed in communal sheds that held thirty or so adults, and I was sent to the children's boarding house. You see, this ghetto was supposed to be a model camp the Nazi's used for propaganda to show the world how good the Jews were being treated." She leaned forward, cupping her chin in her gnarled fingers. "We had so many artists, intellectuals, and musicians in the camp that they allowed us to have cultural activities. A lady artist kept a stash of drawing materials so the children could learn to paint. She asked us to portray things we loved, the life outside the stone walls of the old fortress: my puppy . . . my pink lace frock."

Irene smoothed back her wiry hair with one hand, her bracelets tinkling lightly. She continued, "I'll never forget—one day a guard handed me a crisp white pinafore and told me to shower and then wait for him at the foot of the steps near the dormitory. The showers really were showers there. The dead from disease and starvation were disposed of in ovens, but mass killings did not occur at Terezin. It was a way station for the death camps like Auschwitz-Birkenau, but we did not know it at the time. Anyway, to my surprise, the windows of nearby buildings were stocked with breads and pastries—things I had not seen for the two years I had been there. At first I thought I was dreaming."

The faint drone of the television set in the kitchen intruded on Irene's tale. Rachel figured her mother was probably at the kitchen table watching her favorite talk show, letting her friend do a *mitzvah*, a good deed.

"Irene, I feel so bad. You suffered hell on earth," Rachel said.

"It was bad, but much worse was coming . . . unimaginable evil. So, about twenty minutes after I got to my post at the foot of the steps, the guard, along with a camera crew and some International Red Cross workers, came up to me. They asked if I liked my pastries. I shyly murmured yes and then smiled for the camera, which whirred as I spoke. And then they collected their gear and moved across the cobbled street to document the candy store. After the Red Cross people went away, I was abruptly told to get out of the dress and was left in the street, standing in my ragged underwear."

Why is Irene was telling me such a surreal story about sweet shops and art lessons in a concentration camp? Rachel kept quiet and told herself to let the woman finish what she had come to do.

Irene's milky blue eyes started to glaze over like condensation on glass. "A few days later my parents were sent on a transport to Auschwitz on July 25, 1944. I was told I would meet up with them shortly, but I never laid eyes on them again." Tears rolled down Rachel's face that contorted with anguish as pain welled to the surface. Irene squeezed her hand tightly and said, "I am almost finished, Rachela. Auschwitz was where the extermination took place—where I eventually was sent. The number of Jews murdered there was staggering. And yet I survived. To this day, I do not know how or why. I live with the memory of my damned smile. If only I had cried out that we were hungry and people around us were dying, maybe the Red Cross would have realized it was all a sham. Maybe my parents wouldn't have been sent to their deaths. Maybe I should have begged harder to go with them on the transport. Too many *maybe*s. I could drive myself *meshuge* trying to wish I could change what happened in the past, but I cannot."

Rachel's head felt like it weighed more than the rest of her body, and she sank her face into Irene's lap and cried. Irene's rough voice smoothed to water over pebbles in a brook. She crooned, "There, there, *maideleh*. The dead are gone, and we cannot bring them back." She stroked Rachel's hair as she gasped for air with each heaving sob. "The Mourner's Kaddish says that the deceased live on in the memories and hearts of their loved ones. We cannot change the past. Life is a circle that can either give us a kiss on the cheek or a bite on the *tuchas*. The Jewish religion tells us how to carry on and to live a good life in the here and now."

"Irene, I feel so terrible. You've suffered so much and you're so strong. What's wrong with me?"

"Nothing, *dahlink*. I'm just an old lady and it took me a long time to finally understand—that we cannot totally protect anyone. Of the 15,000 children who were at Terezin, only about one hundred or so survived. I do not know how or why I was one of the few lucky ones. When I was small, my mother used to always say to me that 'man plans and God laughs.' I believe the ultimate design is in His hands."

"Or *Her* hands," Mama said, entering the room. "Here, honey bun, I brought you a nice hot *glezel tai*. By the way, did you know you're out of coffee?"

Before Irene took her home, Mama cornered Rachel in the kitchen. "You've got to pull yourself together. Your grandma Marlena used to tell me that doing something for others would make me happier. She said to shop around at the various charities, try them on until one fits."

"Once a dress shop owner, always a *schmata* seller," Rachel said, rolling her eyes toward the ceiling.

Mama snapped back, "Your grandmother, a *schmata* seller, was a whole lot smarter than your smart mouth. Why do you think I knit booties for the preemies in the neonatal unit at Parkland? Hopefully, they'll get a better start than you did and won't suffer from asthma. Baby Patrick would be alive if he'd been born today."

"Who?" Rachel asked, trying to remember which of her mother's friends had lost a baby boy.

"The Kennedy baby. His little lungs hadn't developed. Now they spray something the March of Dimes came up with into all the preemies so they can breathe."

Rachel began to think her mother had lost her mind.

Mama forged on, "It's time for you to find some group and get out of this prison." She marched out of the kitchen and called to Irene, "Let's hit the road before we get stuck in rush hour on Northwest Highway."

"Fine, you and Irene can just go and talk Yiddish all the way home. That's all you seem to do anyway!" Rachel yelled back.

Mama said, "It wouldn't hurt you to wish us well by saying *gay ga zinta hate*."

"Rachela, dry your eyes and try to *git a schmeykhl*." Irene smiled and blew her a kiss.

DREAM JOB

CHAPTER 25

FOR QUITE A WHILE, Rachel hadn't been able to muster a smile. Not even one for Irene. When she called to get a renewal on the tranquilizers, her doctor insisted upon a follow-up visit. At the appointment, Dr. Silvers advised that she participate in group or individual therapy, after Rachel mentioned her mother's suggestion about taking some action. The doctor also handed her a glossy pamphlet about an organization called the Victims of Violent Crimes Network.

"I don't think I can do this right now—listening to other people's horror stories." Rachel stuffed the brochure into her purse and left the office.

Armed with the filled prescription, she headed directly to bed. She wanted to stop the painful thoughts of Missy lying crumpled with a massive head wound in her car on the roadside of dried weeds and black dirt.

Rachel closed her eyes and images appeared of her daughter's little legs running through the sprinklers. Squealing with delight, Missy loped across the lawn and tried coax her out of the lawn chair to join in the spray. Rachel clutched her book to keep it from getting wet. Missy's cool touch felt so good against her sun-baked skin, but she forced herself to pull back so the child's dripping wouldn't ruin the pages.

Missy begged, "Ple-e-ase play with me, Rachel."

"Call me Mommy, not Rachel," she answered, surprised that Missy had used her first name.

Out of the depths of sleep, Michael was shaking her arm. "Rachel, wake up. Are you all right?"

"I'm tired, so why should I get up? I was dreaming about Missy and I want to go back to her. What time is it?" Rachel strained to make out his face in the room lit only by the hall fixture.

"It's seven o'clock in the evening. Why are you sleeping all day? You've got to get a goddamn grip on yourself."

"Why should I get a grip? There's nowhere I need to be. Where do you want me to go?" She looked away and didn't meet her husband's stare.

"Rachel, just do *something*." His face was red and sunken, ringed with much more silver around the temples than she had noticed before.

She sat up, propped against the pillows and looked at him. "Okay. I've got to get something going. Let's see . . . I'll get on a mission to figure this out. Maybe I'll do telemarketing and bug the hell out of people during their dinnertime or translate Spanish for rich housewives who can't communicate with their maids.

"You could teach." Michael sat on the edge of the bed.

"Or I guess I could be a teacher's aide. I used to teach, so this might be a good way to get back into it."

The glint in his eyes was rekindled. Michael spoke in rapid fire, "Well, that's it! Teaching. Great! If you need a few new clothes, go out and buy what you want. Do you need me to make a few calls?"

"No, I'm just fine by myself. Slow down! Maybe I'll check into working at North Dallas Elementary. It's close to the house. The schools are always interested in cheap or free help."

"That's just great," he said again slower. Michael had that determined 'you-can-do-anything-you-set-your-mind-to-it' look on his face with his jaw firmly set. "Rachel, I'm going downstairs for a while to go over some blueprints. But I won't be down there all night, hon. I'll make it worth your while to wait up for me."

"I'm really tired, so I might not be awake when you come up." Rachel closed her eyes.

As he walked out of the room, he softly muttered, "Great, just great."

A few days later, Rachel called the administrative office at the elementary and was told she was in luck because they had positions open for a cafeteria worker, a girls' basketball coach, and a teacher's aide for after school play. She expressed her interest in becoming a T.A. and agreed to an interview at two o'clock that afternoon.

Rachel washed her hair and pinned it in a French twist. She was fresh out of enough energy to blow dry or style it and hoped the updo would look like an attempt at grooming.

She squeezed into a lightweight dress and decided on a pair of beige low heels. Stockings would make them more comfortable, so she conducted a search and rescue mission through her drawer to find a pair without runs. At one-thirty she left the house for her first job interview in over twenty years.

Rachel was amazed that she remembered the way to the principal's office. The halls still had the same dank smell of when she was a child, only now they were air conditioned in the late August heat.

Mrs. Washington, an imposing woman who appeared to be Rachel's contemporary, emerged from an office. She sported a smart navy pantsuit and wore wide horn-rimmed glasses that set off her chiseled, dark features. "Mrs. Frank, please take a seat."

"Thank you. Just Rachel. What should I call you?"

"Principal Washington isn't necessary; Mrs. Washington will do. So tell me about yourself."

Rachel felt like she had just been reprimanded with a slap on the wrist. She shifted in her chair and dropped the purse that had been clutched tightly on her lap. "Mrs. Washington, I want to work with children."

"I see from your resume that you're qualified for a full teaching position. Why are you applying to be a teacher's aide?"

"I've been out of the classroom for a number of years. This is a good way to get my feet wet, and the hours will work out. I prefer afternoons to mornings." Rachel hadn't seen many mornings in recent months and felt fairly certain she could get herself together to leave the house by three in the afternoon.

"Do you have any children of your own?" the principal inquired, shuffling through some papers on her desk.

Of all of the questions Rachel had rehearsed while driving to the interview, she hadn't anticipated this one. She gasped, taken by surprise. Most of the people with whom she came in contact seemed to know about what had happened to her precious Missy. She tried to breathe, but the air hardened to concrete in her lungs. After a few seconds, her chest loosened and she exhaled.

Mrs. Washington glanced up, raising her eyes above her lowered glasses.

Rachel reached down for her purse. "I might as well tell you now. My daughter was brutally murdered last year, and that's been pretty much my whole life lately. If you don't want me, I perfectly understand."

"Frankly, there's only one thing I see is wrong with you for this job."

Rachel closed her eyes for a second, and then through slits, braced herself to receive the bad news. "Yes, and that is . . . ?"

"Your wardrobe. For after school play, stockings and dresses really won't cut it on the playground. Comfortable clothes and sneakers are fine for the recreation areas."

"Thank you, Mrs. Washington. I'll be sure to buy some new sneakers."

"We view after school play as an opportunity to help children transition from the concentration of schoolwork to a state of relaxation before entering the home. It's a place where they can play, have a snack, and catch up on their homework. Weather permitting, most activities will be outdoors. We'll see you next Monday at 2:45 p.m. Please always check-in for duty fifteen minutes early with Miss Rightwood." Mrs. Washington put her hand on her new employee's shoulder and escorted her to the door.

Later that night Rachel received a call from her sister Hedy, who never started off a conversation with "hello." She just launched into speaking the second anyone answered the phone. "I heard from Mama that you got yourself a little job."

"The family grapevine doesn't waste any time, does it? I start on Monday at after school play at North Dallas."

"You couldn't pay me enough to watch those little 'rugrats' out in the heat."

"You'll be happy to know they barely *are* paying me, so no problem. Thanks for your continued support, Hedy." Rachel wished the phone call would end.

"I don't know why you're getting your nose in such a snit." Hedy started to pick a fight, as usual.

"You're mixing metaphors again. Now my nose *is* out of joint. Look, I've gotta go. If you speak to Lenora, tell her there's no need to congratulate me. She's probably too sauced to think about me, anyway."

"She won't like it that you think she drinks like a chimney. I'll be sure and tell her what you said. Bye now." Hedy hung up, armed with the newest ammunition against her younger sister.

Why the hell do I let her get the best of me? Rachel felt she was already nervous enough about starting to teach again without being aggravated by her sister's taunts.

On Monday afternoon, Suzi Rightwood checked her watch when the new hire arrived at 2:47 p.m. "Miss Rachel, punctuality counts at North Dallas," she said, pursing her lips. She was a pert blonde in her early twenties, and Rachel figured she had probably been a cheerleader at some point in her life.

"I was in the office picking up a copy of my employment agreement."

"Afternoon play starts promptly at three. Teachers from grades three though five will bring the kids who are staying after school. Introduce yourself to the children as 'Miss Rachel.' The key to the equipment room is in the top drawer of my desk. Make sure you always return it when you finish. The mothers will pick up the students at six o'clock. You need to stay until the last child leaves."

"Okay, Suzi, no problem," Rachel said cheerfully, trying to sound cooperative.

"You might as well start calling me 'Miss Suzi.' Consistency counts when you're working with children."

Then a line of thirty wiggling youngsters filed onto the playground. They took all shapes and forms; some giggled, stumbled, pouted, or scratched, but they all stared at the new teacher—the great unknown. A bead of sweat tricked into Rachel's left eye, stinging, making her other eye tear.

One of the smallest girls approached her. "It's all right. The first day of school always makes me cry, too."

Rachel burst out laughing. "Thanks for the advice, honey. What's your name?"

"Miracle Baldwin. My folk say it's a miracle that I don't drive 'em plum crazy. I know Mama really thinks it was a miracle that I was born became I came out real early, and she's really glad to have me."

Miracle was all wiry energy wrapped in a kraft brown package that weighed no more than sixty pounds. Her thick brown hair, tinged slightly golden at the ends, spiraled around her face, like the curly laces on her red sneakers.

"Nice to meet you, Miracle. Now I'm going to say hi to everyone, so please step back with the rest of the group," Rachel said, smiling at the little girl.

Suzi ordered, "Class, stand up straight and dress-right-dress!" Like little soldiers, one by one, the youngsters stood an arm's length between each other in straight formation. "No talking, please. Children, this is Miss Rachel. She's going to supervise your after school play. She's new here, so let's show her how great North Dallas kids are. Welcome her with a big round of applause."

The students clapped half-heartedly as if their batteries had run down. Miss Suzi stepped closer to them and said, "You sound like a bunch of beached seals. Let's show her how loud we can yell hello to Miss Rachel on the count of three."

Upon cue they shrieked in unison. In triumph, she turned to Rachel and said, "They're all yours."

Rachel walked in front of the line of children to introduce herself and cleared the catch in her dry throat. "Hi, I'm Miss Rachel. We're going to have a lot of fun after school. There are a few rules I expect you to follow. Number one: You can tell me anything. Number two: Let me know the minute you don't feel well or have to go to the bathroom." This prompted them to titter like a bunch of cartoon mice. "And number three: Never leave this playground without my permission. Now, let's get started with the fun and games!"

She organized the older children into teams to play kickball. The younger ones followed her to the jungle gym, wrapping their rubbery bodies around the brightly colored metal. She sat on a bench facing the parallel bars and squinted into the searing sunlight. From that vantage point, she could also monitor the progress of the kids running around the bases, dodging the large rubber ball. Rachel tried to memorize their names by using association techniques: Heather was as delicate and pretty as a flower; Ross seemed to want to be the boss or captain of the team, but it didn't work for everyone. Still confused, she hoped to remember to make little nametags to pin on their shirts. It was difficult to absorb everything at once. With so much to remember, Rachel knew she wouldn't be able to forget Miracle, with her bright face brimming with bravado.

Children's laughter and taunts were mixed with the sounds of traffic along the perimeter of the playground. Rachel served as referee on small disputes, dispensed juice and cookies at snack break, and wiped a few noses from the stash of tissues from her fanny pack. The last half hour was reserved for those who had questions about their homework.

The sun hung high in the sky, even though it was a quarter to six. She instructed the kids to gather up the equipment. Rachel counted the balls and the children's heads, and then went with her class to the carpool line beyond the playground.

One by one, they were picked up by parents, nannies, and grandparents—some in carpools and others individually. When the last boy disappeared into a green minivan, Rachel headed back to the equipment area to lock up. She tied the jump ropes in neat bundles and tried to stow the balls in a cabinet, but they kept uncooperatively rolling onto the floor. Suddenly, her head began to throb like someone was bouncing a basketball against her skull, probably from excessive sun exposure and acute dehydration. She hadn't spent much time outdoors in years except lounging beside a swimming pool. Blisters from her new sneakers hurt almost as much as her pounding head.

She didn't hear Suzi enter the room on her soft-soles while Rachel was sliding the keys into the desk drawer. "So, are we going to see you back here tomorrow?" Suzi asked.

Startled, Rachel jumped, banging her knee on the open drawer. "You bet. This is going to be a walk in the park." She hoped her supervisor would respond to perkiness. "Miss Suzi, I have one question: When do we hold after school play indoors?"

"Way after Thanksgiving. It'll give you something to be thankful for," she said with a half-smile.

Rachel found little humor in the remark that Suzi seemed to think was extremely clever, as evidenced by her smug expression. The younger woman still looked as fresh as in the morning, and Rachel bemoaned to herself that she had to drag her weary old carcass to the car, which was scorching hot from baking in the Texas heat all day. *Tomorrow I'll remember to look for a parking spot shaded by a small grove of live oaks.*

THE BIG SHOT

CHAPTER 26

RACHEL HOPED HER young charges were enjoying their time on the playground. She remembered when she was in elementary school, the seemingly idyllic time in life that was actually fraught with playground politics and drama.

Her home had been a roller coaster of emotions when she was young, but after the night of the escape to the Thunderbird Hotel, everyone tiptoed on pins and needles. Rachel was afraid to do or say anything that would make Papa blow up again.

He came home from his job at the plant and headed directly into the den to watch the evening news. If Rachel made the mistake of meeting him at the door, complaining about what newfangled torment Lenora or Hedy had perpetrated against her, he'd explode at all of his daughters—not directing his tirade at any particular target. Mama prepared the meals and kept the cigarette drawer stocked. Her Technicolor beauty faded as the seasons reluctantly began to change, and 1963 turned out to be a year of many losses.

Rachel and her sisters stopped inviting company over to their house, not being able to predict when the shouting would begin. Rachel figured Papa's outbursts probably frightened P.J., but she never gave a hint in her polite refusals. The girls spent their sleepovers in the serenity of P.J.'s white and cornflower blue bedroom.

P.J. also never mentioned that Gypsy was missing, although Rachel had noticed her staring at the shelf and didn't have the heart to confess how she had lost her favorite gift from her best friend.

The opening of the school year held no great surprises. In the sweltering September heat, Rachel's back stuck to the contoured wooden desk in her damp transitional cottons. It was too hot to wear woolens, and the "fashion police" in Texas dictated that white after Labor Day was taboo. Rachel and her friends were clad in heather, eggplant, rust, and chocolate brown cotton skirts and shirtwaist dresses. The boys wore jeans and button downs, while the girls had to stick to knee length skirts all year round; pants or shorts violated the dress code.

Each fall, Rachel would sit in Temple in an outfit that looked like it belonged somewhere in New England instead of the middle of sweltering Texas. In spite of the almost tropical heat, some women wore wool suits with plush fur collars to services, ignoring the soaring Fahrenheit outside. Little beads of sweat glistened on their brows if the air conditioning wasn't set low enough. They fanned themselves with the brightly colored announcements about synagogue activities that were stuffed into the *Union Hymnal*.

November finally signaled some relief. The live oaks and Dutch elms around Dallas transformed into an orange and gold tapestry. Rachel's courses in seventh grade seemed much harder than sixth. She was benched most of the time in PE because she couldn't run the laps around with track without succumbing to an asthma attack that sucked the air out of her lungs.

Math, formerly one of her best subjects, became a source of increasing anxiety. Her grades plummeted toward the end of the term. She was sure her math teacher, Mr. Spears, held a grudge. Hedy had been his former student, and she had taxed all of his patience with her unruly antics and poor aptitude for calculations. Rachel felt persecuted from the start. She thought his stinging, disapproving blue eyes were like her father's.

Perched at his desk, Mr. Spears honed in on her like a falcon snatching a helpless mouse. "Miss Miller, perhaps your parents need to check your homework before you bring it to class. You're just not keeping up. I want to see a signature at the bottom of each assignment for the next two weeks. Young lady, you're riding sidesaddle, if you catch my drift."

The man is utterly insane. "Sidesaddle?" What the heck does that mean? She worried that Papa would scold her if he thought she wasn't giving it her all in math. She felt she was a numerical numskull compared to his being a mathematical wizard and worried that word problems always confused her. The previous year had been much easier, and she never before had to show her homework to her father.

Rachel knew Mama was smart in many ways, but word problems often caused Rosy to burst out laughing. "How many men would it take to do this or that? Just hire some more to get it done faster" was her reply.

In the evening after the dinner dishes were cleared, Rachel waited for the right moment and walked quietly into the den. Walter Cronkite's rich, throaty voice and fatherly face was on the screen of the Magnavox, holding Papa's attention.

From behind the recliner, Rachel spoke above a whisper, "Papa, I need a little help with my homework."

"You really should try to work it out yourself. But what's the problem, Red?" He was the only person who ever called her "Red," which made her feel a little special.

"I can't do word problems. Everyone's having a tough time. Mr. Spears said we should ask our parents for help and then have them sign our papers."

"Okay, but make it snappy. There's a bridge game tonight."

"Here's the one I can't get." She handed him her seventh grade textbook and crouched alongside his chair. "Farmer Jones has a huge red barn that holds 1000 animals. He keeps 40% of his barn for the bulls and 60% for cattle. If on Monday, the barn was 75% full with 200 bulls and some cattle in the barn. How many heads of cattle were there?"

He put on his reading glasses and perused the page. "550 cattle," he answered, hardly missing a beat.

"Papa, I just don't need the correct answer. How'd you figure it out so fast?"

"Anybody can make a simple equation and go from there."

"But how'd you get to the answer?"

"What don't you understand? 75% of 1000 is 750. This is so basic that I did it in my head. Don't they teach you how to do the simplest division and subtraction?" His blue eyes zeroed in on her while he tapped his fingers on the open book.

"Oh, okay, now I get it," she lied. "Just sign my work here."

He scribbled "D. S. Miller," shut the book, and handed it to his daughter without taking his eyes off the evening news.

Mama twirled into the room, like Loretta Young, in a black and white polka-dot dress cinched at the waist by a wide red patent leather belt. She smoothed her freshly dyed mahogany-colored hair in the mirror and spoke to her husband's reflection, "Like it? It's an exact copy of a Valentino. I got it at Margie's Dress Shop for a fraction of the cost. Time to go, Danny. Rachel, your asthma medicine's on the counter. Don't stay up past ten. Call us if you need us. We'll be at the Levine's. You know the number is on the chalkboard near the fridge."

Papa said, "Hedy and Lenora, no visitors while we're gone. That especially means boys! The liquor cabinet is locked for a good reason, you two." His eyes narrowed when he addressed them.

"Yes, sir. I know the rules," Lenora answered.

Hedy twisted her long, straight ponytail and nodded in agreement.

Rachel tried to diffuse the ticking bomb in his head. "Have fun at the card game, and I hope y'all win." Like the plaster model of Mt. Vesuvius that she made in social studies class, Papa left the house without an eruption.

The next day, she dropped her paper on the stack on Mr. Spears's desk. The hour clicked away and he hadn't called on her yet.

"Who wants to go over the first word problem?" he asked. Rachel studied the graffiti scratches on the top of her desk. Pointing in her direction he said, "Miss Miller, I see that you're anxious to share your answer with your fellow classmates. Come up to the board and show us what you've got."

A wave of nausea washed over her. She untangled her gangly legs from the all-in-one desk and chair. Her limbs had been twisted around each other, and the circulation hadn't completely returned yet. She wobbled to the blackboard at the front of the room and picked up a piece of chalk from the tray.

He dictated in halting phrases, "If a train leaves the station . . . in Chicago . . . going 55 miles per hour at 9 a.m. . . ." Rachel scratched 55 on the board. Amid the piercing sound of squeaking chalk, everyone groaned as the hair stood up on the backs of their necks. He continued unruffled, "The other was going 45 miles per hour." The school bell wailed over his words. He looked at Rachel with a crooked smile. "Miss Miller, you're lucky there's been a derailment. We'll pick up first thing on Monday. Class dismissed!"

The students exited in single file toward the cafeteria, heading down the dull gray hallways, shuffling along the speckled linoleum floors. The line dissolved into complete chaos once they entered the cavernous lunchroom with rows of tables. They were free to sit wherever they wanted; the teachers ate in self-imposed exile at a head table that ran across the front of the room near the cafeteria line.

Rachel had forgotten to bring her lunch because she had rushed out of the house when carpool came early. Mama had warned there would be a lot of traffic in town and had told this week's carpool mom to pick up Rachel a half hour ahead of time so they wouldn't get caught in it and be late for school.

Rachel stood in line, inching her way to the hot food counter. She ordered a plate lunch from the dark-skinned, hair-netted ladies who welcomed her with warm smiles and gave her extra portions sometimes, perhaps because she was so puny.

She slid a water-splotched tray along the chrome railing and ordered, "Chicken fried steak, mashed potatoes, and green beans, please."

"Something to drink, sweet thang?"

"A carton of milk, please."

Mrs. Johnson, in her white cafeteria matron's outfit with her silver hair in a neat bun coiled like a Danish pastry, tallied her bill. "That'll be seventy-five cents."

Rachel pulled three-quarters out of her red plastic squeeze pouch. She noticed that the cafeteria servers were all colored, while the lady who handled her money was white.

She grabbed a seat at the table with Christie and Carrie Anne, saving the place next to her for P.J. Christie was already halfway through her homemade sandwich on spongy brown bread. She said that her mother thought whole wheat was healthier than white, but Rachel didn't consider it desirable for lunchtime trading. She couldn't imagine eating bread that looked like cardboard, when she could sink her teeth into Mrs. Baird's brand white bread. Sometimes she pulled the white, soft center away from the brown crust and rolled it into a moist ball and popped it into her mouth. When her family drove down Central Expressway at certain times of the day, she could smell the sweet aroma wafting from the Mrs. Baird's Bread factory. That day at school, she was eating a plate lunch, savoring the mashed potato moat filled with thick brown gravy.

In his thick, rubbery shoes, Mr. Spears walked into the cafeteria late, about twenty minutes after the kids arrived. His eyes were glassy, his nose red and swollen.

"What do you think's the matter with him? Bet he caught a cold all of a sudden. Maddy always says that's what happens when the weather changes," P.J. said.

Rachel rubbernecked to get a better look. "He looks funny doesn't he, like he's been crying."

"'Sharp' Spears crying? Come on. He's too mean to cry," Christie protested.

"Maybe someone in his family is sick or something." Rachel caught another glimpse of Mr. Spears as he leaned toward Mrs. Koch, the old prune of a librarian who always had tissues escaping out of her bodice and cuffs. He cupped her ear with both his hands and whispered. She abruptly clutched her shriveled fingers to her mouth. Then she hung her head and kept her eyes riveted on her plate while he spoke.

"What do you think happened?" Rachel asked.

Carrie Anne answered nonchalantly, "Who knows and who cares? What I want to know is what you're going to wear to Cotillion this week?"

"Let's talk about it outside. I can't breathe in here—it smells like onions, yuck!" Rachel avoided the subject for the minute.

"I'm done. Let's get out of here," Christie said in her high-pitched whine.

Trays and crumpled lunch sacks were gathered and discarded. The girls climbed down the back stairs of the lunchroom and spilled onto the blacktop playground. The sun shone down from a clear blue sky. The fresh, cool air blew Rachel's bangs into her eyes, and her full skirt swirled in the breeze. The chain from a neglected tetherball clanged against its pole.

Carrie Anne moved in close to P.J. "I'm going to wear my new Villager set with the matching knee stocks."

"Mother made me get a navy dress with a white Peter Pan collar when we were at Neiman's last weekend. I'm not so crazy about it." P.J. wrinkled her nose as she spoke. "There was another cool dress that I wanted."

"Your gold circle pin with the pearls will look cool on it." Carrie Anne maneuvered closer, trying to make brownie points with P.J.

"I'm wearing the new dress I got for Rosh Hashanah. It's rust and gold plaid. Mama said it sets off the color of my hair," Rachel said.

Jason Fuller, the boy who sat behind her in math, grabbed Rachel's arm to get her attention. "Guess what, y'all. President Kennedy's been shot!"

The air exploded from Rachel's lungs, as if she had been hit in the belly with the tetherball. She squinted at him in the bright midday sun and asked, "Says who?"

"I heard that Mr. Spears told Mrs. Koch that the president was shot just a few minutes ago at the parade downtown," Jason reported. "He's gonna be okay. Just got winged."

Christie squealed, "Oh, wow, I don't want that ugly old LBJ as my president! He looks like a worn-out boot, and besides, he yanks on his dogs' ears. Him and Her are such cute pups and they don't deserve to be treated that way."

"Jason said he's going to be okay, so don't sweat it," Rachel chimed in.

"My folks say Kennedy didn't know what he was doing with all of the pigs in Cuba," Christie added. Her upturned nose seemed more tilted than usual.

"Oh, shut up, stupid! He knows plenty. Lenora wanted to go to Dealey Plaza, but Mama wouldn't let her skip school today, and she said I was too young to be in such big crowds and all that traffic. I was dying to see JFK and Jackie in person. They're like movie stars, so totally glamorous," Rachel blurted.

The metallic blast of the school bell signaled the end of recess. The students filed into English class and took their seats. Mrs. Braxton balanced her girth on the edge of her desk. "Come in, children, and take your seats quietly. Hurry up, please."

Bing-bong-bing, the loudspeaker played over the sound of dragging feet and shifting desks. "Students of North Dallas Elementary, this is Principal Hightower. May I have your undivided attention. I have a grave and important announcement to make. It grieves me greatly to inform you that President John Fitzgerald Kennedy was killed in downtown Dallas by an assassin's bullet. Governor Connally was wounded, but he's expected to fully recover. Let us bow our heads in a moment of prayer for our country and for our slain leader."

Rachel lowered her head and tears dripped onto the notebook paper on her desk, distorting her childish script.

From the loudspeaker, she heard Principal Hightower's prayer: "Dear Lord, a great tragedy has befallen our nation. Give us the strength to overcome this great loss and to continue the lofty ideals and purpose of our founding fathers. Please bless and give comfort to the Kennedy family, especially our first lady, and pray for the speedy recovery of Governor Connally. In Jesus' name we pray. Amen. I now declare school closed for the day."

"Amen," Rachel echoed faintly, not feeling the least bit guilty that it was in the name of Jesus.

Mr. Hightower's voice had soared over the high-pitched sobs and sniffling all around her. Jason's head was down on his desktop, buried in his arm. Mrs. Braxton was quietly weeping, strolling around the room. She rested her hand on the shoulders of children who were beginning to cry louder and louder—careening toward hysteria.

"Students, your parents have been called to pick you up. Gather your things because you're going home," Mrs. Braxton slowly announced. For a moment Rachel was excited about leaving school, then the dull ache of the president's death came back. Her teacher continued, "Jason and Christie, stay with me until your mothers can get you after work."

Unsteadily, Rachel went to her locker and loaded up her book bag. Mrs. Braxton led the children out the front doors, and they waited in the searing sunshine for their parents to arrive.

Rachel spotted Mama's Fairlane near the end of a long line of sedans and station wagons. Finally, the car pulled up to the curve. She got in and slid next to her mother, burying her head in hollow of her neck, their tears mixing together.

"Let's go pick up Hedy and Lenora at the high school," Mama said.

They drove a few blocks to Preston High where the two sisters were waiting on the steps. Lenora glared at Rachel for sitting in the front, but she didn't make her change places. The older girls dabbed their eyes and asked Mama to turn the radio to KLIF, their favorite rock station.

"How about a few moments of silence without the radio?" Mama said. Then everyone stayed quiet. Rachel thought about President Kennedy and then her crying kicked up an asthma attack. She found it hard to believe that even the president of the United States—the most powerful person in the world—wasn't safe.

By Sunday of the weekend of the assassination, the streets of downtown Dallas were snarled with traffic jams of people trying to get a glimpse of the places where the two surreal killings of John F. Kennedy and Lee Harvey Oswald had taken place, and to pay their respects to their fallen chief. The newscasts showed mounds of bouquets and wreaths piled high on the grassy lawn in front of the Texas Book Depository near the spot where Kennedy was struck down. Rachel and her family mourned with the shell-shocked citizens of Dallas—along with the rest of the country.

During the week of the assassination, Cotillion was cancelled and it seemed like the whole country came to a halt. Rachel sat glued to the television set in the den, watching the black riderless stallion prancing down Pennsylvania Avenue, kicking up his sleek, sinewy legs. He reminded her of the dashing president with the beautiful full head of hair and movie star smile who had captured her heart. The camera zoomed in to show the stirrups turned backward to symbolize the fallen leader.

Rachel had seen the pre-election debates on television without fully understanding the questions—just studying the faces of the two candidates. Nixon was so ugly, shifting on one leg, his beady eyes staring out from a mask of dark stubble. His rough voice sounded like sandpaper to her ears, compared to the melodious, yet unfamiliar, accent of the Harvard graduate John Kennedy. At school, the children mimicked him by saying "*paahk the caah.*" Even though Rachel was too young to cast her ballot, there was no question in her mind that she wanted him to be her president. Although she practiced "duck and cover" drills, crouching under her school desk in case of atomic attack, she knew John F. Kennedy would protect her from the Communist threat.

And now, it seemed surreal that the reporters on television were explaining that he was to be buried in Arlington Memorial Cemetery after lying in state in the rotunda of the Capitol Building on the same catafalque that supported Lincoln's coffin. Rachel sat on the floor in front of the Magnavox while Mama and her sisters were huddled on the couch. She figured that if someone could kill the president of the United States, then no one was really safe.

Mama warned, "Rachel, don't sit so close to the set. It'll ruin your eyes."

"Yes, ma'am." She got up and climbed into Papa's chair. Mama stroked Hedy's hair with one hand and clutched a tissue in the other. Through her tears, she asked, "Do you think Jackie already had that black suit in her closet or did she just buy it? She's always so chic. Girls, let's all try to act like Mrs. Kennedy and be strong and silent when things get tough."

Jacqueline Kennedy walked along side Caroline and John John, her two small children. Her sheer black veil and dark sunglasses hid any evidence of tears, if there were any. Rachel's throat tightened and then released a rush of air that escalated into uncontrollable sobs. She couldn't imagine how the first lady remained stoic, a heroine in the face of unspeakable tragedy.

After a few days, Mama went back to business as usual—picking up her daughters from school, keeping the house, and shopping without ever mentioning what might happen when Papa got home each night.

Rachel cried herself to sleep at night because President Kennedy was dead. *Why is there so much violence is the world—in my world?* Hearing the sobs from the nearby twin bed, Hedy barked at her to grow up and pipe down.

The loss of JFK has never left Rachel's consciousness. Even decades later in November when Missy, Michael, and Rachel were watching the news, images of the assassination peeled away the scabs on her memory of that awful day.

Rachel could never bear to watch the Zapruder film, slowed frame by frame to its sickening conclusion. She considered it fate that Abraham Zapruder stumbled into history, because he hadn't taken his new Bell & Howell 8mm movie camera with the zoom lens to work with him that day in downtown Dallas. A secretary had made him return home and get it after the cloudy morning cleared up in time for the motorcade to pass by his office. Zapruder picked his spot on the plaza, perched on a pedestal that gave him a panorama view of Elm Street. The footage of the assassination never affected Missy and Michael as adversely as it did Rachel.

"Mom, why can't you watch it?" Missy asked.

"What's the matter with you? It's not some action movie! It's the real deal in living color."

"I know, but that was ages ago."

"How can you look at it?" Rachel asked, thinking it's the worst twenty-six seconds ever caught on film—American's loss of innocence. All 486 frames of the silent movie chilled her to the bone.

"Rachel, Missy's too young to really understand. You act like you were personally injured, but we all felt grief and pain in '63," Michael said.

"It's all that movie violence! You've both been numbed. That's it! Missy, no more action films for you. Maybe that goes for us, too, Michael," Rachel proclaimed, feeling wounded from his lack of support.

To this day, the Zapruder film still turns her stomach. Rachel averts her eyes from the gruesome moment when the top of President Kennedy's handsome head is blasted wide open, and split seconds later, Jackie climbs on the trunk of the limo on her hands and knees to retrieve parts of her husband's skull.

Rosy hadn't let her three daughters attend the parade for the Kennedys because she was afraid it would rain. She said Hedy couldn't afford to miss even one day of math class and decided Rachel was too young to contend with the crowds in Dealey Plaza. As it turned out, Rachel knew her mother had spared her from being an eyewitness to one of the greatest tragedies in the nation's history.

Jackie Kennedy had always been Rosy's role model for the meaning of "class."   Over the years, Rachel concluded that very few really possessed it. Rachel's list of people with true class was very short: Jacqueline Kennedy Onassis and Fred Astaire—and her best friend, P.J.

Astaire made her list because he knew when to stop performing in public while still at his peak. Rachel was stunned when she saw Fred Astaire starring posthumously in a vacuum cleaner commercial, dancing around the ceiling and walls of a room, busting dust. She hoped to never live to see Jackie Kennedy in a feminine hygiene spot, confiding the real reason she always looked so poised and cool.

She remembered the first lady at the funeral in a black veil and oversized sunglasses. Rachel felt she'd never forget the strength and composure Jackie exhibited in the procession that she watched on television with Mama and her two sisters.

Papa had tinkered with the car in the driveway and missed it all. He also was absent from the important times in Rachel's life: her high school and college graduations, her wedding, and the birth of her only child.

LOST AND FOUND

CHAPTER 27

BY THE END OF of the first month of teaching, Rachel was pleased she was falling into a routine. She had memorized the names of about two-thirds of the children, met the parents in the carpool line, and in some cases, could have picked them out of a line-up with no problem matching them with their offspring. The most unruly children often had mothers who arrived late from their tennis games or ones who gave her a list of instructions about their child's particular likes and dislikes.

The dragon's breath heat still took its toll on her, but she hoped to eventually acclimatize before fall. Her freckles had amassed into one dark patch on her nose because she failed to bother to protect her face with makeup or sunblock. Regardless of the soaring Fahrenheit, the kids played hopscotch, tetherball, kickball, and softball. Rachel helped a handful of them with homework at a table in the shade of the building at the end of the day, because some parents didn't bother with their children's studies.

Late one afternoon, Miracle pulled her third grade math textbook out of her book bag. Her forehead scrunched when she admitted to struggling with her homework. Rachel watched while the girl flipped through the pages until she pointed to the source of her misery. The tip of her caramel-colored thumb was as dark and discolored as the "blue-thumbed carpenter" Russell Rutherford used to joke about at the ranch.

"How'd you do that?" Rachel asked, picking up Miracle's hand to examine it.

"Caught it in a door. It's nothin'. My biggest pain is problem number three."

"You'll probably lose that fingernail. Let me know if it gets any worse and we'll send you to the nurse," Rachel said.

She picked up the math book and scanned the page for the problem. The words began to blur when Rachel read aloud: "A farmer raises chickens and sheep, and he keeps track of his animals by counting their legs. If there are twenty legs in total, what are the most chickens or the most sheep he can have at any given time?" Rachel began to sweat, realizing she had no earthly idea of how to begin. "Let's see . . . chickens have two feet, and how many feet do sheep have?"

"Four," Miracle answered, looking a bit more hopeful.

Rachel stared at the numbers, pausing before speaking again. "You have to make an equation to get the answer. Where should you start? Think about it while I check on the class."

She stood and did a quick headcount, only tallying twenty-seven students. Ice water coursed through her veins. She counted again, straining to see if she had overlooked a student. Twenty-seven again. Someone was missing.

"Attention, children! Fall in, dress-right-dress!" Rachel shouted. The youngsters dropped their balls and jump ropes, and lined up outstretching their arms. "Now, everyone, look around and tell me who's missing."

They lowered their arms and turned their heads from side to side. Manuel shouted out as if he had just won at bingo, "Ross!"

"Okay, I want all of you to stay right here while I search for Ross." Rachel walked to the edge of the playground and then broke into a run, passing the jungle gym and the softball diamond. The boy was nowhere in sight. On the perimeter of the grounds, the parents were beginning to line up in their cars to pick up their children. Rachel yelled, "Ross, Ross Jamison. Come out from where you are. Time to go home!"

She prayed silently, *Please let him be all right. Lord, don't let something horrible to have happened.*

Only the rustling oaks answered her shouts. It was five minutes until six o'clock and she grew increasingly sure he might be in danger. Leaving the other children to get help, Rachel ran past the older students and flew into Suzi's office. Out of breath, she managed to blurt out, "Ross Jamison is missing! I've looked everywhere." She envisioned him dead, lying crumpled in a thicket of bushes.

"You go to the carpool lane, now! I'll handle this." Suzi darted out of her office and then sprinted around the grounds with the speed of a track star. She slowed enough to direct a sharp glance at Rachel and then ran back into the school building.

In a few minutes, the chimes of the loudspeaker cut through the air. Mrs. Washington's voice blared, "Ross Jamison . . . please report to the principal's office. Ross Jamison . . . report to the principal's office immediately."

One by one, the children disappeared into their parents' cars. They flashed Rachel worried looks from the backseats. To calm them, she smiled bravely and waved goodbye. Out of the corner of her eye, she spotted a softball lodged between the branches of a mesquite bush along the fence. She stuffed it into her fanny pack, planning to return it to the equipment room later.

Suzi approached her after the last child was picked up. Dread had made Rachel's mouth taste bitter and acrid, wondering if Ross was safe. She fretted, *I knew I never should have taken this job.*

"Miss Rachel, Ross is okay at home. I called his mother. She said she picked him up when she saw him sitting outside the playground fence at the carpool line."

"What the hell was he doing there?" Rachel stood still with clinched fists.

"You're in enough trouble as it is, so watch that potty mouth, Miss Rachel! He went to retrieve a ball that flew over the fence, when his mother saw him. She told him to get into the car because she was running late to get her clothes from the dry cleaners before it closed."

"But it's against the rules to leave the playground. I warned the children on the very first day. His mother should have known better than to take him without notifying me."

"Mrs. Washington will sort things out. She wants to see you in her office, pronto," Suzi said with a hint of satisfaction.

Rachel followed the gray linoleum corridor to the principal's office. The image of a condemned prisoner came to mind.

Mrs. Washington ushered her inside and closed the door. She pointed for Rachel to take a seat. "A serious infraction has taken place, Rachel."

"I know. How should I submit my resignation?" She inched forward in her chair.

Mrs. Washington removed her glasses and rubbed her temples. "Rachel, you're over-reacting. The child is safe, and it wasn't entirely your fault he was missing. His parent should never have collected him without proper notification—clearly violating school policy."

Rachel stared forward, willing her eyes to stay dry. "But I'm supposed to protect them. It's *my* job. I failed, and it's only the beginning."

"As it turns out, this was the best of all scenarios. You've got to continually do head checks. While you're working with one student, you must be aware of where each and every one of your charges is at all times. This incident was potentially very serious, but now that it's resolved, and we can move on from here. And forget about handing in your resignation!"

Rachel let out a deep sigh and a torrent of tears streamed down her face.

"You have a future working with children." She reached across the desk and handed Rachel a tissue. "As Abraham Lincoln once said: 'The best thing about the future is that it comes only one day at a time.'" She opened her office door.

"Thank you for giving me a second chance." Rachel resisted the urge to hug her supervisor, trying to be professional.

Mrs. Washington smiled and gave her a warm embrace. "Rachel, lesson learned. Thankfully, it all worked out. It's late now, so go home, and we'll see you tomorrow afternoon."

CHAPTER 28

RACHEL BEGAN TO LOOK FORWARD to weekday afternoons. The children presented new and interesting challenges every day, and they constantly amused her with their never-ending antics. At night, she would tell Michael anecdotes about a few of them—if he ever returned home before she went to bed. He seemed pleased to hear that Mrs. Washington had said Rachel had a future in teaching.

The weekends were still a dark abyss. Rachel was overwhelmed by the number of hours on her hands. She and Michael were on a more even keel, but they still didn't spend much time together. During the week she was too tired after school to cook, so they usually each fended for themselves or resorted to take-out Chinese.

One Saturday night, Michael came home with a bag stuffed full of groceries from the Simon David. Rachel took it from him and unloaded the items one by one as if she were opening a gift: two thick filets, a couple of artichokes, a box of strawberries, whipped cream, and a little jar of caviar. He donned one of her aprons and took the fruits and vegetables to the sink to wash them. She ripped open the package of meat and began to sprinkle it with seasonings.

"Not too much garlic on the steak tonight, hon."

"Why, are you planning on kissing somebody?"

"You never know," he said, smiling. Michael waved a wet strawberry in front of her.

Rachel leaned over and slowly sank her teeth into the juicy red berry and ran her tongue across her lips between exaggerated bites.

"Looks good enough to eat," he said softly while he dried his hands on the dishtowel. "How about a late dinner?"

Rachel stowed the filets and whipping cream in the fridge and left the rest on the counter. Then she put her arms around his waist to untie the apron from behind and pulled it off.

He grabbed a few strawberries in one hand and playfully took her wrist in his other, leading her out of the kitchen to the stairway. Rachel climbed the stairs to their room with the same excitement she had felt on the first night they met and ended up in bed together at the Driskill Hotel. He scattered the berries on his night table and lifted her loose shift over her head. His fingers slowly ran across her breasts in small circles narrowing to her nipples. It was first time he had seen her naked in months. "You're looking good, babe. How about trashing that old sack you always wear?"

"Well, how about losing some of your clothes right now?" Rachel said with a sly smile.

He undressed quickly and dove into the bed, next to where she was already lying with the sheet over her.

"Let me get another look, Rachel. Don't cover up. Let me enjoy this."

He took a bite of the strawberry and then kissed her so the sweet juices mingled in their mouths. Rachel took another taste and kissed his chest and then his stomach. He stroked her hair and inhaled deeply, sighing while she began pleasing him. He muttered, "You're the next course."

She ran the strawberry across him and savored their intimacy. Right before his excitement was at its peak, the phone destroyed the moment. "Just let it ring," he moaned. It continued three times until the machine picked up.

And then another woman's voice filled their room. "Hi, Michael, it's Susan. I hit some snags on the project and I need to go over them with you. Give me a buzz when you get a chance."

"Why the hell is she calling you on the weekend? Don't the two of you see enough of each other during the week?" Rachel asked, abruptly sitting up, covering her nakedness with the sheet.

"Look, I didn't tell her to call. Things are getting heated up at work and we're under the gun." He peeked under the sheet and frowned. "Hon, it looks like the only thing I'm up to right now is dinner. Sorry, but do you want me to take care of you now?"

She pulled the sheet up to her chin and turned on her side away from him. "No, my appetite's been spoiled. And I'm beginning to think that you've been eating out way too often lately."

A chilly breeze played toss with the russet and gold leaves on the playground. Mrs. Washington called Rachel into her office when Rachel was packing up to go home after the children were picked up. On the way down the corridor, she searched her brain to remember what she'd done wrong. She sat in the chair and chewed on the hangnail on her index finger. The studied the portrait of Martin Luther King Jr. on the side of the principal's credenza.

"Rachel, Miss Rightwood has a bad case of the flu and can't chaperone the field trip tomorrow morning. I'm in a tough bind to replace her because the state requires two adults for this off-campus outing. We'll have to cancel if we can't get a substitute. I know it's short notice, but can you fill in?"

Rachel removed her finger from her mouth and buried it in her closed fist. "Sure, I'll help out. Will we be back in time for after school play?"

"Yes, it's only a two-hour field trip downtown to the Sixth Floor Museum."

Rachel was furious at herself for agreeing to go before finding out the major detail that the outing's destination was the museum commemorating the assassination of JFK. She frantically tried to backpedal. "I'd better check my schedule, just to be sure."

"Sorry, but I need your answer now so I can notify parents if we're forced to cancel. They've already signed the consent forms to take the children off site. I wouldn't ask if it weren't an emergency."

Rachel relaxed her hands that were balled in tight fists, pausing to examine her raw nail quicks. "Okay, count me in. What's the drill?"

"The bus leaves at ten o'clock sharp. Check in fifteen minutes early to help with boarding. You and Jan Burnett from social studies will supervise the fifth and sixth graders," Mrs. Washington said.

When Rachel arrived at school the next morning, Jan firmly shook her hand when they met. The energetic spring in Jan's walk made Rachel look at her sneakers to see if they had air pumps. Jan's taut frame reminded her of Pecos from Camp Rio Bravo.

"Nice to know you. We've seen each other passing in the halls, but I haven't had a chance to stop and say hi. Thanks for pitching in today," Jan said warmly.

"No problem. All part of being on the same team."

"Right, I'll take the sixth graders and you watch the fifth. The older ones are a bit more of a handful. Somehow a year can make a big difference."

Rachel remembered the change in Missy when she turned eleven. Her frame began to elongate and little breast buds poked out from beneath her t-shirts.

Jan said, "One little kid complained to me that his older sister was being moody and mean to him. Then he informed me in all seriousness that his mother told him that it was just a stage that would pass, because she was going through *poverty*."

The two women laughed together, and Rachel quickly realized she was going to enjoy spending the day with Jan. For one thing, she didn't insist on being called "Miss Jan."

After a forced potty stop, the children tumbled into the bus. Jan and Rachel assumed a pair of seats on the first row across from the driver. Mr. Sherman, a massive guy with haunches spilling over the worn-out leather driver's seat, smiled at them, flashing a big gold front tooth. His shirt was tucked into his pants. Rachel was thankful she didn't get a shot of a butt crack that was probably the size of the Grand Canyon. Jan stood up to take a final head count—forty on the button. She turned to the driver and said, "All right, Mr. Sherman, let's get this pop stand rolling." The children giggled. Jan steadied herself on the back of the seat and faced the bus full of little bodies writhing like worms stuffed into a can. She tested the microphone with a few sharp taps and began, "Good morning, students. We're going on a very important field trip. Does anybody know the name of the place where we're headed?"

One little girl with a head full of cascading blonde ringlets raised her hand, wildly waving it into the aisle.

"Yes, Sara."

"I know—to the Texas Schoolbook Suppository!"

Jan shot her fellow chaperone a look, and Rachel covered her mouth to stifle the laughter. She recalled that Hedy used to refer to the building in the same way, causing her mother and Grandma Rosy to crack up at her constant malaprops.

Jan continued, "Well, almost—we're going to Texas Schoolbook Depository and to the Dealey Plaza Historic District. As we learned in social studies, George B. Dealey was a civic leader and publisher of *The Dallas Morning News* about the time your grandparents were little. And who was the founder of Dallas who had a log cabin and cornfield on that site?" For the first time, dead silence spread like a blanket over the bus riders. "It was John Neely Bryan in the 1840s. Okay . . . moving on, some of you know Miss Rachel from after school play. She's going to stay with the fifth graders. The rules for the day are that we stay together as a group, and no one strays. A guide, called a docent, is going to show us around the museum. Remember, you can look—but don't touch."

The bus chugged on the highway toward downtown Dallas. Jan led the kids in endless rounds of "The Wheels on the Bus Go Round and Round." The last time Rachel had sung on a bus was when she returned from Camp Rio Bravo, sobbing while reading her autograph book all the way home.

When the school bus approached the triple underpass at the entrance to Dealey Plaza, Jan grabbed the microphone. "Did any of you know that the area around the overpass used to be the banks of the Trinity River? In the 1930s, they moved the river a mile away because it kept flooding downtown Dallas. Can you imagine how anybody could move a river?"

All Rachel could think about was how she didn't want to see evidence of death and violence at the museum. She kicked herself for having agreed to go on this outing, especially since she rarely ventured out beyond her world of school and home, feeling paralyzed by fears and grief.

The bus followed the Kennedy parade route down Elm Street until it reached a boxy, seven-story red brick building. Rachel searched for the familiar name on the façade, but it now was called the Dallas County Administration Building. Mr. Sherman waited for a long black Lincoln convertible to pass by before maneuvering the bus into the parking lot. He cut the engine and announced, "Here we are, gang— 411 Elm Street."

The group entered the building through the Visitor Center, an addition to the original Book Depository. The docent John Adams ("no relation to the president," he apologized) welcomed them. His cardigan sweater with a logo patch on the pocket made him a dead-ringer for Mr. Rogers, the children's television host. Rachel wondered how he was going to put a positive spin on a space dedicated to one of history's most heinous crimes. *One heck of a day in the neighborhood.*

He clasped his hands together and began: "Welcome, kids. Many of you have heard of John Fitzgerald Kennedy, our thirty-fifth president. Dealey Plaza and the Sixth Floor Museum were created to commemorate his life and to provide an informative setting for the details of his assassination on November 22, 1963. Like Pearl Harbor, the National Park Service has designated this site as a National Historic

Landmark. I'm an employee of the Park Service, but I don't look like a forest ranger, do I?" A few girls in the front giggled. "The Dallas Historical Society created The Sixth Floor Museum to educate the public about these events, with over four hundred photographs, several documentary films, and many nonviolent displays. We'll skip the introductory film and move right along into the exhibit halls."

The students listened attentively, and Rachel did a quick head count while they were gathered during Mr. Adams's introduction.

"As many of you know, a very bad man named Lee Harvey Oswald crouched behind boxes of textbooks that were stored when this was a warehouse rented by a private business called the Texas Schoolbook Depository Company. Oswald was at work when he shot the president from the far window in the corner. We've recreated the setting so you can see where he was hiding. Follow me and we'll get a closer look at what we call the 'sniper's perch.'"

Rachel and Jan herded the children in single file to a section of the room where cardboard boxes sealed with packing tape were stacked to create a screen for the gunman. Enclosed in glass to protect the original flooring, the setting was based on crime scene photos of the area where the rifle and three shell casings were found. Suspended on display was the actual window that had been removed during renovation of the building, which Rachel considered an artifact of death. Flecks of pink paint peeked through the dark green trim that was used in reconstruction to return the building to its original 1901 façade when it housed farming equipment. The children quickly filed one by one past the glassed-in area, looking on with seemingly little interest.

Rachel stood fixated on the "sniper's perch," imagining Oswald carefully unwrapping his rifle from its brown paper bag and assembling it behind the boxes. Her flesh prickled when she looked out the window and stared at the same view where the killer had marked Kennedy in his sights from his urban deer blind.

The students moved on and encircled a model of Dealey Plaza. Tiny figures represented the victims and witnesses, and plastic trees lined the Grassy Knoll. Rachel figured that the boys were itching to play with the toy cars and buildings strategically positioned around the detailed miniature. Lilliputian cars were attached to strings, originally used by the FBI during the Warren Commission investigation to re-enact the procession of the presidential motorcade. A custom-built Lincoln Continental convertible limousine, complete with a U.S. flag, was stopped at the precise point where the third rifle shot scattered Kennedy's skull while Governor Connally lay wounded bleeding next to his wife, Nellie. Rachel peered closer to get a look at the tiny figure of LBJ in his vehicle that was surrounded by several little motorcycles. While the students chattered and jockeyed to get a better view, she thought they seemed more enthralled with the model than they had with the piles of boxes and an old window frame.

Rachel glanced around at the photos on the gallery walls, into the faces of John F. Kennedy and Jackie, looking radiant upon their arrival in Dallas at Love Field airport. The first lady beamed at the crowds while the president basked in the hopeful sunshine that had just peaked out from the morning clouds. Connally waved his large hand from the jump seat in front of the Kennedys while a secret service officer in front intently eyed the bystanders, like a hawk scanning for prey. Rachel felt dizzy looking at the moments before all their lives would be shattered. A photo caption described Mrs. Connally ironically saying to JFK as the motorcade turned into Dealey Plaza seconds before the fatal blasts: "Mr. President, you can't say that Dallas doesn't love you." Rachel shuddered at the thought of how the world changed in a matter of split seconds.

She felt a gentle tapping on her shoulder. "Rachel, be a good girl and stay with the group." She turned around to find Jan standing behind her. "Are you all right? You look a little green around the gills?"

"I'm fine. I just need a little air," Rachel said, mustering a weak smile.

"Grab some water and hang in there, girl." Jan scooted back to the front of the line with the docent.

Rachel caught up with her group clustered around a display case with thirteen cameras: old Polaroids, 8mm movie cameras, and 35mm single reflex models lined up neatly in a row with labels describing their former owners. The children inched forward to get a better look at the antiquated, unwieldy contraptions from the 1960s, in contrast to the sleek video recorders and compact point-and-shoots of today.

Mr. Adams addressed the group: "Boys and girls, many of you have heard or seen on television the footage of the assassination shot by Abraham Zapruder. He didn't act alone. In fact, there were two professionals and ten amateurs who captured the events in Dealey Plaza on film. The showpiece in this collection is the Bell & Howell home movie camera that documented the whole course of events from beginning to its tragic end. Most people with cameras in the Plaza came to take souvenir snapshots of a historic day when the president was in town." The children began to fidget and kick their feet on the baseboard of the display.

He continued, "The group that captured it on film included an Associated Press photographer, a postal worker on his lunch break, a clerk from the nearby county courthouse, and even a schoolgirl with her parents who came to watch the parade—with an excused absence from school, I might add." The children settled down and focused on Mr. Adams. He pointed to the boxy camera in the case. "Little Tina Tower ran her father's movie camera while he captured the events on stills. She even had enough film left to cover the Grassy Knoll and to pan the Schoolbook Depository after the shooting. All of the photographic material was used to piece together the course of events on that fateful day."

Rachel was lost in her thoughts about how Tina Tower's parents had made a family outing to the site of the presidential visit to Dallas. Her own mother had refused to let her and her two sisters get caught up in such a spectacle amid over two hundred thousand people.

Rachel had been angry that Mama thought she was too young to be there. Her mother never expected the trauma such a day would reap on everyone who attended and on people all over the world in the aftermath. Rachel figured little Tina's dad must have thought a great deal of her to let her handle his expensive camera. She marveled that the girl's parents even gave her a note to skip school.

A dead weight lifted from her spirits when she heard Mr. Adams say the Zapruder film would not be shown because it was considered too violent for children. It was difficult for her to be at the museum, and she had worried all morning, wondering how to handle seeing the assassination footage without bolting.

She paused to watch a video monitor suspended from the ceiling with a tape rolling in a continuous loop of a badly shaken Walter Cronkite haltingly announcing the official news of Kennedy's death at 1:00 p.m. Central Standard Time, 2:00 p.m. Eastern Standard Time, over and over—like a recurring nightmare.

Even the nation's voice of authority and truth couldn't hold back his grief. His glassy eyes and broken delivery made Rachel weep quietly as she watched the screen.

She rushed to catch up with Mr. Adams and the kids at the Legacy Wall covered with photos of the Kennedy administration. They were in front of the famous image by New York Times photographer George Tames, titled *The Loneliest Job*. Shot from behind, it depicts the young president standing stoop-shouldered in front of a table between windows in the Oval Office in 1961.

Mr. Adams explained, "President Kennedy seems to be bearing the weight of the world on his shoulders, but he was actually reading the newspaper standing up, as he preferred to do because he had a bad back. Even so, this faceless, shadowy portrait symbolizes the gravity of being the president of the United States."

The school group passed through galleries with hundreds of color, and black and white photos of both better and darker days.

When they reached the end of the collection, Mr. Adams concluded the tour by saying, "We used to hold annual observances at the Memorial on November 22, but at the request of the Kennedy family in 1986, we now commemorate the anniversary of JFK's birth on May 29." He smiled broadly. "Thank y'all for coming, and be sure to tell your parents and friends about us."

The two teachers encouraged their students to applaud by clapping in broad, sweeping motions. Rachel stopped to sign the guest book near the exit and wrote: "Thank you for giving us a painful, but necessary, lesson from the past.—The 5th and 6th grade classes of North Dallas Elementary."

The path to the exit led directly into the museum gift shop. Rachel and Jan warned the children that they could have only five minutes to browse. There were racks of tote bags silk screened with smiling faces of Jackie and JFK. As Rachel wove through the aisles of mugs and t-shirts, she spotted her student Sara playing with a toy viewfinder, rotating the wheel of photos. The girl was watching tiny illuminated transparencies of the assassination.

Rachel snatched the toy out of Sara's hand and hurled it back into the display pile. The child stood frozen, wide-eyed and shell-shocked, but didn't utter a word.

"It's time to go, honey," Rachel said, trying to keep Sara's tears from erupting, an imminent possibility. "Time's up, class! We'll gather in the Plaza for a short walk before we board the bus," she announced.

Rachel counted heads again: everyone present and accounted for. All of the North Dallas Elementary group stopped, looked, and listened in preparation to cross the street. They waited for the black stretch convertible to pass by—the same one that had rounded the curb from Houston Street onto Elm when they arrived. Rachel thought its vintage chrome grill looked like a toothy grimace. Seated next to the driver, a young woman in jeans topped with a pink wool jacket and pillbox hat waved to her. She called out, "Wanna ride? I'll even let you wear Jackie's hat." The limousine stopped and two tourists piled into the backseat for a catbird view of the parade route.

Rachel cursed under her breath, "Assholes!"

Jan whispered to her, "Who, the driver or the passengers?"

"Both!"

They snaked along the sidewalk that skirted the Plaza. Jan pointed out to the children the Grassy Knoll where picnickers were sprawled on the lawn enjoying the Indian summer day. Although it could have been a public park anywhere, with rolling greens and inviting benches, to Rachel, it was part of a monument to violence. After about ten minutes, she rounded up the kids and herded them into the bus. They filed into their seats with a minimum of confusion. Mr. Sherman set down his Dr. Pepper and hit the ignition, unleashing a numbing vibration from the rumbling engine. He took one look at Rachel and said, "Tough day at the salt mines, huh, kid?"

She mustered a fake smile and sank into the seat next to Jan. A deep sigh escaped from the depths of her soul.

"Don't worry. I'll do the final head count. This field trip's harder on the adults than on the kids. We know what that day meant and how it changed the world. You were fine, Rachel. Couldn't have done it without you," Jan said warmly.

"No need to thank me. We make a good team." This time Rachel's smile was a real *schmeykhl*. She closed her eyes and slipped away into a well-deserved afternoon nap.

THE ANNIVERSARY

CHAPTER 29

AT FIRST, Rachel had looked forward to October, with the hope of a respite from the unrelenting Texas heat, but then she began to dread it. It was the month of the anniversary of Missy's death—the unveiling of her headstone.

Almost a year ago, she had gone with Michael and Mama to Saltzman's Funeral Home to order the monument. Sitting in Mr. Jenkins's office, they had flipped through a leather-bound photo album of carved marble funeral markers. Michael made the final decision because he was more accustomed to choosing building materials and signage. Rachel had no stomach for it, but she knew they needed to honor Missy's memory in a tangible way. She would always remember her daughter with her whole body and soul.

Rachel had poured through texts of funerary poems to make a meaningful selection and handed Michael a note with an inscription. Sullen and stone-faced, she sat staring at a reproduction painting of Adam reaching out to touch the hand of God, while Mama and Michael discussed type fonts and graphic embellishments for the plaque. They debated over whether to use seraphs, like the chiseled letters on Roman pediments, or elegant, flowery scripts?

Mr. Jenkins announced that a tasteful decision had been made: a simple marker with a single rose bud centered between two Stars of David etched out of white Cararra marble. Along with the dates that bookended Missy's life, the words on the piece of paper would be carved in a contemporary script:

> "Perhaps God tires—always calling the aged to His fold,
> And so He picks a rosebud before it can grow old.
> God knows how much we need them and so He picks but few;
> To make the land of heaven more beautiful to view."
>
> —*Anonymous*

MELISSA JANELLE FRANK
Beloved Daughter, Granddaughter, and Friend

They planned to follow the Jewish custom of waiting to view the headstone until the unveiling near the one-year anniversary of her death. Although Rachel knew the short tribute was meant to be a way of getting a handle on the grieving process and a time to ponder the meaning of life and death, it sounded like torture. She dreaded October 14 and feared it would rip open her wounds instead of healing them.

She stopped by the administration office at school to put in a request for two personal leave days. For the reason, she wrote on the form, "Memorial Service." No one asked her any questions, which led Rachel to wonder if somehow word had spread that she had lost her only daughter. Mrs. Washington swiftly granted her request.

The day before the planned absence, Rachel gathered the children around her right before time for carpool pickup. They stood on the blacktop playground in the Indian summer sunshine. "Class, I won't be here with you tomorrow or Friday." To her surprise, there was an outburst of low groans. "Don't worry, Miss Suzi is going to show you some special games, and I know you'll have fun."

Ellen, a third grader with thick glasses held by an exercise band around her head, called out, "Are you sick or something?"

"No, honey, I'm just fine."

"My mommy has to miss work because she's got cancer and goes to see the doctor all the time to get rid of her hair."

"No, I'm really fine. I have to be with my family for something special. It's time to go home, so be good, and I'll see you next week."

Only two kids were left: Joseph and Miracle. Rachel began to wind up like the tight springs of a clock when she fumed about how Miracle's mother was increasingly tardy picking her up. The three waited on the cold bench, watching the end of the driveway for oncoming cars. The breeze tried to snatch the homework assignments off Miracle's lap, but she used both hands to anchor her work to her khaki overalls. She inched closer to her teacher so Joseph couldn't hear her whisper, "Miss Rachel?" She stopped and looked down at her books.

"What is it, Miracle? Is something wrong?"

"Can I go with you and your family?" she blurted out in one breath like she had been holding it in for a while.

"That's so sweet, but this is only for my family and not for the class. Remember to say *may* instead of *can*," Rachel replied, trying to sound like a real teacher.

"So you don't want me at your party?" Her little lip jutted forward.

Rachel felt sorry she had corrected the grammar. "Honey, it's not a party. It's something sad in honor of my little girl."

"You got a little girl? Where's she now?" Miracle's hazel eyes widened.

Rachel bit her upper lip, gathering her thoughts. "She's in heaven with the angels." Angry with herself that she had let down her guard and told the child about a personal matter, Rachel sensed the slightly metallic taste of blood.

Miracle cupped her teacher's ear with her soft hands and said, "I think my real daddy's in the other place."

A short blast of a car horn startled them. Homework papers flew in the wind like a flock of sparrows in an updraft.

"Let's go, Miracle. Get in the car!" her mother called out.

The child scrambled to catch the airborne pages in her little hands.

Rachel marched over to Latisha Baldwin's dented blue Toyota and leaned down toward her window. "Mrs. Baldwin, could you please try to be on time? The after school program ends at six."

"Get in the car right now, Miracle. I mean it!" The woman glared at Rachel and quickly rolled up her window. Miracle ran to the passenger side and sank down in her seat. Latisha gunned the engine and the car spewed gray exhaust that fouled the crisp fall air. Rachel watched a page of loose-leaf notebook paper trail down the street but didn't chase after it.

The next morning, she and Michael arose at the same time. They managed to get ready, stumbling around each other in the bedroom. Mama said they wouldn't have bother with picking her up because Irene would drive her to the cemetery.

Rachel worried about how her sisters would behave but knew she had to include them, following the rules of Jewish funereal etiquette. Hedy and Lenora always annoyed her—acting so superior about their kids.

When Rachel called Rabbi Sachs to make the appointment to officiate at the unveiling, she leveled with him, "Rabbi, would it be such a sin if I didn't include Hedy and Lenora?"

He paused and then replied, "The answer to that question is best said by one of my favorite quotes by William Walton: 'Carrying a grudge is like getting stung to death by one bee.'"

"Ouch! I'm beginning to get your point. I was expecting instead something a little more Talmudic."

"Rachel, soften your heart and tell them they can recite brief passages, if they wish. Including the actual unveiling, the whole ceremony will last about thirty minutes, God willing. It will do all of you some good to let them share their grief with you and Michael."

Rachel and Michael drove to the cemetery in silence. She thought he looked handsome in his dark suit, but his eyes were static as a statue. The hillsides were still verdant along the winding road that led them to where several cars were parked.

Rachel found her place on the row of chairs in front of a marker covered with a burgundy velvet cloth embroidered with a gold Star of David, with a tasseled drawstring.

Hedy and Walter, Lenora, and Mama sat together on the second row. Hedy's two kids were away at college in the East, and Rachel figured they would have come if they could have. Jack, Hedy's oldest, liked to think of himself as Missy's big brother. Jenna was five years younger and also felt close because Missy used to baby-sit for her to earn some extra cash. Michael and Rachel had tried to teach their daughter the value of a dollar by encouraging her to earn a little money she could spend as she wished. It dawned on Rachel that she still hadn't closed out the savings account where Missy had kept her modest savings.

Rachel's oldest sister, Lenora, was in the midst of divorcing her third husband and was currently dating her Mercedes service attendant, but she came solo. Her kids from her first marriage didn't show up at the unveiling either, and she didn't bother to explain their absence.

Rachel detected Mama's perfume behind her. Rosy had switched to Joy when they stopped making My Sin. She reached over and gave Michael and her grieving daughter a kiss. Rachel barely turned to look at her, but the touch of her mother's lips was like a soothing balm. After a few minutes, a warm hand brushed her neck, causing her turn around to acknowledge P.J.'s delicate touch. In her own fog, Rachel hadn't noticed the arrival of her best friend, who leaned forward to whisper that Juan couldn't attend because he had to supervise the casting of one of his statues at a foundry in San Antonio. He sent his condolences and regretted that P.J. would have to represent both of them.

The smell of fresh grass and decaying leaves blew in small gusts. When most of the twenty guests arrived, the rabbi stepped forward. The bottom of his black robe was bordered with morning dew.

Everyone stood while he recited, "The Lord is my shepherd; I shall not want."

Rachel's knees turned to cotton, and she sank onto the white folding chair that chilled the back of her legs. After the psalm, the rabbi lowered his hands to signal the rest of the mourners to be seated.

Michael's shoulders shrugged as he unfolded a piece of paper from his suit jacket. "I have heard this prayer in services for years, but unfortunately, now it has taken on new meaning. Please indulge me by changing the group refrain to 'She is with me.'" His voice quavered slightly:

> When I rise each day at dawn
> *She is with me.*
> When I take my evening rest
> *She is with me.*
> When I walk along the path
> *She is with me.*
> When I strive to do my best
> *Missy is with me.*

Irene's raspy refrain could be heard above the others' voices and sniffles. When Michael recited Missy's name at the end, Rachel had to force herself to realize that everything had not been a bad dream. The rabbi announced it was time for close family members in mourning to come forward to offer a few words.

Rachel's siblings stood up together. Walter and Hedy wrapped their arms around Lenora to steady her. Rachel had detected a whiff of alcohol on her oldest sister's breath before she pulled out a pack of Juicy Fruit. She thought Lenora looked almost as bad as Rachel felt. Lenora's nose was red and covered by a web of tiny spider veins where she had wiped off her makeup with her hanky. She said in a shaky voice, "Everyone handles pain in different ways and we suffer for the losses in our lives. I hope y'all will reach out for comfort in your grief. We miss her so very much."

Rachel silently mouthed "thank you" from her seat.

Hedy spoke next, while Walter stood mutely at her side. Her sleek black hair was pulled back into a neat bun at the nape of her neck, and she looked like a respectable matron in her suit and heels.

When did we stop being young? Rachel wondered.

Hedy spoke clearly and deliberately: "Hopefully, the unveiling will mark a time when your grief is not so palpable. Although you probably don't believe me, Walter and I and my kids are here for you now and will always be there. We're family, and we need to stick together . . . like Scotch tape. How's that for a proper simile, teach?"

Walter wiped his eyes with his handkerchief and added, "As a parent, I know you've been going through the worse thing possible. Our hearts are with you."

Rachel managed to smile at them amid her tears, wondering if over the years, she had erected an impenetrable wall against her sisters. She hadn't even stopped to notice if they had tried to connect with her.

The siblings remained standing while it was their mother's turn. Rosy must have forgotten to put on her lipstick. It was one of the few times Rachel had seen her mother with pale, chapped lips. Mama held Hedy's and Lenora's hands while she spoke. "Remember at Missy's baby naming how I sprinkled bits of thyme into her spice box and asked that she have courage for the rough times? That's what we all need to help us through this tragedy. It doesn't get much rougher than this." Her sniffles punctuated her words. "Missy had bucket loads of spunk and courage in her short, but exquisite, life. We've all heard it said before that there is a season and a time to live, and a time to die. Believe me when I say, we've got to remember that it's not how long we're on earth, but how we live each season to the fullest."

The four of them filed back to their chairs, after they each stopped to give Rachel and Michael a kiss.

Rachel rose to make her remarks, finding it difficult to catch her breath. She steadied herself on the back of the chair, but the legs teetered and sank deeper in the sod. Michael stood up and put his arm around her waist in support. She said softly between sobs, "Thank you, all of you. You can't imagine how much your kind words mean to us." Rachel turned around and faced the draped headstone and whispered, "Mommy loves you and always will, honey bun."

Rabbi Sachs requested that those who wished to recite the Mourner's Kaddish remain standing. Rachel's friends and family incanted the Hebrew prayer for the departed, accompanied by the chirping of birds and buzzing of a lawn mower on a distant hillside of the cemetery. "*Yit-ga-dal ve-yit-ka-dash she-mey ra-ba* . . . "

The rabbi closed the service with a prayer for universal peace. When the group uttered "amen" in unison, no sound emanated from Rachel's lips.

She watched Rabbi Sachs approach the plot and pull the chord that drew back the velvet drape, revealing the headstone. He stooped to select a pebble from a small pyramid of river rocks and carefully placed it on the grave. Michael reached for his wife's hand and led her to the stack. They bent down and collected their smooth stones. Rachel rubbed a few between her fingers until she found one that felt right in palm of her hand. Together they each placed one on the mound of turf, as if they were setting a precious diamond in a mounting. Mama was next, followed by Irene, Rachel's sisters and brother-in-law, and then P.J. Everyone filed past, leaving the stones as small visible markers that Missy was loved and remembered.

NETWORKING

CHAPTER 30

THE AFTERNOON SUN hung lower in the sky than when Rachel had started working at North Dallas Elementary in late summer. She felt that the children liked her, and she looked forward to the ball games and also the quiet moments when she helped them with schoolwork.

Playground warriors battled furiously in a heated game of kickball. Miracle adjusted her stance to kick when the pitcher sent the large rubber ball rolling in her direction. She drew back her foot and made a valiant effort—but missed the ball. She tumbled backwards onto the blacktop, landing on her arm and twisting her leg.

Rachel watched in horror as she fell, as if seeing it in slow motion. She dashed over to inspect the girl's injuries. Miracle was sprawled on the playground, crying while Rachel unfolded her leg from under her like a broken toy. Rolling back the crimson-blotched sleeve, Rachel found a trail of blood mixed with brown grit collecting on Miracle's scraped forearm. When she pushed the torn fabric farther up, to her alarm, she discovered a large greenish bruise tarnishing her slim upper arm. "I'll get Nurse Ellen. Stay here. Don't move while I find someone to watch the rest of the class!"

The students surrounded Miracle, admiring her wound.

Suzi stepped outside of her office to watch the group. Rachel alerted the nurse and then stopped by the administration office to request that the assistant call Miracle's mother.

The school nurse arrived on the scene and inspected the child's injuries. Miracle was declared free of any broken bones and then dutifully went to the infirmary to get her wounds dressed.

The ball game resumed, but Miracle was benched for the remainder of the match. She sat silently watching every move on the field. Flocks of geese flew in formation overhead, casting V-shaped patterns on the playground. At the end of the afternoon, the children were swallowed up by the vehicles that had lined up to collect them—with the usual exception. Rachel and Miracle sat on the bench near the pick up area waiting for her mother. The air felt cool against Rachel's face, and she secretly relished the opportunity to spend extra time with her favorite student. The girl swung her legs back and forth to the beat of the music from her headphones, so Rachel figured her injuries really were superficial. She was haunted by a remark Miracle had let slip the last time they were waiting together.

"Miracle, could you turn down your music for a minute?" She pulled the headphones out of her ears and smiled up at her teacher. "A long time ago you mentioned something about your real father. Do you have another father now?"

Her face clouded over quickly. "Not really. Me and Mommy live with Hank, and I have to call him 'Daddy,' but he's not really my daddy."

"I know your father passed away. I'll bet it was hard on you." This time Rachel refrained from correcting her grammar, letting the "me and mommy" slip by.

"Kinda hard, I guess. Sometimes I wish that me and Mommy could . . . "

She stopped talking when the old blue compact turned the corner into the school grounds. It pulled up next to the pair, and Miracle jumped into the car and strapped on her own seatbelt. Rachel approached the driver's side and leaned toward the window.

"Ms. Baldwin, I'd like to have a few words with you"

"Not now. I gotta go to work and Hank's waitin' for me to drop Miracle off."

"Really, only a minute. You've been getting here late and it's against campus policy."

"We'll do better, Miss Rachel," Miracle called out.

"Sit still, girl." Letisha shifted the pile of Miracle's books and papers that were teetering on the seat next to her.

"Ms. Baldwin, could you please at least do me the courtesy of looking at me when we talk?" Rachel coldly reprimanded her, as if she were one of her students.

Latisha snapped her head in Rachel's direction, swinging her hair away from her face to reveal her bloodshot right eye, encircled by a swollen, discolored ring.

Rachel's own eyes welled up with tears. "My God, you really need help."

"Why don't you just butt the hell out? I banged into a tray full of food at work. Everyone saw me do it, so just mind your own damn business!" she shouted.

"Miracle *is* my business, and it's my duty to make sure she's safe. If I suspect she's in danger of any kind, I'm mandated to call social services!"

"Well, Miss Rachel, you'd just better be careful about who's accusing who of doing what. Miracle told me your daughter's dead. How 'bout if I start asking questions about that at school? I'm not so sure I want you in charge of my daughter!"

She gunned the engine and drove off. Rachel choked on the fumes and then sat frozen in pain on the bench, crying until evening fell.

That night she tossed in the bed, flailing across the empty space next to her. Michael still was keeping late hours. Finally she heard his steps on the stairs. The light on her nightstand threw a soft shadow in the hall.

"Why are you still up?" he asked.

"Because I'm worried sick about a little girl in my class. I think she's in danger and her mother could be, too. Miracle's finger looked . . ."

He threw his wallet on the dresser. "I thought you said you were enjoying school these days. It seemed like you were coming out of your funk, even though you still haven't done a damn thing around here."

"I do like it. And what am I supposed to take care of? You're never around much anymore to notice," she quickly shot back.

"It's always *something* with you, Rachel. Your depression has escalated into full-scale paranoia now. Maybe being around kids isn't the best thing for you, after all."

Instead of pain, numbness spread across her body. She lay there unable to utter a word in her defense.

The pitch in his voice steadily rose. "You don't enjoy anything these days! Now I'm supposed to stress with you over some problem you *think* some little girl is having. I've got enough on my plate these days."

"Oh, so you'd just close your eyes?"

"How about opening yours for a change? You know how to play by the rules: If you really think there's a problem, report it to social services. Have you conveyed your suspicions to Mrs. Washington yet? Or did you just come home and dump on me?" He paced up and down the room near his side of the bed.

"I didn't know what to do."

"Well, do you expect me to save every child on this planet when I couldn't even manage to help our own? I'm sick to death of it, Rachel!"

"Easy for you to say. Nothing ever gets to you, 'Mr. Man of Stone.' You've been around buildings so long, I think you've turned into one!"

"I'm not the one who's having a problem coping. At least I can get the job done and don't fall apart every other day. Why are you so damned resistant about getting some help, Rachel?"

"I think someone in this room needs to take a good look in the mirror and not be so enamored with his holier-than-thou reflection that stares back," she screamed.

The phone rang, cutting through the thickness of their tension. Michael lunged for it. His tone softened when he spoke into the receiver. "No, it's okay. It's never a good time. . . . I'll see you in a little while. . . . I've got a key, so don't worry." He hung up.

"Who was that?" Rachel got out of bed and stood in front of him, blocking the doorway to the hall.

"You already know the answer to the question, so why ask? I'm going out and I don't know when I'll be back."

"Now that's original!" she hissed. He sidestepped her and walked out of the house. Rachel began to cry. *Everything I touch turns to shit.* She climbed across the bed and reached into her purse on the nightstand for a bottle of pills. Instead of the plastic container, she felt the crumpled surface of a booklet. She pulled out the Victims of Violent Crimes Network pamphlet and stared at the twenty-four hour hot line number in bold red type on the cover.

Rachel became convinced that everything was reeling out of control. After a few minutes, she dialed the ten-digit number to register for the program. After leaving the receptionist hanging on hold while she gathered the information, she provided Missy's police case number, nature of the crime, and social security number. The appointment counselor suggested that Rachel and her husband both attend the workshops on Tuesdays—starting tomorrow. She assured her that they were excellent candidates for help because many marriages and jobs suffer after such emotional trauma. Rachel jotted down the time and date of the session on the cover of the pamphlet and dropped it on top of the pile on her desk in the kitchen, which was beginning to resemble Macchu Picchu.

Rachel figured Michael must have stayed out most of the night. She knew he eventually had been home because the next morning the shower was damp. They were like two strangers maneuvering around each other. She wondered why he even bothered to come back at all, since he probably got everything he needed from Susan Lovett. Rachel called his office, but his assistant wouldn't patch her through, shakily reporting that he was with a client and couldn't be disturbed. Rachel imagined Michael standing in front of his assistant, pantomiming that he didn't want to speak to his wife.

During the next day, Rachel tried to hide her anxiety from the kids by working them at full speed. By evening, her tension built to a point where she was too nervous to eat dinner before her appointment. The frustration of not being able to reach Michael gnawed at her gut.

After a brisk shower to rid herself of the playground grime, Rachel put on a pair of jeans and a crisp white t-shirt with a navy blazer. She couldn't imagine dressing up to discuss her child's death in front of a bunch of strangers. But she needed to feel comfortable, and to her amazement, the jeans bagged at the hips. Rachel figured she must have shed a few pounds from chasing the children at after school play. Her "fat jeans" were relegated to the back of the closet. She grabbed the "next-to-the-largest" pair, and miracle of miracles, they zipped easily.

She drove to the Dallas County Municipal Building, five miles north of downtown. A uniformed guard at the desk waved her through and directed her to the elevator bank down a drab corridor. She waited impatiently for the creaky doors to finally close. After a spasmodic ascent, she exited the graffiti-scratched elevator in which someone had tried to clean up "Don't Fuck with Texas," but the outline of the curse word remained visible on the faded paneling. The greenish fluorescent fixtures cast a sickly glow down the hallway with stained government-issue carpet. She looked at the arrows on the wall pointing to room numbers and turned down the wrong corridor. Finally, by circling the whole floor, she located Room 202.

After fumbling with the stuck door handle, Rachel entered a lobby where a handful of people were waiting in mismatched chairs. From a quick head count, she spotted six people: an elderly white couple; a twenty-something woman with stringy purplish black hair; a pale middle-aged woman wearing designer flats, along with her businessman-type husband; and a black teenager in pants that showed more than the tops of his boxers and dragged in shredded fringe on the floor.

A tall, thin man with a name badge on his corduroy jacket entered the room and sat on the edge of a table in the front. He addressed the group: "Thanks for coming. We're all here to help you get past a difficult time in your life. Some of you've been victims of violent crimes and others have loved ones who've been violated. Let's go around the room and introduce ourselves." Everyone seemed suddenly frozen. "Don't all jump in, y'all. Hey, I'll go first. I'm Edward James. It's okay to call me Eddie. I have master's degrees in criminology as well as in social work and family counseling. I've been with Dallas County Social Services for seventeen years. We've heard a lot of stories in this room and have helped a lot of folks."

He looked around at the group seated in a semicircle and nodded to the young woman. "How about you? Tell us who you are and why you're here."

The girl tugged on her greasy locks. "I'm Regina. I was assaulted leaving the movies." She twirled a few loose strands and looked down at her lap.

The boy sitting beside her handled his hair pick, like a tennis player fingering the strings of a racquet. "My name's Ikey. I was popped by a drive-by in the parking lot of Northpark. I really don't need to be here, but my rent made me."

"He means 'his parents.' They'll be here in subsequent sessions. Okay, thank you, Ikey. Now the two of you, please," Eddie said.

"Hilda here, and he's Manny. We were mugged by a couple of *schwartzes* in our driveway coming home from the Safeway."

"What's up with that, honky?" Ikey shot back.

Every instinct told Rachel to bolt, but she remained steadfast in her seat.

Eddie said, "Now, let's get some ground rules straight. Inside these walls, we treat *everyone* with respect. This is a safe place for all of you, so please refrain from using hurtful phrases."

Ikey settled back in his chair, crossing his thickly muscled arms, exhaling loudly in protest.

With Rachel's turn approaching, the constricting feeling about unloading personal information in front of a group of strangers made her cough. Eddie handed her a bottle of water from a small cooler on the back table. The couple to her right was next.

"My name is Celeste and this is my husband, Sterling. Our daughter was murdered after she broke up with her boyfriend in college in Lubbock. She didn't tell us what was going on, but he was stalking her. He broke into her apartment and cut up her sofa. The police later found threatening emails that said he'd do the same to her. Then one day, he showed up and stabbed her and shot five of her sorority sisters. Two died, including Lark."

Rachel vaguely remembered reading about the murders in the newspaper. She continued to regret her decision to attend the session.

Celeste paused to dab her eyes with the handkerchief Sterling produced from his pants pocket. She delicately blew her nose and continued her story: "He was executed last week. I got a call from a victims' rights organization asking if I wanted to attend, but I passed. They said seats were limited for the families of both the murderer and the victims. Believe me, I was glad he was going to be punished, but it's not an image I want to carry around with me for the rest of my life. His death didn't bring closure—because I'll always miss Lark. Sterling went for the two of us."

Rachel shifted her weight to soften the pain from the hard metal seats. The glaring lights made her think about the sizzle of the electric chair. She wondered if there were laws prohibiting comfortable seating in government buildings.

Then it was her turn, and the collection of unfamiliar faces stared expectedly, waiting to hear her tale of woe. A rush of heat rose to her cheeks and her heart raced in a new, frightening rhythm. And then her thoughts crystallized: *I just can't do this. I can't talk to these strangers. There's no way they could understand how much I miss her.* She reached down to get her purse to leave, when the door handle clicked and jangled without opening.

Eddie walked toward the door. "I don't know when the county is going to fix this dang knob. Everyone who's registered is present and accounted for, but I'd better get it. Besides, we might find ourselves stuck in here."

He wrestled with the door handle until it finally opened. Silhouetted against the harsh fluorescents in the hall was a familiar outline. Michael walked into the room and took the empty seat next to Rachel.

Eddie stood near him and asked, "How can we help you?"

"I'm Michael Frank, Rachel's husband. Sorry to interrupt. Am I too late?"

"No, you're fine. We're getting started with introductions. Just in time. Rachel, why don't you begin, and then Michael can say a few words afterward."

"How'd you know to come here?" she whispered to Michael.

"I guess you could say I climbed Macchu Picchu. The pamphlet was on the top of the massive pile of papers in the kitchen."

Rachel leaned back with closed eyes and said, "Okay, to begin with, I'm a friggin' basket case, and my daughter Missy was murdered last year." Avoiding a glance at Michael, she could hear his shallow breathing. She opened her eyes, startled when Eddie brushed his hand across her shoulder as he walked back to the center of the group.

"Can you tell us a little about what happened?" He took his seat, picking up his coffee cup.

"Yeah, Michael was angry at our daughter right before she went back to Austin for school. We should have driven her ourselves."

"What do you mean?" Sterling asked.

"I mean she was being charged with possessing a fake ID, and we sent her back before we all went to a lawyer. On the way, someone forced her off the road and shot her and her best friend." Rachel burst into sobs and then focused on the Rorschach test of coffee stains on the carpet. "I'm sorry, y'all. This is just too hard for me."

Michael's voice cracked when he jumped in. "It's classified as an unsolved crime." He cleared his voice and continued, "The police have just officially closed the case because there weren't any viable leads after all this time. It happened about a year ago."

Out of the corner of her eye, Rachel saw Celeste wiping her tears.

"Thank you, Rachel and Michael. Now, let's get back to Regina . . ." Eddie switched the attention to the details of the young woman's assault.

Rachel exhaled deeply and slid lower in her chair.

She and Michael left the meeting in separate cars. Rachel clutched the steering wheel tightly and tried to drive away her thoughts of dread and regret. She clicked the garage remote and saw Michael's car parked in its spot in the garage. When she opened the back door, he was sitting solemnly at the kitchen table, looking like a jury foreman waiting to pronounce a guilty verdict.

Before she retrieved her key from the door, he asked, "Why'd you accuse me in front of all of those people? No one could stop it. Just like you couldn't stop the violence in your home when you were growing up."

"What violence?" Rachel was shocked that Michael brought up something he knew nothing about.

"Do you think I've been blind all of these years? I'm talking about the beatings that scarred your mother's face and your blasted psyche. I never asked you because I respected your privacy about something you seemed to have put behind you—until Missy died. Years ago, I questioned Rosy about it, and she told me how your father had abused her."

"You knew and didn't say anything?" she asked in disbelief.

"Rachel, you held on to that damned secret of yours. You wouldn't let me in one little bit, even that night of the charity dinner for Hideaway Hotel. I tried to get you to open up, but you never gave an inch."

"You wouldn't understand. What happened to Mama was my fault. I didn't protect her," she confessed, leaning against the kitchen counter to steady herself.

"Protect her—how? You were only a child. What could you have done?"

"I could have stayed home with her that summer instead of going off to camp. I knew things weren't good, but I wanted to escape the war zone. If I'd been there, he wouldn't have beaten her to a pulp." The dam of pain split open, and Rachel sobbed hysterically.

Michael grabbed her by the shoulders and tried to lift her face to look into his eyes. "You weren't responsible. *She* was the adult and Rosy put you in harm's way by staying with your father. But your mother didn't feel she had any other choice. And I'm not responsible for Missy's death!"

"I know you aren't. And I'm sorry I said it."

"But you meant it! I came down on her that day because she'd done something wrong. Do you think there isn't a minute that goes by that I wish I'd held her before she left our house? Or wish to God I'd waited an hour before I picked up her car, and then she wouldn't have been on the road when that madman was there? I could make myself so damn ill that I couldn't function if I took all of the blame on myself." He broke down crying and crumbled to the floor, sitting on his knees like a little boy.

"Oh, Michael, you never showed me you were in so much pain." She reached down to stroke his thick hair.

"No, Rachel, you never bothered to look. You were too busy with your own grief and blaming me." He pulled away and struggled to stand up.

"So that's why you turned to Susan instead of me?"

"You're still too blinded by your own neuroses to trust me and to know what kind of man I am. I've upheld our marriage, although you really haven't by shutting me out of your heart—and our bed."

"But I thought you and Susan . . ."

"Well, you thought wrong; I wasn't having an affair with Susan. We've been involved together on a project for the past year. I wanted something good in my life instead of drowning in the sea of depression at home that's greeted me every day since Missy was murdered. I wanted to do a *mitzvah* that would make a difference for someone in need and might also change things for us, too." He clutched his jaw tightly.

"What about me? What project would be good for us that has kept you locked up in that den, working nights and weekends, I'd like to know? What is it—another high-rise in downtown Dallas that's taller than the last one?"

He moved closer so their faces were only a breath away. "Your selfishness and myopia never cease to amaze me. If you must know, it's a recreation center and serenity garden for Hideaway Hotel. After I do my on-the-clock shit-load of work, it's a charity project I've been handling during off-hours to get it ready for the opening scheduled on first day of summer."

Rachel had mixed feelings of relief and rage at how he could have kept such a secret from her.

Michael's face was flushed with anger. "I want to make sure there's a place where women like your mother can escape from violence until they can make new lives. Of all of the evil in the world, this is one type I feel I can help get a handle on. Maybe I can save someone else's child."

"I'm so ashamed. Michael, I didn't know." She reached out to touch his arm.

He pulled back slightly. "Rachel, it's a little too late for 'I'm sorry.' I've tried and tried, and you've kept your pain to yourself like a hidden treasure. You never once thought about me. Did you ever think I might want a decent meal at home or a little sex with the woman I loved?"

"No, and it makes me sick to admit it. What can I do to begin to show you how sorry I am? I was so wrong and selfish. Just tell me what you want." She tried again to touch him.

Michael stood to unzip his pants—then he tucked in his shirt. "Rachel, I'm going to take a drive right now and check out the construction site. I don't know when I'll be home, so don't wait up."

CHAPTER 31

THE MONTHS PASSED BY SLOWLY after Rachel's meltdown in the kitchen. Michael spent even longer hours at the office. She worked at school in the afternoons and religiously attended the Victims of Violent Crimes workshops on Tuesday nights. Gradually, Rachel began to care about the people who shared their most intimate thoughts with her.

Michael never went back to the sessions and she never asked him to. They buried the hatchet and lived with an unspoken truce, careful not to upset each other, but also kept a safe distance from any real closeness.

P.J. called and Rachel detected a slight hesitation in her voice. "Michael told me that he let you know about the recreation center."

"The two of you are talking behind my back again, but this time, I don't mind. P.J., I'm so ashamed of how I've treated him. I had no idea." Rachel sank into the chair at her kitchen desk and prepared for a long, overdue conversation. The polished wooden desktop was finally visible, devoid of the stacks of papers. She doodled on a grocery list while her friend spoke.

"You and Michael are good for each other. You've been though something most marriages can't survive. Don't worry, pal. You'll get past this. Michael's project at the shelter has been good for my life, too."

"What? Don't tell me that you and Juan have hit a snag?" The pencil point snapped to a dry nub on the page of concentric circles.

"No, I'm talking about Mother. Michael persuaded her to fund the addition to Hideaway Hotel as part of the company's community service project. She forked out most of the bucks to sponsor the new vocational and physical rehab center with a therapeutic pool. Mother especially sparked to the idea of a solitude garden and was going to dedicate it in memory of Daddy."

"Oh yeah, your so-called friend Rosemary used to tell me about the healing power of green spaces. I wonder why didn't she paint her front door green instead of that satanic red."

P.J. laughed. "But then Mother decided there are already enough glass and steel monuments with Daddy's name on them. Finally, she took to the idea of a meditation garden within the protected confines of the women's shelter. You could have knocked me over with a feather when she asked Juan to create a sculpture for it."

"I'm surprised your mother doesn't think meditation's a weird cult thing."

There was a beat of silence on the line. "Hey, between the two of us, I'm the only one who's allowed to diss my mother. You know how that goes. It's only all right to rag against your own kind, but heaven help anyone else who does."

"Forgive me? I never know when to keep my smart mouth shut." Rachel began to worry that she had really upset P.J. It was difficult to tell because she couldn't look into her friend's eyes.

"*No problema.* Anyhow, Mother and I have gotten much closer to each other because of this project. We even talked about her use of DES and my infertility, for the first time in our lives. She's felt guilty all these years, and I guess I secretly held it against her. It really wasn't her fault; she was only doing what she thought was best and what the doctor ordered."

"Now that's an awesome breakthrough," Rachel said in true amazement.

"She also asked me to help the kids at the shelter paint a mural that will be unveiled at the opening. Will you be there?"

"Of course, wild horses . . . and all that." Rachel picked up a fresh pencil.

"Catch you in a couple of weeks. And Rach, don't beat yourself up so much. Oh, I almost forgot to tell you—Juan and I are fed up to here with Rosemary!"

Rachel could only imagine P.J. gesturing by swiping her hand across her forehead. She listened with heightened interest.

"At her latest book signing, Rosemary cornered him while I was in the john. She had the nerve to roll her tongue around in her cheek and ask if he wanted her to give his barn a few licks of paint for old time's sake. He, of course, repeated to me what she said, which after I stopped laughing, made me see red—like that damn door of hers!"

"Sounds like a typical two-faced thing Rosemary would do. Having a couple of divorces under her turquoise belt, I guess she doesn't respect the sanctity of marriage much."

"He told Ro that she'd better permanently lock her barn door because the bull escaped years ago and wasn't coming back. There were a few things I wanted to tell her myself, so I barged in front of her adoring fans lined up at the book signing," P.J. said.

"Poor, misguided souls looking to that fake for advice."

"So I said to her, 'Ro, even though your old sidekick Andy Warhol claims everyone's entitled to fifteen minutes of fame, in my book, your time's up!'"

"Sw-e-et!" Rachel said approvingly. "I would have loved to have added that her book should have been titled *Some Women Are Like Douche Bags*. Just like Rosemary, they pump you up at first, and then drain the hell out of you."

They snickered like schoolgirls, delighted at their petty acts of revenge.

"See you in a few weeks. Hugs to Michael."

"Same to Juan."

GIMME SHELTER FROM THE HEAT

CHAPTER 32

THE SUN BEAT DOWN in the cloudless sky on the morning of the grand opening of the recreation center. Michael was already on his way to Hideaway Hotel before Rachel awoke. They took separate cars because he wasn't exactly sure of the demands of his schedule before or after the event. He had asked her to be a part of it, and she agreed to be a hostess in the therapeutic pool area.

She noticed a note sitting on his pillow. In his crisp architectural lettering, he had written:

Rach,
This is our big day! Thanks for sharing it with me.
I did it for both of us.
Love,
Michael

She slipped on the fresh yellow polo shirt with a Hideaway Hotel logo patch on the breast pocket he had laid out on the empty side of the bed. Following the shelter volunteer dress code for the ceremony, Rachel neatly tucked the size-medium shirt into her khaki shorts.

She drove toward downtown to the Harwood exit and turned left past old deserted garment factories and run-down houses. Winding her way through unfamiliar territory, she finally spotted a high gray metal wall with number 33 etched in a black plaque. It was easy to miss because there wasn't any obvious signage to alert husbands and boyfriends to where their women and children had fled. She pressed the intercom button and a female voice answered, "Hideaway Hotel. We're here to help."

"I'm Rachel Frank, here for the opening."

The metal wall slid open, revealing a path of commemorative bricks that led to the front door. Rachel stopped to read some of the words pressed into the clay: "To a Future Without Violence," "Pray for Peace of Mind," "RESPECT," and "For my beloved daughter." Inching along, she was moved by the inspirational sayings and then scanned the names of corporations and individuals. She figured the bricks were really dollar signs that represented valuable donations that funded the shelter.

The glass front doors were wide open. Usually they were locked for round-the-clock security. A large arrangement of lilies, roses, and hydrangeas bursting with color at the reception desk made the facility look more like a hotel lobby than a safe haven. A young woman with "Louise" on her name badge on her HH polo greeted Rachel and checked the guest list again. She plucked a nametag from several neatly arranged rows and smiled broadly.

"Oh, Mrs. Frank, your husband is really something! He's put his heart and soul into making this a great place. Thank you so much!" she gushed.

"It was really his baby. I had nothing to do with it," Rachel replied while looking around the room.

"You're too modest. Welcome to Hideaway Hotel. Are you going to take a little tour before you report to the pool area? Some of the clients' rooms are available for viewing. They're great because they have their own private bathrooms so moms and their kids can stay together in one room, including the boys. The day school and psychological workshop spaces are open, too."

"I'd like to, but I don't have much time. Where should I start?"

"Your husband is in a meeting with Mrs. Rutherford and Dr. Clara. Do you want me to get him for you?"

"No, I really don't want to bother him. I'll just find my way around," Rachel told Louise, fearing they might not be the picture of the perfect couple, if Michael showed up to greet her.

She ambled toward the back of the lobby, pausing at framed inspirational sayings. She lingered at one penned by a woman who seemed to keep sending her messages from beyond. Amid the floral border that looped and swirled around the rainbow-colored calligraphy, a quote filled the frame:

> "You gain strength, courage and confidence by every experience
> in which you really stop to look fear in the face. You are able to
> say to yourself, 'I lived through this horror. I can take the next
> thing that comes along."
>
> — *Eleanor Roosevelt 1884-1962*

Louise called out from the reception desk, "You might want to step through those glass doors to the garden before you head to the recreation center."

Rachel opened the sliders and entered an interior courtyard. Its lush beauty stunned her. The profusion of plants reminded her of an Impressionist canvas come to life—with crepe myrtles, foxgloves, and orange day lilies ringed by beds of yellow roses and black-eyed Susans. She found it incongruent that a flower with such a violent name could be so cheerful and vibrant. The horticultural sign near the patch indicated rudeckia hirta, equally forbidding.

Enveloped by the serenity of the garden, Rachel sat on a wooden bench carved like a tree branch, nestled within the dense green canopy. The careful pruning of the flowering shrubs gave her a perfect view of the garden's focal point—a bronze sculptural fountain of a girl romping in the sprinklers—her baseball cap tipped jauntily to the slide and her ponytail flying skyward. Metallic water droplets hung in the air, almost imperceptibly suspended from the cast figure of a child. A faint spray of water kept the sculpture gleaming with moisture. Rachel's hands began to shake uncontrollably when she realized she was looking at Missy—the essence of pure, childish delight. Almost unable to feel her legs, Rachel willed herself to stand and walked over to touch the smiling face of her little girl, burnished with a greenish gold patina. Then she kneeled to get closer to read the plaque nestled in the soft green sod:

MISSY'S GARDEN
A peaceful place for women and children to feel young again.
Donated by the Russell and Lynda Gayle Rutherford
Charitable Trust
Sculpted lovingly by Juan Miguel Siguieros

In the bittersweet mixture of sadness and joy, Rachel felt like she was swirling in a vortex. After a few seconds, a sensation of warmth flowed over her when she determined that this monument to her precious daughter was much more fitting than the cold marble headstone she and Michael had erected at the cemetery. She squeezed back her tears and thought of the comfort the image of little Missy would bring to women on the edge, on their way to a new life—free from the grip of violence.

Louise stuck her head through the opening to the garden. "I think they might need you at poolside. A few visitors arrived while you were in Missy's Garden. How'd you like the statue?"

"More than you can ever imagine," Rachel answered softly.

"Please follow the signs and keep going right."

Rachel followed a hint of chlorine down a corridor and then walked through the double doors into the pool area where the dedication was about to commence. Deep breaths of the moist air calmed her nerves while she watched the water glisten, as smooth as glass on the freshly plastered surface. She spotted P. J. balancing on a stepstool, trying to attach a canvas tarp over the children's mural. Focused on her task, she was unaware of her friend's arrival.

Rachel listlessly shifted her weight from one leg to the other while waiting for the ceremony to begin. Minutes later, Lynda Gayle Rutherford strolled through the double doors, trailed by her assistant, Mitzi, followed by Dallas Mayor Delfina Ramirez, members of the City Council, and other guests. Then Michael entered with Dr. Amparo and Susan Lovett. Michael winked at Rachel from the far end of the pool deck where he was standing in the center of the group.

The adult residents of the shelter—women of all shapes and colors—filed in and stood along the sides of the pool. Some used canes and others slowly crawled along, leaning on metal walkers. Rachel was shocked to see young women with medical devices usually needed by the elderly and hadn't expected to see so many arms in slings and bandaged wounds. Then the children marched in, congregating in a tight bunch in front of the draped mural.

Dr. Amparo's dark eyes sparked with enthusiasm as she began her opening remarks: "Welcome to Hideaway Hotel. Our center is a very special place that serves each and every district of the city. We provide shelter and counseling to women and children at risk from spousal abuse. This addition to our facilities couldn't be possible without the generosity of Mrs. Lynda Gayle Rutherford and the Russell Rutherford Charitable Trust. The children are delighted with the new recreation center and want to show their appreciation of your support."

The boys and girls giggled, excited about being mentioned.

Dr. Amparo waved to the children. "Also, special thanks to P.J. Siguieros for her artistic supervision. In a few minutes, we'll gather in the serenity garden to dedicate the magnificent sculpture by her husband, Juan, who is waiting for us there. But now we have a wonderful treat for you." She turned to the little ones and said, "Okay, kids, now!"

On cue, the children tugged on a rope, and the canvas tarp tumbled to the ground, revealing a swirling scene of sea creatures: breaching whales, smiling dolphins, and all manner of fishes—real or imagined. Everyone, including the kids, gave a round of applause. P.J. finally spotted Rachel and nodded a welcome from across the room.

Rachel, in turn, responded with a "thumbs up." Preparing for an onslaught of speeches, she sat on the edge of the shallow end of the pool.

Dr. Amparo addressed the dignitaries, occasionally turning to include the residents at poolside. "Hideaway Hotel is a safe haven for victims of serious domestic abuse—both mothers and children. It's a dirty little secret that many women don't share, with even their priests or rabbis. We've learned that about seventy-five percent of men who become abusers watched their fathers beat their mothers. Battering is a learned behavior that we want to reverse and prevent. The injuries sustained are emotional as well as physical. That's one reason we're so thankful for our new recreational and rehab facility. The pool is therapeutic for the healing of bruised bodies and spirits as well as respiratory problems, such as asthma."

A physical therapist ushered a few of the children into the water. Instead of an orderly procession, they broke ranks and plunged in, splashing Lynda Gayle's silk suit. Unruffled, she shook Dr. Amparo's hand and then turned to Michael, thanking him for his hard work and dedication. Rachel took pride in watching him standing there in his shelter polo and crisp khaki slacks, looking handsome and humble.

She slipped off her sandals and dangled her feet in the delicious water; she felt something like a little fishy lightly pinching her toes. Floating below her, Miracle bobbed up and down in a light blue swim cap that corralled her thick hair. She clung to Rachel's submerged feet and begged, "Ple-e-ase come play with me, Miss Rachel."

"Miracle, oh my gosh! Honey, I'd love to, but I really can't because I'm supposed to welcome the guests. Besides, I don't have on a swimsuit."

"Please, Miss Rachel. Just for a little while." Miracle gazed up with her wide hazel eyes.

I never could resist that precious little face I cared about—even loved—so why should I now? Rachel stood up and leapt into the pool, clothes and all, lingering at the bottom. *Have I really lost my mind this time?* When her lungs felt like they were about to explode, she burst to the surface. Wiping the water from her eyes, she spotted Michael starting to run toward her, but then Susan caught the crook of his arm.

Rachel dove back under to the bottom, and when she came up for air, flung her head back to slick down her hair.

Miracle appeared, splashing and swimming around her like a playful dolphin rescuing a drowning sailor. "Now, you close your eyes, spin around and count to three, and I'll hide, Miss Rachel."

"Okay. Whatever you say . . . Ready?" Rachel stood in the shallow end, twirling around with her eyes squeezed shut, not really caring who was watching her making a complete fool of herself. "One . . . Two . . . Three . . . Marco!" she shouted over the shrieks and giggles of the children in the pool.

Then from somewhere far away, a voice called out, "Polo!"

EPILOGUE

MICHAEL HAD A HECK OF A TIME getting rid of his ear infection. A few insidious drops of chlorinated pool water lodged in his ear canal and wreaked havoc on his equilibrium. He didn't complain about his loss of balance and religiously took his medicine to combat the vertigo. Rachel suspected that he actually enjoyed his short-lived malady as a badge of courage and devotion.

The sight of Michael plunging into the pool in his crisp khaki pants and Hideaway Hotel polo shirt will always be, in Rachel's mind, his finest hour. When he shouted her name from across the recreation pavilion, she opened her eyes, which had been tightly shut while she was "it" in the watery game of hide-and-seek. He wrenched his arm away from Susan and jumped into the pool, loafers and all, and headed toward Rachel. In amazement, she watched him, with the water barely lapping at her chin.

He swam a brisk crawl and then planted his feet on the smooth pool bottom, standing before his wife with droplets collected on his lashes. Rachel put her arms around his neck and wrapped her legs around him, hanging on—not for dear life—but for the sheer fun of it.

She planted a dripping kiss on his lips and then announced to her husband, "It's your turn to be 'it,' Michael. Start counting!"

ACKNOWLEDGMENTS

I GREW UP IN DALLAS, Texas, and was touched by JFK's assassination in "my own backyard." A senseless act of random violence against an acquaintance, along with the dirty little secret of domestic violence in households throughout America, inspired this work of fiction.

Many thanks to those who helped me prepare for this journey to become an author. The novel was created in an advanced fiction workshop led by Carol Lee Lorenzo at Callanwolde Fine Arts Center in Atlanta, Georgia. In addition, excerpts were critiqued in graduate school at Kennesaw State University, where I received a Master of Arts in Professional Writing degree in creative writing.

Friends who either love literature and/or the state of Texas offered their comments and suggestions. Many thanks for the support and encouragement of Laura and Walter Levy, Terry Spector, Walter Lawrence, John Turman, Mark and Tina Landers, Kay Watson, Joy Greenberg, Dominique Greve, Bill James, Carolyn Wills, Debbie Harris, and many others not mentioned here who shared their time.

My late husband, Simon, was a generous and supportive force behind my creative efforts. He hoped *Shelter from the Texas Heat* would make its way into print.

I have great respect and admiration for those who run women's shelters and for the brave women who escape from domestic violence. Special thanks to Paige Flink, executive director of A Family Place in Dallas, who gave me an inside look at a safe haven.

Thanks to Rabbi Ronald Segal for inspiring some of the passages with religious rituals.

I am thankful for my pal GiGi, my poodle pup, who patiently waits to play while I put the finishing touches on my manuscripts.

Thanks to the book team: Ahmad Meradji for production supervision, Sara Strish for the cover illustration, and Angela DeCaires for copyediting. My photo portrait was made by J. Reneé Photography.

And almost last, but never least, much appreciation goes to my mother, Polly, who has cheered my progress and offered support and advice about reaching goals in life—and to my stepfather Amnon, who also shares a love of writing.

And thanks to Willie Nelson . . . just because!

DICUSSION QUESTIONS

1. Rachel was ashamed to tell anyone about the spousal abuse in her family. Has anything changed over the years to reduce the stigma?

2. What do the recurrent symbols of swimming pools, yellow roses, stars, and the Texas heat mean?

3. Several of the characters in the novel were deeply affected by the JFK assassination. How did it impact Rachel's family and the American public in general? Where were you when it happened or what have you read about it?

4. Which incidents best showed the depth of Rachel and P.J.'s friendship?

5. What types of prejudice were shown in *Shelter from the Texas Heat*?

6. What did Rachel learn from Irene, the Holocaust survivor? Have you met survivors who have shared their stories to help others?

7. Rachel's mother, Rosy Rosenshein Miller, often gives unsolicited advice. Is there any truth in the *bubbameisters* (wives' tales), such as catching a cold from wet hair or sitting too close to the TV?

8. Rachel feared that Miracle and her mother were being abused. Was it her responsibility to report her suspicions to the authorities?

9. Maddy goes to the March on Washington for Jobs and Freedom to hear Dr. Martin Luther King Jr. How did the protest change life in America?

10. Do you think Rachel and Michael will reconcile and be happy again?